THE STRENUOUS AGE
IN AMERICAN LITERATURE

THE
STRENUOUS
AGE
IN
American
Literature

BY GRANT C. KNIGHT

COOPER SQUARE PUBLISHERS, INC.
NEW YORK
1970

Originally Published and Copyright © 1954 by
University of North Carolina Press
Published by Cooper Square Publishers, Inc.
59 Fourth Avenue, New York, N. Y. 10003
Standard Book No. 8154-0351-8
Library of Congress Catalog Card No. 75-129461

Printed in the United States of America

FOREWORD

I t is likely that many well-read persons if asked to name the capital works of American literature for the first decade of the twentieth century would give answers so tentative as to be nearly guesses. For that decade is, if not exactly *terra incognita* in our literary history, at least an area that has been little explored, and reports upon it have been fewer and less sympathetic than might have been expected. The historians and biographers have, as a rule, slighted it, and the critics have been equally neglectful in favor of other periods which at present have an imperious call. It may be noted as one consequence that there is room for critical-biographical studies of Robert W. Chambers, Winston Churchill, Margaret Deland, John Fox, Jr., Mary Wilkins Freeman, Ellen Glasgow, Henry Harland, O. Henry, Robert Herrick, Emerson Hough, Mary Johnston, Meredith Nicholson, Booth Tarkington, Maurice Thompson, Brand Whitlock, and Owen Wister, and that an analysis of our humor of the decade, a history of the American political novel, and many investigations such as that which might determine the relation of Sinclair Lewis to the muckrakers and to David Graham Phillips would be of considerable help to scholars and to serious readers.

The reasons for this inattention are as easy to discover as they are on the whole unconvincing. For one, the writers, including the reviewers and critics, of the early 1900's were inclined to belittle their own achievements and to look backward with understandable nostalgia to the effulgence of the Golden Day, not much more than a generation past. To cite

v

an extreme example, H. L. Mencken in his first critical article contributed to *Smart Set* in 1908 complained that "American manufacturers of fiction, having the souls of fudge-besotted high-school girls, behold the human comedy as a mixture of a fashionable wedding and a three-alarm fire with the music of Chopin"; and in the Fourth Series of his *Prejudices* (1924), writing about the American novel, he remembered the decade as a "time of almost inconceivable complacency and conformity" and went on to state too sweepingly that "the American novelists most admired by most publishers, by most readers, and by all practising critics were Richard Harding Davis, Robert W. Chambers and James Lane Allen."

The severity of Mr. Mencken's strictures may be attributed to his Shavian fondness for badgering dwellers in the lowlands of Philistia. But the authority back of those opinions was not much questioned by the young men who were to become the chroniclers of our literature and who through reading them had acquired prejudices of their own which the years have not entirely eroded. Quite recently one of the most competent and respected of American critics, addressing a college assembly, declared that

From 1900 to 1910 American literature was in about as dull a state as it has ever been since the New England revival. . . . Almost all of the books that we now consider of literary merit or interest were either written in this country and privately printed, or written abroad. . . . There were a few serious writers here—Ellen Glasgow perhaps, although her work during that decade was in the fashionable manner of the time—but there were very few.

The measure of truth in this disparagement is at once undeniable and challenging. It must be conceded that *Mont-Saint-Michel and Chartres* and *The Education of Henry Adams* were privately printed, that *The Wings of the Dove*, *The Ambassadors*, and *The Golden Bowl* were written abroad, that Miss Glasgow had not attained artistic maturity, that *Sister Carrie* was suppressed, that Edwin Arlington Robinson was not sufficiently appreciated by critics or public. Yet it would seem that a rejoinder can easily and fairly be outlined. Copies of Henry Adams' books were sought for; James's fiction was more popular in the United States than in England and it was in our country that the New York Edition of his novels and tales got under way in 1907; Ellen Glasgow was already orienting herself in a realism new to the South; *Sister Carrie* found a publisher in 1900; and the chief executive of the nation publicized Robinson's first volume of poetry. Moreover, a decade which produced *The Octopus* and *The Pit*, *The House of Mirth*, *The Jungle*, *Captain Craig* and *The Town down the River*, *The Deliverance*, *The Call of the Wild* and *The Sea-Wolf*, *The Hungry Heart*, *The Crossing*, *Cabbages and Kings*, *The Son of Royal Langbrith*, *The History of the Standard Oil Company*, *The Life of Reason*, *Folkways*, *Pragmatism*, *The Memoirs of an American Citizen*, and "An Ode in Time of Hesitation" cannot be rightfully dismissed as an arid one or as one lacking in seriousness. And the interval which saw the attempt of Percy MacKaye, Cale Young Rice, Josephine Preston Peabody, and Olive Dargan to restore poetic drama to the place from which it had declined may no more be termed unadventurous than the same interval, turning out the stories, sketches, and columns of O. Henry, Gelett Burgess, Finley Peter Dunne, George Randolph Chester, George Ade, Oliver Herford, Charles P. Loomis, Will Irwin, Ellis Parker Butler, Irvin Cobb, Marshall P. Wilder, Simeon Ford, John Kendrick Bangs, and Carolyn Wells, and supporting the weeklies *Puck*, *Judge*, and *Life* may be shrugged off as dull unless the word is to have special definition.

The decade has also been slighted because both the 1890's, which witnessed the resolution of the struggle between "romanticists" and "realists," and the 1920's, which uncovered some brave new talents, appear by contrast more stimulating. In 1900 the question was no longer whether realism might be accepted in American literature but how far and in what direction that realism would go, so that the following ten years constituted a period of transition with shifting currents not easily traced. The history of literature does not invariably lend itself to examination in ten-year intervals, but the period from 1890 to 1900 was so decisive, and the Theodore Roosevelt era so prophetic of literary and social evolution, that both decades may properly be scrutinized with some closeness and in relation to each other. Since this book intends to continue that examination and is therefore a sequel to *The Critical Period in American Literature* (1951) it seemed best to employ for it the same approach to the subject; that is, to give literature position in the social panorama, to try, without subtracting from it any of its peculiar values or any of the affection we hold for it, to integrate literature with the social history of the time, so that it might become a transparency through which we may catch glimpses of other art forms, of politics, of philosophy, of science. From this point of view it can be seen that our writings for the eleven years from 1900 to and including 1910 had their share of esthetic qualities and that, like the American people of the time, they were concerned as they never had been before and never have been since with the image of the Strong Man who consciously battled for power and who threatened to develop into a cultural hero. That he did not attain such an apotheosis, that our national politics went on for good or ill to the New Freedom, the New Deal, and the Fair Deal is largely because the way for these experiments was made straight by the career of Theodore Roosevelt and by the productions of novelists, poets, dramatists, and journalists whose effect upon history was on the whole more pronounced than their triumphs in art, but who for that very reason do not deserve to be forgotten. Books, like persons, need not be great in order to be respected or loved.

Because Mr. William T. Stafford of Purdue University and Professor John L. Cutler of the University of Kentucky, and Professor Lyon N. Richardson of Western Reserve University read and made helpful suggestions for the chapter on Henry James, I wish here to acknowledge their kindness and to register my appreciation. And to Professor W. S. Ward,

Dean M. M. White, President H. L. Donovan, and the Trustees of the University of Kentucky I express my full thanks for that practical encouragement without which the completion of this volume would have been much delayed.

GRANT C. KNIGHT

Lexington, Kentucky

CONTENTS

THE STRENUOUS AGE
IN AMERICAN LITERATURE

I

Peace and Prosperity

The leading article in *The Atlantic Monthly* for March, 1901, probably meant to come to the attention of the newly inaugurated William McKinley and Theodore Roosevelt, was entitled "Democracy and Efficiency." Its author began with an arresting observation: "It is no longer possible to mistake the reaction against democracy." Then Professor Woodrow Wilson of Princeton University proceeded to expound that the nineteenth century had been a triumphant one for democracy but that disturbing portents were now appearing, even in the United States. He called the roll of our "errors": too many riots and disorders, a frequent failure of justice in the courts, unceasing contests between capital and labor, inequitable laws of property and marriage, the worst governed cities in the world outside those of the Turkish Empire and Spain, a high rate of crime, and an inability on the part of our citizens to achieve a "monopoly either of happiness or of enlightened social order." But he relieved this depressing *dossier* by asserting that democracy is not a matter of forms but of principles, and he pointed out that our new responsibilities acquired along with our new island possessions gave us the opportunity to illustrate the worth of those principles, for "this change in the order of the world [a frontage toward the Pacific] came, so far as we are concerned, at the natural point in our development." And he ended the essay with a plea for responsible leadership, fidelity to ideals, and freedom for the Philippines as soon as possible.

Eloquent though his language was, Professor Wilson wrote

so cautiously as to suggest that he had not considered, though he certainly knew about, the formidable social factors that had long thwarted the spread of Jeffersonian democracy, that he had not fully assessed the appearance in the nineteenth century of such Strong Men as Cavour, Bismarck, Palmerston, Alexander I, General Boulanger, and Napoleon III, that he did not understand that the Industrial Revolution had set in motion forces which by the end of the century were prophetic of catastrophes in western civilization which might seem in line with the predictions of Karl Marx. The paper indicated, indeed, that the Princeton professor of Political Science did not measure the gravity of the time or foresee the perils democracy was to encounter within twenty-five years.

Some Americans did. Before the opening of the twentieth century Henry Adams told Poultney Bigelow that the Latin nations, including France, were finished as great powers; that England would survive on its fat for ten years; and that in the new century the world would belong to the United States and Russia. His younger brother Brooks developed this view more analytically in *America's Economic Supremacy* (1900), thereby making some of the most interesting prophecies in our literature.

Everywhere [he wrote] society tends to become organized in greater and denser masses, the more vigorous and economical mass destroying the less active and the more wasteful. Thus Latin Europe has rotted from end to end of the Continent, China is disintegrating, and England seems destined to lose her preëminence as the heart of the world's industry and finance. On the other hand, Germany has grown to be the center of an entirely new economic system, Russia is rapidly absorbing all Northern Asia as far as the Yanktse River, and the United States has been converted from the most pacific of nations into an armed and aggressive community.[1]

1. Brooks Adams, *America's Economic Supremacy*, New York, 1900, pp. 26-27.

After noting the concentration of power and wealth in the United States Brooks Adams further declared that a tug-of-war was on between an "Anglo-Saxon" coalition and Russia; that it was in effect a struggle between maritime and non-maritime nations for the trade of the world; that stupendous battles would be fought, West against East; that this country would fail to capture and exploit Chinese markets; that in the end Russia would lose because it was corrupt and inefficient; and that here in the United States either the trusts would own the government or the government would be obliged to own the trusts.

This prescient thesis rested upon events just prior to its publication and could have drawn support from what followed. The strong European nations and the United States, constrained by the pressures of their economic systems, had recently been and were after 1900 briskly engaged in a rivalry for colonial prizes, the richest of which were to be found in China and in Africa. In 1900 the British, who fought forty wars in Victoria's reign, were still suffering reverses in South Africa despite Lord Roberts's proclamation in September of the annexation of the South African Republics to the Empire; in fact, the reverses were so humiliating that some Frenchmen feared lest the English attack their homeland in order to recover military prestige, and in June Lord Salisbury, addressing the Primrose League, called upon Englishmen to defend their shores while Andrew Carnegie mistakenly thought that the continental powers would shortly combine against England, whereupon that nation would ask help of the United States and get it. The French, wishing to consolidate their positions in North Africa, were fighting the Berbers and clashing diplomatically with the British.

Of the nations that made up the Triple Alliance, Germany at the beginning of 1900 was voicing its need for colonies through a speech by Prince Bernhard von Bülow; later the Chancellor tried to obtain the friendship of Great Britain only to learn that British policy envisioned a war between Germany and Russia, and abandoning his first plan he watched the growth of a hostile feeling between his own people and the English. Italy, having withdrawn from Abyssinia after the defeat at Adowa, was busy with the administration of Eritrea but did dispatch some two thousand troops to join the allies in China; Austria, comparatively unambitious, did no more at the opening of the century than send its popular Franz Joseph to Berlin on a visit of friendship.

The remaining European great power, Russia, was playing a free and devious hand on that continent but at the same time was deeply concerned over the obvious intention of Japan to achieve first class status as an Asiatic empire. All through 1900 and 1901 commentators on international affairs remarked upon the warlike preparations of the rivals, the Japanese showing special resentment over the presence of Muscovite soldiers among the relief columns in China and special alarm over the completion of the Siberian railroad in November of 1901. In the same year Russian touchiness set off a tariff war against the United States.

The latter country meanwhile was assuming a larger rôle in the feverish global politics of the era. Our attempts to pacify the Philippines were having little more success than those of the British to subdue the Boers, but the appointment of William Howard Taft in February, 1900, to head a commission charged with setting up civil government in the islands, the succession of General Arthur MacArthur to the command in April, and the capture of Emilio Aguinaldo in March of 1901 and his taking of an oath of allegiance in the following month made it fairly certain that this imperialistic venture would presently pay off. Americans began to puzzle over such place names as Taku, Tientsin, and Pekin as they followed on their maps the march of General A. R. Chaffee's men to the Chinese capital to aid in suppressing the Boxer Rebellion, and to read shamefacedly that the "Oregon" had run ashore in June, 1900, in the Gulf of Pe-chi-li; they read also Mr. Dooley's opinion that the fighting represented a combat between "westhren and easthren civilization," with the west winning because of its machines. In that year the United States was pressing Turkey for the payment of an indemnity and ordering two warships to the Isthmus of Panama to protect our interests in Colombia, where civil war was imminent; in the same year the battleships "Wisconsin" and "Alabama" were added to the navy and in 1901 the "Illinois" and the new "Maine" were launched. To make this navy more mobile and to use it as a possible deterrent to Japanese expansion—Japan was already being spoken of as the Yellow Peril—arguments for an isthmian canal became insistent.

By the end of May, 1901, the foreign troops which had put down the rebellion were withdrawing from China but elsewhere in the turbulent world of the twentieth century dissension and bloodshed went on: Björnstjerne Björnson agitated for a separation of Norway from Sweden, Abyssinia waged a local war in January, Colombia and Venezuela clashed while the former coped with a civil war in mid-summer, and in the fall Turks and Albanians were shooting each other in Serbia. Other evidences of a violent temper from 1900 to 1902, evidences of nationalistic feeling, of lawlessness, of human daring are to be found in the spirit of the Celtic Renaissance, in the polar expeditions of the Duke of the Abruzzi, Fridtjof Nansen, and Robert E. Peary, and in the report of over two thousand murders a year in the United States.

In 1900 and 1901, then, the globe or the maps in the library might have been dotted with pins to indicate the presence of armor on land and sea, armor being deployed to conquer territories, to put down insurrections, to overawe smaller nations, to police lands already wrested from native populations, and to counter maneuvers made by competitors in the deadly game. Some of the keener minds were able to see that although the balance of power in Europe would still be sought, perhaps with sanguinary consequences, the balance of power throughout the world was shifting. The fortunes amassed by Americans in the nineteenth century and the seemingly inexhaustible natural and technological resources of the United States made it inevitable that the money center of the world should move from Threadneedle Street to Wall Street; our need for markets had made us an empire, deeply engaged in the Pacific and determined to maintain John Hay's Open Door policy in China while we fortified ourselves against two contingent foes in the East. For the first time a majority of Americans began to realize that we had the might of which we had long boasted. They realized it dimly, being politically immature, but they could not escape the knowledge that we had easily defeated a European army and navy in 1898, that we had acquired a protectorate over Cuba, that we had taken over the Philippines and other islands in the Pacific, that our soldiers had fought under our flag in China, that we were now a united, vigorous, young people operating under a dynamic politico-economic system which had brought freedom and great national wealth. They could not overlook the fact that we had stirred from hemispheric containment and had stretched out strong arms to east and west.

Naturally most of them exulted in these evidences of our health and most of them, judging from contemporary records of all kinds, considered more openly than ever before the virtue of being strong in a world still ruled by force. The total circumstances of colonial and pioneer life in America had created the self-reliant man and the ideal of self-dependence, easily to be transformed in the nineteenth and twentieth centuries into the Strong Man of business, war, and politics, and into the Will to Power. The average American did not use that last phrase, but he subconsciously recognized its meaning and its presence. Darwinism, which he was not sure he could accept, was nearly comprehended for him in the catchword "the survival of the fittest," and this seemed to give scientific justification for the use of power in self-interest. Nietzsche's Superman had got into his more thoughtful speech, and although he probably misinterpreted the meaning of the German's *Wille zur Macht*, it too seemed to provide a rationale for the unscrupulous wielding of force. The last serious war in Europe, he could reflect, had been won not by a nation dedicated to *la gloire* but by one devoted to mechanical and personal efficiency, and from it had come the slogan about blood and iron. Georges Clemenceau's *Le Mêlée sociale* (1895) had emphasized man's unending war with man for food; Alexander Del Mar's *A History of the Precious Metals* (American edition 1896) described the world scramble for gold and silver; the partial tendency of naturalism in literature, of pessimism and decadence and satanism as moods or fads, of Higher Criticism of the Bible, and of the competitive nature of life as he experienced it, confirmed the American in his opinion that this planet was most likely to be inherited by the hardy and cunning and that the Strong Man was something of a demigod. In the early nineteen-hundreds colored prints of the Snuffbox portrait of Napoleon could be purchased in many of what were called "ten-cent stores," a bust of the Corsican might be found sitting beside one of Lincoln in the Art Center, and biographies of the Little Corporal were widely read. Allusions to Napoleon were so numerous as to have plain significance in any reading of American psychology: President McKinley was caricatured as having the height, dress, and aspirations of the first Emperor of the French; the opening paragraph of David Graham Phillips's *The Deluge* (1905) introduced that conqueror; the perusal of a book about Napoleon gave Jethro Bass in Winston Churchill's *Coniston* an authoritarian to emulate; in the *Atlantic Monthly* for June, 1903, Goldwin Smith blamed Bonaparte and his cult for a "recrudescence of militarism," for Caesarism, for dazzling examples of immoral success and renown; in 1912 Henry Adams wrote that he still saw Theodore Roosevelt as "a rather droll Napoleon." [2] And so on.

Some of this conditioning of the American public to an acceptance of imperialism had been effected by Rudyard Kipling, the idol of a host of young writers and readers in the nineties. His championing of the philosophy of the white man's burden had made him a target for anti-imperialists: Robert Buchanan called him the voice of the Hooligan, and Madame

2. *Letters of Henry Adams, 1892-1918* (ed. Worthington C. Ford), Boston, 1938, p. 603. All future references to Adams' letters will be to this volume.

Blanc, writing in the *Revue des Deux Mondes* for the first of April, 1900, vowed that he had had a bad influence upon English character. More heatedly, Charles Edward Russell declared in the *New York Journal* for 20 July, 1901:

> ... it came upon me as in a flash that this was the thing he had always meant and always apotheosized—the strong arm, the dominance of brute instincts, the coarse, hard fiber of mind, the gross and material view of life, and love of cruelty and savagery, the negation of sympathy and brotherhood, the right of might, the cynical indifference to justice, the burden of strong races upon the weak, the thirst for preying and plundering.

But literate Americans went on enjoying his stories, and pondering the nationalistic editorials in their newspapers, and noting that the respected and tolerant Dean of Canterbury, Frederic Farrar, had written in *The North American Review* for September, 1900, that war against evil was a Christian duty.

Moreover, some authoritative Americans had recently spoken up energetically for the use of our strength to extend our influence around the globe, among them the president, Senator Henry Cabot Lodge, the vice-president, and Senator Albert J. Beveridge. Lodge and Roosevelt had for years been frank imperialists and had rejoiced in the Spanish-American War, upon which the latter capitalized successfully. Speaking before the Hamilton Club in Chicago on the tenth of April, 1899, Roosevelt exhibited the manner and the ideology which he wished associated with himself, and after vehemently defending American and British expansion and eulogizing the soldier and the mother in near-Nietzschean fashion, went on to say, "Let us therefore boldly face the law of strife ... for it is only through hard and dangerous endeavor, that we shall ultimately win the goal of true national greatness." [3]

In January, 1900, his biography of Oliver Cromwell, a sign of the popularity of the Strong Man, began as a serial in *Scribner's Magazine*. As for Beveridge, he had proclaimed in a speech

---

3. Quoted in Theodore Roosevelt, *The Strenuous Life*, New York, 1900, pp. 20-21.

entitled "The March of the Flag," delivered in Indianapolis on the sixteenth of September, 1898, that the conflict we had just won was "the most holy war ever waged by one nation against another," and in another address, "For the Greater Republic, not Imperialism," given before the Union League in Philadelphia, 15 February, 1899, that God "has made us the lords of civilization that we may administer civilization." On the ninth of January, 1900, his plea for the retention of the Philippines was so stirring as to be rated for years among the best specimens of American oratory. Lesser authorities also helped lull the American conscience. Professor Washburn Hopkins of Yale University argued in *The Forum* for January, 1900, that a large nation's aggression against a small one might be of advantage to God and man; ex-Senator W. A. Peffer of Kansas conceded in *The North American Review* for August, 1900, that "The course of Americanism has been in the natural order, a little rough sometimes, it is true, but that, too, is the nature of things."

This naturalistic view of politics could not completely dispel a sense of misdoing; the contradiction between the morals taught to the average American householder and the practices of the nationalists of the western world was too apparent, too pervasive, and too exacerbating to be ignored. Any American who debated the matter found it difficult to reconcile the teachings of Friedrich Nietzsche and Jesus of Nazareth. Looking at the times from one angle, he was justified in believing that he was witnessing a world-wide reaction not only against Jeffersonian democracy but also against Christian ethics. The Boer War, the Philippine Pacification, the cruelties of the French in Madagascar, the torturings of Negroes in the Belgian Congo, the exaltation of the Blond Beast in terms of biological supremacy could hardly be filed under the workings of the Golden Rule, and to some sensitive observers it seemed that in 1900 western man was for the first time since the dawn of the Christian Era trying to live without God. The Deity, Nietzsche had written, died of his pity for the human race, and when the prophet of the Superman died on the twenty-fifth of August, 1900, his detractors derived a lesson from the shadowing of his last years.[4] Too much attention had been given this "dead lunatic," wrote H. M. Alden in the *New York Times* (20 October, 1900).

To set up a man [he continued] like Nietzsche as a philosopher... is as preposterous as is the devil-worship which is practiced in Paris by men who believe in neither God nor devil, but whose chief desire is vainly to try to shock the sense of decency which they once knew.

Yet no condemnation of one thinker could exorcise the guilt that settled down upon the West or banish the suspicion that churches were not assuming the moral leadership which the times needed.

An Anti-Imperialist Conference in Philadelphia during February of 1900 opposed McKinley's policy in the Philippines; Olive Schreiner temperately told magazine readers about the Boers; some influential papers like the *Philadelphia Times* assailed our Pacific enterprise as the "very worst phase of imperialism"; Dr. Charles Parkhurst of the New York Anti-Imperialist League condemned our actions in China as well as in the Philippines. William Jennings Bryan employed his matchless voice in denunciations of our expansion program; William Dean Howells, a pacifist by virtue of temperament and of the reading of Tolstoi, opposed it; James Lane Allen, not a pacifist, disapproved it on the grounds that the islanders of the Pacific had as much right to liberty as we had. The Reverend Charles Wagner, by publishing *The Simple Life* in 1901, offered an antidote to Roosevelt's *The Strenuous Life* of the preceding year, but in spite of its being syndicated by newspapers it made less impression. None of these objectors, however, equalled the spleen of Mark Twain when he derided the hypocrisies which did not cover the purposes of British

4. Some others dying in 1900: John Ruskin (20 Jan.), R. D. Blackmore (20 Jan.), H. D. Traill (21 Feb.), Richard Hovey (24 Feb.), Stephen Crane (5 June), Charles D. Warner (20 Oct.), Max Müller (28 Oct.), Arthur Sullivan (22 Nov.), Oscar Wilde (30 Nov.), Moses Coit Tyler (28 Dec.).

and American colonialism: "The Blessings-of-Civilization Trust, wisely and cautiously administered, is a Daisy. There is more money in it, more territory, more sovereignty, and other kinds of emolument, than there is in any other game that is played." [5]

Such mockery cut into the quick of consciences already aware of the paradox created by an ethic of compromise but the prevailing attitude here and abroad was to accept the "fling and swing" of the day as unavoidable and in the long run productive of good; to arraign public figures like David Lloyd-George and Bourke Cockran, who were pro-Boer; to stigmatize socialists, with their cry of "Workers of the World, Unite," as anarchists. Elbert Hubbard called in *The Independent* (27 June, 1900) for "The Church of Man," but a whispering campaign alleged that he was scarcely the person to take a high moral tone, and it was more comfortable to read Ralph Connor's tale of muscular Christianity, *The Man from Glengarry* (1901), or to believe with Thomas Hardy, as reported to William Archer (the April, 1900, *Critic*), that war was doomed and that one might intelligently if saturninely be a meliorist. Consolation could be gained, too, from Ernst Haeckel's *The Riddle of the Universe* (English translation 1900), which concluded that despite the struggle for power the love of others is as natural as love of self, and that though we had lost the concept of an anthropomorphic god, belief in freedom and immortality, goodness and truth and moral beauty remained as the religion of an educated man. To a small degree, at least, dissatisfaction with institutionalized Christianity—dissatisfaction with Christian principles has been rare in the United States—accounted for an interest in the occult, for the attention given to hypnotism and mesmerism and telepathy, for the reading of Jack London's "Planchette" (1900), for visits to the séances of Helen Smith and Leonora Piper, and for the respect given to Professor James Hyslop's adherence to spiritualism. Out of the same discontent came the appeal of

5. Mark Twain, "To the Person Sitting in Darkness," *The North American Review*, CLXXII, 165.

James Lane Allen's *The Reign of Law* (1900), which attacked
a fundamentalism that drove a would-be clergyman from his
church.

As the twentieth century got under way the American lover
of belles-lettres, informed though he was by newspapers,
magazines, and orators, could learn very little in his favorite
books of the contracting and explosive world in which he was
living. He could discover in the public prints that Charles
G. Fitzmorris had in 1900 gone around the world in sixty
days and that there was fighting in Colesburg and in Luzon,
but American essays, poems, plays, and fiction seemed almost
isolationist, thus departing from a tradition which from the
beginning had made them generously international in aims,
taste, and outlook. The essay was chiefly personal, even when
it dealt with nature: Agnes Repplier, John Burroughs, Stewart
Edward White, and John Muir were representative and popular in the type. Poetry had not recovered from the slump
which followed the War between the States; no one had succeeded to the place of Whitman; and readers fell back upon the
romantic masters and upon the English Victorians, especially
Tennyson. However, the most promising American poet,
William Vaughn Moody, was an exception to the evasiveness
of his fellows. His "The Quarry" was a protest against the
imperialistic spoilage of Asia, and "On a Soldier Fallen in the
Philippines" (*The Atlantic Monthly*, February, 1901) also
anti-imperialistic, accused the dead man's "darling land" of
stumbling and sinning in the dark.[6] Most ambitious in this
criticism was Moody's "An Ode in Time of Hesitation" (*The
Atlantic Monthly*, January, 1900), the final word in the title
alluding to the debate over the absorption of the Philippines.
The poet accepted the liberation of Cubans and Filipinos as
just, but shrinking from the "sounds of ignoble battle" that
came "sullenly over the Pacific seas" and reminding our leaders that the people might forgive blindness but would smite

6. "The Quarry" was first printed in Moody's *Gloucester Moors and
Other Poems*, Boston, 1901, pp. 22-23.

baseness, he exhorted them not to convert a righteous victory into a selfish gain. One of the best American poems on a topic of national urgency, the "Ode" is surcharged with idealism, is kindled by a controlled imagination, and is linked to a vocabulary and to verbal figures somewhat on the bookish side.

The entertainment world of music and mimicry in 1900 and 1901 was almost wholly enveloped in romanticism, with small intent to offer social criticism. *The Boston Transcript* alleged on the last day of January, 1900, that interest in opera was waning in New York City but did not add, as it might have done, that Leslie Stuart's tunes in "Floradora" drew audiences that might not have enjoyed the music dramas of Richard Wagner, the most popular in the current Metropolitan season.[7] It is possible that the vogue for the Ring operas had some relation to contemporary heroics, as Maurice Grau's production of operas in English had some connection with nationalistic feeling, but more likely music-lovers flocked to the opera house to hear the last American performances of Jean de Reszke.

Writing in the April issue of *The Criterion*, Charles H. Meltzer regretted that our theater was at a standstill, Clyde Fitch, Augustus Thomas, and Guy Carleton having made no advance upon the output of their predecessors. Fitch, with the brightest name in the theater then, received publicity in 1900 through the arrest of Olga Nethersole, leading lady in his translated "Sapho," on the charge of having performed in an indecent play. In 1901 his "The Climbers," with some tepid satire on New York society and centering upon the truism that all persons climb toward happiness, was really the drama of a weak man, with characters having so little inner life that they bring the play to the brink of farce, with flat comic speeches, and with a happy ending arrived at through a suicide, a feature which could not have pleased all who saw it. Thomas's "Arizona," still running in 1900, was highly thought

7. In Clyde Fitch's "The Climbers" Trotter boasted that he had seen "Floradora" thirty-six times.

of for its western speech, chivalry, and code, yet was fundamentally a run-of-the-mill melodrama carpentered to the
Broadway design.

Otherwise, and even though the dramas of Ibsen and
Maeterlinck were being briskly debated along with Hauptmann's "The Weavers," the American theater was almost
monopolized by plays based upon the favorite historical
novels, thereby provoking Howells to allude scornfully to
"the matinee school of fiction." The outstanding actors and
actresses of the period bent to the phenomenal fashion for
these romances; in 1900 and 1901 John Drew and Ida Conquest played in "Richard Carvel," Viola Allen in "In the
Palace of the King," Mary Mannering and Virginia Harned
in "Alice of Old Vincennes," Julia Marlowe in "When
Knighthood Was in Flower," Robert Lorraine in "To Have
and To Hold," Blanche Bates in "Under Two Flags," Richard
Mansfield in "Monsieur Beaucaire," Kyrle Bellew in "A
Gentleman of France," and E. H. Sothern in "If I Were King."
Besides these were associated productions: Otis Skinner appeared as Stevenson's introspective Prince Otto; Julia Marlowe
was seen in "Barbara Frietchie" and Henrietta Crosman in
"Mistress Nell"; "Ben-Hur" continued to pack theaters in
cities large and small, but "The Choir Invisible" failed on the
boards; two companies offered "Quo Vadis" in New York
City; and Mrs. Leslie Carter won admirers in "Du Barry."

This liberal use of historical novels highlighted the craze
for a kind of fiction which had nothing to say about the contemporary struggles for power and which threw little light
upon them. In the nineties the "realists" had won their place
in the sun and had by their detractions forced the historical
novel out of the hand of the first-rate author into that of the
merely skilfull one, but the debate over the worth of this kind
of fiction had not ended and the public went on buying hundreds of thousands of copies of costume narratives. In a sense
the historical novel was, although Woodrow Wilson had not
remarked its implications, a revolt against democracy, against
the routine and commonplaceness of everyday living in the

crowd, against standardization of houses and clothes and furnishings, against the tame and mediocre. Viewed with unnecessary seriousness it was a turning away from the mass-man and a search for the leader, the Superman. Howells, whose brand of realism had valiantly illustrated and supported democracy in being, was especially caustic in his comments upon the most popular school of narration:

When I see people reading the nine hundred and ninty-ninth thousand of the latest historical romance, my heart sinks; but I do not lose my faith that, when some great novelist divines how to report human nature as truly as such romances report it falsely, people will read him too in the nine hundred and ninety-ninth thousand.[8]

Writing in "The Easy Chair" of *Harper's* for April, 1901, his disapproval was more testily worded, but his deepest feeling, a combination of his dislike for romance and bloodletting and imperialism, emerged in an essay printed in 1900 in which he declared that "the accumulation of riches and the explosion of wars has brutalized the popular mind and spoiled the taste" and that the favored books rank below the writings of Scott, Manzoni, Hugo, Dumas, Thackeray, and Cooper.

I find duels and battles set forth as the great and prevalent human events; I find pride and revenge worshipped as right and fine, but no suggestion of the shame and heartache which have followed the doers of violence in all times and countries since the stone age. There is such spilth of blood that you might almost expect to see it drip from the printed page.[9]

Instead of reminding Howells that the story-tellers he preferred recounted their share of deeds of mayhem and slaughter the apologists for this kind of fiction, serene in their general approbation, almost ignored him, and they paid little if any attention to Sidney Reed's amusing short burlesque of the historical romance in *The Independent* (5 September), or to

8. In *The New York Evening Post*, 16 May, 1900.
9. "The New Historical Romances," *The North American Review*, CLXXI, 939-40.

Richard Burton's assertion in *The Criterion* for May of the same year that bad as the novels were the plays based upon them were worse. E. H. Sothern, indeed, had written exactly a year before in the same periodical that those plays were increasing culture among actors, and Charles Major, speaking up for the kind of tale he wrote, pointed out in *Scribner's Magazine* for June, 1900, that the historical novel relies upon genuine documentation, and somewhat later an editorial in *The Independent* took the position that this type of narrative was after all democratic. Furthermore, wrote Maurice Thompson in that magazine (9 August, 1900),

> ... the return to romance is simply a young, strong, virile genera-
> tion pushing aside a flabby one. The little war we had with Spain
> did not do so much for us; the thing was already done by our
> schools, churches, gymnasiums, outdoor sports. . . . We had almost
> lost in the stagnation of "realism" that prime element of a good
> story.

Robert Neilson Stephens, who understood that the book which supplies vicarious adventure and transports the reader to an age in which he fancies he might have been heroic and happy needs no humble excuse, prefaced his *Captain Ravenshaw* (1901) with a temperate denial that Howells had jurisdiction over the case of the contemporary novel and accused him of illiberality. "Herewith," he stated mildly, "is offered mere story, the sort of thing Mr. Howells cannot tolerate."

At the turn of the century the historical novel, not yet a Heptameron of boudoir exploits, had evolved an easily recognizable formula to which, however, there were numerous and good exceptions. For one thing, it had dash and gayety and innocence—things much out of favor a generation later— things that still make it refreshing reading for whoever can momentarily lay aside his sophistication. Robert Neilson Stephens' lengthy *Philip Winwood* (1900), a tale of our Revolution, had it is true a priggish husband whose wilfull wife ran off to England with another man, and Mary Johnston's *Audrey*, beginning as a serial in *The Atlantic Monthly* for May, 1901, moved somberly to its close, but usually this kind of novel sped high-heartedly through scenes of dancing and laughter, duelling and intrigue, courtship and hair-breadth escape, with the fate of a continent, perhaps, depending upon the flirt of a lady's fan or the note she concealed in her satin slipper. As a rule the historical personages took minor parts, but in Mary H. Catherwood's *Lazarre* (1901) the hero was the last Dauphin of France, and in Maurice Hewlett's *Richard Yea-and-Nay*, a best-seller in 1901, the British author after an acceptable analysis of the personality of England's lion-hearted king took unpardonable liberties with the facts of the Third Crusade.[10]

The heroine of the historical romance was invariably an idealized, fetching young lady but the fashion was also to have her capricious and headstrong to the point of being something of a madcap. An excellent example of this maiden is found in the Silver Heels of Robert W. Chambers' *Cardigan* (1901). Chambers had begun his literary career in the 1890's with short stories of a bizarre and original quality and with historical novels treating the time of the third Napoleon. Now, turning to New York state of the colonial and revolutionary periods, he wrote a series of historical romances of which *Cardigan* is first and best. Chambers knew the region near Johnstown intimately, for he was an outdoor man as well as a painter and writer; he did not deviate too far from the chronicles, though he made Walter Butler more satanic than the known facts warrant; he understood something of the language and the ways of the Iroquois, whom he made credible; he invented easily; he wielded a graceful, lively style; he captured what seems to be a fair approximation of the idiom of the century. Anyone compiling a list of the more readable American historical novels would do well to include

---

10. Alice Payne Hackett's *Fifty Years of Best Sellers, 1895-1945*, New York, 1945, consists largely of tables of annual selections and brief comments. For fuller historical and critical treatments see Frank Luther Mott, *Golden Multitudes*, New York, 1947, and James D. Hart, *The Popular Book: A History of America's Literary Taste*, New York, 1950.

Cardigan; to one kind of reader few episodes can give more satisfaction than the one, beginning with Chapter IX and the words "My first three weeks in the forest were weeks of heaven," in which Michael Cardigan sets out alone and afoot through the wilderness from upper New York to Fort Pitt. The whole book has the rare faculty of recreating a raw and stirring era together with the reds and whites who peopled it. Its one weakness is an unending sentimentality, for though writers of Chambers' generation had a license for sentiment now revoked he went too far under its protection, and in later years quite bogged down in the emotions of some of his magazine serials. Throughout *Cardigan* this fault manifests itself not only in the tenderness of phrasing but also in the plot management whereby Michael inherits a title and the haughty Felicity Warren is brought to low degree, to be rescued, of course, by marriage to the hero.

If the heroine of these novels was regularly bewitching of face and figure and whim, the hero *a la mode* was a young and manly gentleman, not likely to be much of a scholar but sure to be a swordsman best not crossed. The protagonist of Robert Neilson Stephens' *Captain Ravenshaw* (1901), however, is a mature swashbuckler who fights his way through the coils of Elizabethan London to win the hand of the spirited Millicent Etheridge, and the hero of the widely read *The Helmet of Navarre* (1901), Felix Broux, is an awkward stripling when he leaves home and gets caught in the whirlpool of events swirling about the efforts of Henry of Navarre, of the Catholic League, and of the Huguenots to gain control of Paris. This, the first of Bertha Runkle's books, was one of the novels said to keep reviewers and readers up all night, and the compliment is understandable for the tale races from one danger and escape to another, from one moment of suspense to a greater one. Possibly Miss Runkle had read Stanley J. Weyman with respect, for like the Englishman she showed a generous acquaintance with French history, she relegated the love element to the background, she used the point of view of a lad— all of which are reminders of *The House of the Wolf* (1890)

—and when it was time for the story to end she cast Henri Quatre in the rôle of a merciful *deus ex machina*, something which Weyman and his imitators had a habit of doing. But the American writer's romance does not pale even if it lives in a shadow.

The villain of Mary Johnston's *To Have and To Hold* (1901), properly named Lord Carnal, might serve as model for all rascals in the historical fiction of those days for he was Machiavellian, daring, and desirous of the heroine. The ingredients of this novel fall into such a mixture as to illustrate nicely what readers of the *genre* wished, which explains the huge sales of Miss Johnston's specimen. *To Have and To Hold*, once picked by William Lyon Phelps as a major contribution to the American historical romance, opens with the selling in colonial Jamestown of a shipload of women for wives and continues with the expected wrangles, perils, duels, and misunderstandings until a happy ending. Its lively characterizations, historical accuracy, and exciting story have given it a long life in the library; it also served for a screen play, though it failed on the legitimate stage.

The Jocelyn Leigh of *To Have and To Hold* turned out to be not a common wench but an English lady, and this use of the Cinderella *motif* exemplified one more device of the period piece in 1900 and 1901. Often there was such a difference in station between man and woman as to make a match between them seem impossible until the time when a title was inherited or an incognito lifted. In Booth Tarkington's sparkling *Monsieur Beaucaire* (1900), for one, the hero, a powerful French nobleman masquerading as a barber in Bath, was scorned by the proud Lady Mary Carlisle until the dénouement, when she had a proper comeuppance. This novelette has also continued to please, having been adapted to both photodrama and musical comedy.

Winston Churchill's *The Crisis* (1901), likewise still read, bowed to the Magnolia Tradition by giving its southern belle, living in St. Louis at the time of the War Between the States, two suitors, one an impulsive southerner, the other a steady

Yankee, and by having the war serve as a barrier to the course of true love. One of the best novels dealing with the struggle between North and South, *The Crisis* is memorable for its judicious handling of the issues involved, for the strategic placing of its main plot within a border state, and for its sympathetic portrait of Abraham Lincoln.

Francis Marion Crawford's *In the Palace of the King* (1900) was a romance of the time of Philip II of Spain; George W. Cable's *The Cavalier* (1901) was another novel of the War of 1861, and Sarah Orne Jewett's *The Tory Lover* (1901) laid its scene in the American Revolution; none of these rose to the level of their authors' better writing. Maurice Thompson, however, will be longest remembered for *Alice of Old Vincennes* (1900), dominated by the personality of George Rogers Clark.[11]

From this much abbreviated descriptive catalogue of historical novels published in 1900 and 1901 it is clear that a reader then could get but the meagerest insight into the international frictions which were to make the century fateful. Most oddly, he received his plainest inklings from an inane variation of the historical romance—the tale of the imaginary kingdom which kept presses turning out hundreds of thousands of copies of such books as Harold MacGrath's *The Puppet Crown* (1900) and George Barr McCutcheon's *Graustark* (1901), each a best-seller in its year. Anthony Hope's *The Prisoner of Zenda* and Richard Harding Davis's *The Princess Aline* had achieved the same distinction in 1894 and 1895 respectively, MacGrath had issued the threadbare *Arms and the Woman* in 1899 and John Oxenham the equally shabby *A Princess of Vascovy* in the same year, but it was McCutcheon's brisk story which established a vogue that lasted for nearly ten years and which gave a name to the species.[12] Arthur W. Marchmont contributed the duchy of

11. See Ernest E. Leisy, *The American Historical Novel*, Norman (Okla.), 1950, for a fuller discussion of these and other historical romances.

12. For an account of the origins, formulas, and social ramifications of Graustarkian fiction see Grant C. Knight, "The 'Pastry' Period in Literature," *The Saturday Review of Literature*, XXVII, 5-7, 22-25.

Saxe-Lippe to the atlases of fancy by publishing *For Love or Crown* in 1901 and Margaret Bryant did the same for a kingdom called Romanza in her *The Princess Cynthia* (1901), but neither of these approached in narrative skill or in popularity McCutcheon's recital of the deeds of Grenfall Lorry in the charming, turbulent Balkan principality of Graustark.

The causes of the liking for these fictional vagaries were several but essentially they provided a satisfaction in fantasy for the Will to Power, in as much as they permitted association with royalty and the winning of a comely princess by an American. Like the historical romance the Graustarkian variation evolved a formula, one which became so inescapable as to defeat itself in the end. Altenstein or Corconia or Frivonia or Rhaetia or whatnot would be situated in southeastern Europe; its ruler would be a beauteous princess about to be forced into a distasteful marriage with an unscrupulous rake; a venturesome American, appearing by chance, would save and wed the princess after at least one duel and many other vicissitudes, or perhaps, as in *The Puppet Crown*, he would meet a violent death. How seriously the readers of these narratives took them it is impossible to know, but it is reasonable to believe that they put them down with the feeling that the Balkans were the powder-keg of Europe; that Austria, Germany, and Russia were troublemakers whereas England and France were anxious to preserve the *status quo;* that the European gentleman was undersized, dissipated, and treacherous; that the American male was invincible; that we should have as little to do with European politics as expediency might allow. How far this feeling influenced American public opinion before and after 1914 no one can say, but millions of American readers must have realized more or less vaguely after taking a course in Graustarkian fiction that the balance of power across the Atlantic teetered uneasily. If they wished to learn more than that they must thumb the pages of newspapers and certain magazines.

World politics comprehended only one area of activity in which the Will to Power functioned energetically. The class struggle was another. For the harsh, world-wide, age-long contest between the haves and the have-nots went on with such intensity that no sane adult American in 1900 and 1901 could have been completely unaware of its rigors. He was still living in the day of the Robber Barons, in the era of John D. Rockefeller in oil, Henry Frick and Andrew Carnegie in steel, E. H. Harriman, Collis P. Huntington, and James J. Hill in railroads, of William A. Clark and Meyer and Daniel Guggenheim in smelting of silver and lead and copper, of J. P. Morgan in banking, of Henry Havemeyer in sugar and John Arbuckle in coffee, of the Armours in the packing industry, of executives of insurance companies who milked stockholders and policyholders alike, of the iron-willed masters of economic might who nodded to presidents, bought senators, looted treasuries, suborned juries, and mocked the ermine of the bench. It was the time that Charles Francis Adams, Jr., had foreseen in 1869, the time when the centralization of wealth, progressing inexorably in the evolution of the economic order, would produce a super-state controlled by the heads of great trusts.[13]

It was the era when too many men turned their backs upon the principles they had been taught in the *Eclectic Readers* of William Holmes McGuffey, the era of Thomas C. Platt, Chauncey M. Depew, Boies Penrose, Matthew S. Quay, Nelson W. Aldrich, Joseph W. Bailey, William McKinley, of a Tammany Hall and a Richard Croker so powerful that Gustavus Myers had trouble finding a publisher for a history of their doings in 1901. It was the era of Orison Swett Marden's uplift editorials in *Success* (founded 1897) and of Alois Swoboda's promises to build strong muscles for his correspondents. It was the era when matrons, living in a society of privilege, enjoyed exercising power over their servants. It was the era of the promised full dinner pail and of Hearst journalism. It was the era when many a laborer with an

13. See his classic contribution to journalism, "A Chapter of Erie," *The North American Review*, CIX, 30-106.

average daily wage of $1.25 condoned much of the shrewd dealing he heard about because he believed that he, too, might someday be rich and because he shared the American admiration for bigness. Naturally he and his wife enjoyed Alice Hegan Rice's *Mrs. Wiggs of the Cabbage Patch* (1901), whose lovable protagonist prayed for her children: "Make 'em thankful fer whatever they've got, even if it ain't but a little," and who whispered at the end of the novel: "Looks like ever'thing in the world comes out right, if we jes' wait long enough." [14] It was the era when the right and ability of the American people to rule themselves was being tested at every point, with results that were, as Woodrow Wilson affirmed, disquieting.

The current toward economic monopoly, of which the Adamses had given fair warning, had a partial sounding in March of 1901 in the Morgan announcement of the formation of the billion-dollar U.S. Steel Corporation, which in that year produced 66% of the steel manufactured in the United States. Encouraged by a favorable tariff and by the benign political philosophy of the president, trusts were growing to gigantic size, controlling the means of production and distribution, fixing prices and wages, and building such enormous private fortunes that even the *Journal of Commerce* of New York deplored the behavior of some of them. In 1899 the profits of Carnegie Steel were $21,000,000; in 1901 Mr. Carnegie revealed that his income would be about $15,000,000, or $28 a minute; and the *New York Herald* estimated in that year that there were 3,828 millionaires in the United States. But in 1900 the Salvation Army fed 40,000 Christmas dinners to the poor of New York City; mining troubles continued in that "hell on earth," the Coeur D'Alene; the number of lynchings increased from 115 in 1900 to 135 in 1901; coal miners making from $40 to $60 a month in Pennsylvania struck for higher pay; three thousand street car employees struck in St.

14. Gertrude Atherton is reported to have remarked that Mrs. Wiggs was the widow of David Harum.

Louis; and race riots, by-products of the battle for bread, occurred in New Orleans, New York City, and Akron.[15] In 1901 a Miss Nellie Auten, investigating sweatshops in Chicago, found only twelve Italian workers earning more than $300 a year, forty-three receiving less than a dollar a week.

The violent anarchistic reactions to a system creating wide disparities in earnings and obvious maladministrations in social justice had somewhat subsided by 1900, both abroad and in the United States, largely because of better times, partly because resistance to the course of unhampered exploitation took the milder forms of socialism, of governmental supervision and reform, and of unionism.[16] The first of these, appealing to many warm-thinking persons as well as to those whose pocketbooks were part of the dispute, mustered its greatest voting strength in this country between 1900 and World War I and put the name of Eugene V. Debs into American history; the second prompted Governor Theodore Roosevelt, with Jacob Riis at his elbow, to try to improve tenement conditions in New York City and led to an anti-trust conference in Chicago in February of 1900 with John P. Altgeld as one of the speakers; the third brought the names of John Mitchell and Samuel Gompers into American homes and made possible a fairly peaceable and steadily successful means of getting a larger share of what Woodrow Wilson later called "prize money" into the pay envelope. But beneath a comparatively calm surface in the prosperous years of 1900 and 1901 passions still ran high between the two classes, one

15. Theodore Roosevelt was strongly censured for having Booker T. Washington to dine with him at the White House in October of 1901.

16. However, King Humbert of Italy was assassinated 6 July, 1900; an attempt was made to kill the Shah of Persia in Paris, 2 Aug., 1900; the Prince of Wales was shot at in Brussels, 4 April, 1900; two attempts were made to kill Kaiser Wilhelm, one on 16 Nov., 1900, the other 6 March, 1901; on 26 March, 1901, a mine of explosives was discovered beneath the palace of the Czar. Tolstoi, writing of the submission and misery of the workers and the rapacity and cleverness of the rich ("The Root of the Evil," *The North American Review*, CLXXII, 481-503) blamed a "doctrine called Christianity." For this heresy he was excommunicated by the Russian Orthodox Church.

of which had too often subscribed to the motto that the public might be damned, the other often too violent in enforcing its demands for a greater social responsibility on the part of those with power and money. Both the surface and the deeps of society were being troubled into rapid change in the twentieth century. Chivalry, *noblesse oblige*, delicacy, privacy, Christian faith, and gentleness seemed to be disappearing into the maelstrom of the Industrial Revolution.

"If," Maurice Thompson wrote in *The Independent* for 17 May, 1900, "the map of the world and the atmosphere of civilization are changing radically, a corresponding change in art should not be surprising," and Cornelia Atwood Pratt in *The Critic* for July, 1901, envisaged the epic novel supplanting the novel of character. The theater, which must have disappointed Mr. Thompson, held to its old ways. American painting had taken on some of the vigor of the new day in the work of William Glackens, George Luks, and John Sloan, all of whom were using city streets and squares and their denizens for subjects, but on the whole it did not reflect the social changes Thompson had observed. Architecture had taken a lead in that respect, for the skyscraper was not only the child of necessity but also the sign of our strut before the world. William Vaughn Moody's "Gloucester Moors" (*Scribner's Magazine*, January, 1900) did state the apprehension of a sensitive, helpless onlooker as he noted the division of men into those who "sat gorged at mess" and those "cursing and sighing" from the "noisome hold," but this impeachment of *laissez-faire* ended in a question instead of an affirmation. And since no one could expect historical romances to treat the problems of the new century the question for this study is rightly, what were the realistic novelists, who had won their battle in the 1890's, doing to interpret the mood of a nation in which there was more and more of everything, in which giants and titans struggled for the mastery over each other and over the countless pygmies?

The answer is that much was being done, but chiefly by the younger realists, some of whom are now almost forgotten.

Mark Twain's disillusionment produced in 1900 the well-known *Man that Corrupted Hadleyburg*, whose thesis is that everyone has his price. Howells, sensible of the waning of his creative powers and perhaps feeling the weariness which age can bring to an idealist, occupied himself after 1900 principally with light comedies and reminiscences, writing only one good novel after that year.[17] Henry James's readers, decreasing in numbers as American chauvinism increased, might have bought in 1900 his *The Soft Side* (containing among other tales the subtle one called "Paste") and in 1901 *The Sacred Fount*. James, writing of the profits returned by intellectual and moral capital, was still the historian of the conscience of the upper middle class as his brother William was to be the philosopher of the middle class, but preoccupied as he was with good and evil, with virtue in the stoic sense, he showed so much repugnance for commonness as to lay himself open to the charge of being over-refined, of being too remote from his time and fellows. His growing complexities of style heightened this impression and alienated many of his would-be readers, so that if Americans wished to sample expatriate products in 1900 they were much more likely to take the repartee in Henry Harland's *The Cardinal's Snuff-Box* than to attempt "The Real Right Thing." In so doing they would likely feel, as a writer did in *The Independent* for 14 March, 1901, that James "kicks up too much literary dust for the size of his caravan."

Mary E. Wilkins, however, did try to face up to the changing civilization upon which Thompson had commented, and her *The Portion of Labor* (1901) was one of the better fictional studies of the New England factory town. It would have been still better if Miss Wilkins had had more conviction and less sentiment; like Elizabeth Gaskell, whose Christian socialist novels she may have read, she had pity for hunger and unemployed persons but saw only the surface of the class struggle as she saw only the outside of the mills, and she found herself distressed by the "turbulent spirits" of laborers not

17. *The Son of Royal Langbrith* (1904). It handles a personal, not a national, problem.

satisfied with the terms of their jobs. Not really qualified to write a labor novel, Miss Wilkins wisely wrote one about a working man's daughter, Ellen Brewster, who sacrificed a college education to support her family and her love for her employer's nephew because of pride. Ellen, like the author, believed that only money was capital and that its possession gave employers the right to set wages. Yet when those wages were reduced by ten per cent Ellen fomented a strike, only to lead the men back to work when starvation threatened the community. The riot which ensued so shocked both sides to the dispute that a compromise was reached, with happy results for all survivors. The moral of the story can be found in the reflection of Ellen's father on the last page: "...labor is... for the growth in character of the laborer." Such a conclusion cannot be said to guarantee that Miss Wilkins had conscientiously applied herself to either the social or the craft problems of her subject.

Sarah Orne Jewett, the other outstanding New England writer of fiction then, had turned to the historical romance. Hamlin Garland, memorialized by Mme. Blanc in the *Revue des Deux Mondes* for the first of January, 1900, as a "radical of the prairies," had abandoned his Main-Travelled Roads themes and become allied with a group of more romantic midwestern writers like Octave Thanet, William Allen White, and Booth Tarkington. Ambrose Bierce, settling down as a Hearst newspaperman, was practically finished as a writer of fiction. Harold Frederic was dead.

Stephen Crane, too, the prodigy and portent of the nineties, was dead before summer arrived in 1900, with H. G. Wells eulogizing him in August as "the first expression of the opening mind of a new period...beginning...with a record of impressions, a record of a vigor and intensity beyond all precedent." [18] But Crane, for all his brilliance and well-nigh pathological sincerity, was not equipped to explain the big new world to itself, and there is a cruel fitness in his dying at

18. This famous judgment is in Wells's "Stephen Crane, From an English Standpoint," *The North American Review*, CLXXI, 233-42.

twenty-eight. For he saw and pitied and grew angry at his America without understanding or trying to understand the huge forces which were transforming it; his reaction to the milieu was emotional and esthetic, never intellectual, and the rising cult of the Strong Man could have provoked only his scorn, with no wish to probe to its origins or to ponder its fictional potentialities. Crane's publications for 1900 support this opinion. His *Great Battles of the World* was a potboiler incited by his fame as author of *The Red Badge of Courage;* "The Great Boer Trek," printed in *The Cosmopolitan* for June, was obviously timely reporting; *Whilomville Stories,* a collection of matchless stories about children, revealed his retreat from adults to the young whom he loved; and *Wounds in the Rain,* concentrated upon the mysterious heroism of the little man in Cuba and containing the best stories and accounts of our invasion of the Pearl of the Antilles, produces an overall romantic impression.[19]

Of the elder realists, then, those who held aloft the standard of their cause in the *fin de siècle,* only Frank Norris was going to write of the newborn America and he was going to write of it with great pith, great gusto. But there were younger authors, some of whom tried to come to grips with the politics or the sociology or the whole spirit of their time. Gertrude Atherton's *Senator North* (1900) was too much a love story to have enough to say about Washington, but Ellen Glasgow's *The Voice of the People* (1901) told, with the edged undertones that aristocracy gives to a realist, how Nicholas Burr, son of the Virginia soil, "walked roughshod where his abilities led him" to the governor's chair, thereby dramatizing the rise of a new class to power in the Old Dominion. Upton Sinclair's *King Midas* (1901), another love story, was also a protest against "mercantility." Isaac K. Friedman, a Chicago student of politics and economics, published *Poor People* in 1900 and *By Bread Alone* in 1901, both of them heralds of the novel's bourgeoning interest in the city

19. I have discussed Crane's 1900 publications in *The Critical Period in American Literature,* Chapel Hill, 1951.

proletariat. The first announced immediately that "... the struggle [in tenements] is cruel, fierce, and terrible," but the author's endeavor to prove this staggered under an amateurish plot, too firmly controlled and given a narrative point of view quite unworkable, and under a sentimentality which rewarded an idealistic sister and punished a covetous one. Socialism was tepidly introduced by Adolph Vogel, the hero watch-maker, who married Ida Wilson and despite "inherited" alcoholism came to improbable success through the writing of a play with the same title as the book. Friedman's story had none of the heartbreaking simplicity of Dostoevski's novel of that title and deservedly won little attention. *By Bread Alone* showed improvement. Its hero, Blair Carhartt, resigned his pulpit to become a steelworker, preached socialism, led a strike vividly described, and lost his leadership when the strike failed. Edwin Lefèvre's eight anecdotes in *Wall Street Stories* (1901) created a mild sensation because of their literalness in showing how speculative fortunes were made and lost; two of them, "The Break in Turpentine" and "The Lost Opportunity," were almost manuals of instruction in how to play the market. Lefèvre's Napoleons of finance were not so inhuman as the public imagined them; some betrayed a sense of humor and now and then abode by sturdy principles or even philanthropic impulses.[20]

The name of Robert Herrick, which some critics were to adjudge the most promising in the field of the American novel through the early 1900's, was attached to two books in the years under consideration: *The Web of Life* (1900) and *The Real World* (1901). The first, a cheerless story laid against the Pullman strike in Chicago as background, was a solemn exploratory indictment of the American way of life; beyond that it was a doubting exploration of life itself, which, declared Dr. Sommers, "is based on getting something others haven't,—as much of it as you can and as fast as you can."

20. Characters identified in *Wall Street Stories:* Samuel Sharpe was James R. Keene; Col. Treadwell, Roswell O. Flower; John F. Greener, Jay Gould; Daniel Dittenhoeffer, Charles Woerischoeffer; Silas Shaw, Daniel Drew.

This indignant mouthpiece of Herrick's ideas rebuked wealth and class distinctions and marriages for money; he saw that most men were out for "plunder"; and in a pre-Arrowsmith gesture he left a prospering clinic because he could not subscribe to the creed of Success. Yet Herrick wished it understood that this act was idiosyncratic and solved nothing. "Most people," Sommers informed Louise Hitchcock, "are best off in the struggle for bread, but the few who see how—unsatisfying that end is, should be willing to work without profits." And washing his hands over the quest for teleological truth Herrick reflected at the end: "In striving restlessly to get plunder and power and joy, men wove the mysterious web of life for ends no human mind could know."

The story of *The Real World* is the timeless, engrossing one of the entrance of a young man into the world, and its excellent opening chapters have the poignancy of all truth-telling about human relationships. More exactly, it is the story of an idealist's search for the great illusion, the Blue Flower, which will take the sting from life and help him adjust himself to a society founded upon what Thorstein Veblen had called a protracted predatory culture. At first Jack Pemberton, under the tutoring of one of those ambitious, conscienceless women who were to become numerous in fiction as the century got under way, saw the world as Clyde Griffiths was going to see it. "Can you make money [Elsie Mason asked Jack], and make the little man buckle down to you, and the women give you what you want? That's what it is to be a man! ... a man who is a man wants to triumph, to fight with his fellows." And she remarked of a big westerner: "... power will out, and the power in our country lies with just such men." Further on, Isabelle Mather, Pemberton's good angel, exclaimed over a woodchopper: "I love to see power more than anything in the world! Force, force!" she repeated in rhythm to the axe. "Oh, for more power, like that!" Notwithstanding all this lust for strength, in which Jack had been well coached by both women, he rebelled at the crux of the plot when a group of eastern financiers schemed to reorganize a small western railroad so as to squeeze out its helpless stock-holders. The novel ultimately belongs, therefore, to the money-is-not-everything school, with rewards for the good and punishment for the evil, the rulings being based upon principles essentially Christian. The real world, the hero and Herrick concluded, is one of peace of mind created from the will to "character"; that is, from the will to preserve integrity by being just and strong and virtuous. Despite its typed per-sonae and a dimness in detailing business matters *The Real World* is a valiant novel, searching, four-square. It, too, found character.

David Graham Phillips's *The Great God Success*, published in 1901 under the pen name of John Graham, was held to-gether by two themes which the author was going to employ constantly and more expertly thereafter: the temptation of a young man to surrender ideals so that he may obtain money and fame, and the effects of the marriage relation upon hus-band and wife, especially if they are harnessed to the struggle for power. The protagonist, fresh from Yale, was a newspaper man who entered journalism with dreams that may properly be quoted because they have an autobiographical ring:

... journalism offered the most splendid of careers—the develop-ment of the mind and the character: the sharpening of faculties; the service of truth and right and human betterment, in daily combat with injustice and error and falsehood; the arousing and stimulating of the drowsy minds of the masses of mankind (p. 17)

and

How to avoid hysteria; how to set others on fire instead of only making of himself a fiery spectacle; how to be earnest, yet calm; how to be satirical yet sincere; how to be interesting, yet direct—these were his objects... (p. 89).

Unlike Phillips, Howard with sporadic misgivings became an apostate, gave up principles, gave up simplicity and probity, and ended a rich newspaper owner, an influential voice in the land, a devotee of the God Success, and a loveless and unloving man, his marriage having collapsed from a weight of superfluities and a weakness of substructure. Like Phillips, perhaps, Howard was a self-centered individualist, craving freedom more than anything else, cold and hard-driving where ambition was concerned. Only in the first third of the story wherein Howard was willing to be poor and to love Alice without marrying her is he an attractive person, and Phillips came close to saying that a liaison is preferable to marriage since the latter compels a man to join the procession that honors Mammon. To underline the already obvious morality the author manufactured a Dorian-Gray ending for his novel.[21]

None of the above books made so much of the essential mercilessness of the struggle for existence, the fierce exultation in brute strength, the thirst for power as did a collection of nine short stories published on the seventh of April, 1900. Jack London's career, as hard and as exciting as that of any American writer, had taken him to the frozen north where he found not only many stories but also corroboration for his belief, derived from his reading of Herbert Spencer as well as from his own adventures, that only the physically fit can meet the test of living. *The Son of the Wolf* shouted forth this conviction in its infatuation with the strength and endurance and "blood" which spell supremacy when man strives with nature and man. The title was an appropriate label for this conviction, for the Son of the Wolf was the white man, superior to the Indian and the Eskimo in cunning, cruelty, greed, and stamina, and therefore justified in robbing the native of his women and his riches. In four of the stories we meet the Malemute Kid, who was "capable of felling an ox at a blow," who traveled twenty or more sleeps on the Long Trail and was therefore a "man whom the gods may envy," and who played his hand in "the hoary game of natural selection." In "The White Silence" the Kid shoots the slowly dying Mason so that he himself and Ruth may have their chance to live; in

21. Phillips is said to have had Joseph Pulitzer in mind while writing *The Great God Success*.

"The Men of Forty-Mile" he prevents a duel by threatening to hang the survivor; in "To the Man on Trail" he helps Jack Westondale escape the Mounted Police on Christmas Eve; in "The Wife of a King" he employs a shrewd stratagem to reunite a white man and his Indian wife. The *mise en scène* for the deeds of this Strong Man could hardly be better: a land of perpetual snow and ice and long periods of darkness, of intolerable loneliness, of little food; a land where human beings and dogs eat each other when starvation removes fear; a land where the law makes itself felt only at long intervals and where men must drink and fight and make love or go mad with boredom. Here the white man sloughs off inhibitions: Scruff Mackenzie in "The Son of the Wolf" battles the Bear with knives for a chief's daughter, Carter Weatherbee and Percy Cuthfert learn to hate because they have to spend a winter together in a cabin. Here, too, Sitka Charley in "The Wisdom of the Trail" kills a fellow Indian who violates the law of all for one, one for all, and Naas in "An Odyssey of the North" leaves for a world-wide journey to track down Axel Gunderson, the blond giant who stole his wife. In these and many stories that were to follow, London, rousing atavistic impulses dormant in civilized readers, was a primitive bard, a scald who sang of valorous men who fight and kill and surmount hunger and pain. With sentences and pictures often as crisp and relentless as the air his characters breathed he transported the homedweller from an armchair to a forlorn region where he could plow through waist-deep snow, woo a dusky sweetheart, strangle a wolf, trade cuff for cuff. The popularity London earned with this kind of tale has waned but little; in 1949 UNESCO reported that he was the most-translated American author even in Russia and other Iron Curtain countries.[22]

The young Jack London had been thrall to the ideal of physical prowess; the maturing London learned that brain

22. According to an item in *Time*, LVIII, 84. American authors who followed London were in sequence Cooper, Upton Sinclair, Mark Twain, Erle Stanley Gardner.

rather than muscle fitted modern man to survive, and in his almost superhuman striving to lift himself from poverty he had read not only Nietzsche and Darwin and Spencer but also Karl Marx. Thereafter he began to write and speak in behalf of socialism. His "What Communities Lose by the Competitive System," printed in *The Cosmopolitan* for November of 1900, argued that there was loss in farming, in trade, in natural and commercial selection, in esthetic values because of this system; his "The Minions of Midas" (*Pearson's Magazine*, May, 1901) was a story about a band of intellectual proletarians who determined to meet force with force, to fight capitalists who crushed "wage slaves" into the dirt and caused strikers to be "shot down like dogs." Their method was a gruelling kind of blackmail which led to two suicides but was otherwise inconclusive. "The Impossibility of War" (*Overland Monthly*, March, 1900) contended that modern war was so deadly, so expensive, with famine and revolution as threats no matter what the end, that it had become unthinkable, and "The Dignity of Dollars" in the same magazine for July, 1900, stigmatized moneyed men of leisure as vampires and bloodsuckers whose "very existence is a sacrilege and a blasphemy." But London's attitude toward the underdog was to remain equivocal to the end of his career. In spite of a misty gospel of brotherhood he was always to see life in terms of force. Not the force that Henry Adams was studying, but human force, so that he could not, any more than Frank Norris or Robert Herrick or most other writers of that generation divest himself of a deep-lying esteem for the man of brawn and implacable will. It is a quandary in which many a leftist has floundered.

There can be no question of the strength of Ward Bennett, hero of Frank Norris's *A Man's Woman* (1900); he beats the heroine's horse to death with a hammer, he lets his dog kill and eat a farmer's dog, he leads an Arctic expedition with almost maniacal resolution in the enviable first chapters of the novel, and he wages a contest of wills with the heroine in which no quarter is given on either side. Norris's description of him deserves quotation:

> ... the rugged, unhandsome face; the massive jaw, huge almost to deformity; the great, brutal, indomitable lips; the square-cut chin with its forward, aggressive look; the narrow forehead, seamed and contracted, and the twinkling, keen eyes so marred by the cast, so heavily endowed by the shaggy eyebrows. When he spoke the voice came heavy and vibrant from the great chest, a harsh, deep bass, a voice in which to command men, not a voice in which to talk to women.[23]

This account of a gentleman who would have existed uncomfortably in a novel by Howells or James must not betray the reader into believing that *A Man's Woman* is, as it has been alleged to be, a thriller. The internal evidence is that Norris meant it to be a serious commentary upon contemporary relations between the sexes, an undertaking for which he was not equipped. The bulk of the book is given over to a crucial combat, with personal and professional angles, which shall decide whether before marriage man or woman will be supreme. When Lloyd Searight eventually subordinated possessive love and sent her husband back to the Arctic because a man must do a man's work Norris proclaims his Nietzschean conclusion about the issue: in a healthy culture man is the warrior, woman the homemaker and nurse.[24]

In *The Boston Transcript* for 13 November, 1901, Norris wrote that men were better novelists than women because of superior physical strength, a contention that must have irritated many of the sex that Charles Dana Gibson was drawing in *Life* with firm chins, too, with tennis rackets, with a clear eye for the main chance, and with talent in the management

23. *The Complete Works of Frank Norris*, Garden City (N.Y.), 1928, VI, 85.

24. "The struggle for sex supremacy had a thrill for one who was so consciously, unwaveringly master in his own house," wrote Juliet Wilbor Tompkins in the Preface to Vol. IX of *The Complete Works of Frank Norris*.

of males. The American woman was changing rapidly with the changing times. Under her own power she was rounding Cape Turk. Blanche Sterling in Fitch's "The Climbers" said to her husband, "Doll wives are out of fashion," and the new fashion in the spinster was also a bit startling to the conservative. She went outdoors now, and she trained for a career, and she sat side by side with man in his office or at the ball park. Young or old she was proud of the agitation of Elizabeth Cady Stanton and Lucretia Mott and Susan B. Anthony, and she debated her right to vote. Sometimes she read Ellen Key. In the person of Carry Nation she thought to destroy the saloon with a hatchet, but it was remarked that the tensions of modern living increased her consumption of liquor. Possibly the death of Queen Victoria on the twenty-second of January, 1901, removed some of the burden of the old propriety.[25] Certainly the turmoil of the decade, the accent upon the Will to Power invited women to a self-assertion that gave our novelists, especially the western ones, a new subject and a new heroine: the progress of love after marriage, and the *belle dame sans merci* who is voracious and climbing. Robert Grant, not a westerner, used both subject and *femme fatale* in *Unleavened Bread* (1900), casting Selma Wright as an unscrupulous, ignorant, "refined" social climber who married and ruined first a manufacturer, then an architect, and finally a lawyer whom she egged on to dishonesty that he might become a United States senator. Although the time of the story was the 1870's the application was immediate and so understood.

Uncovering the roots of the American woman's discontent is a task that may be left to the psychologist. It is a task that Theodore Dreiser had no intention of assuming in *Sister Carrie* (1900), yet that novel has more to say about the friction of the female personality upon that of the male, and

25. Some others who died in 1901: Ignatius Donnelly (1 Jan.), Giuseppe Verdi (27 Jan.), Benjamin Harrison (13 March), Charlotte M. Yonge (24 March), Walter Besant (9 June), Robert Buchanan (10 June), John Fiske (4 July), William McKinley (14 Sept.), William E. Channing (23 Dec.).

Dreiser is more important as a psychological novelist, than American criticism has yet conceded. *Sister Carrie* did, as all commentators reiterate, owe much to Zola in its adoption of an amoral point of view and in its recital of the degeneration of Hurstwood, but it would seem to owe even more to Thomas Hardy and Arthur Schopenhauer in its use of the blind striving of the will, of the fascination which the female exercises almost unwittingly over the bemused male. This is not to say that *Sister Carrie* is a literary novel or a novel of ideas. It is a novel that unfolded from Dreiser's moods and observations, from the experience of one of his sisters, from tramps he had seen on New York streets, and from many pictures he had stored in a retentive memory. It was meant to be and it is an honest Breughel-like but humorless panorama of American life.

All the world knows that Frank Norris read the manuscript of this novel at his cabin on Greenwood Lake, that he recommended its publication by Doubleday, and that someone behind the scenes—Dreiser thought it was the wife of the publisher—took steps to have it suppressed. Before copies of the book were stored away in the cellar of Doubleday's Norris had sent out some hundred to reviewers, and the word went about that *Sister Carrie* was sufficiently wicked; Howells snubbed the author on the sidewalk. Dreiser, who had centered his hopes in publication, was so upset by the suppression that he ceased work on the projected *The Rake*, and although he continued to write on *Jennie Gerhardt* he suffered a nervous breakdown and a paralysis of confidence, so that the latter did not appear until 1911.

In view of the importance of *Sister Carrie* it may be ungrateful to find fault with it. Yet no respect for the book can conceal its awkwardness in plot rhythm, its inferiority in taste and style, often on a level with those of a contemporary confession magazine. As rhetoric the novel is a failure. Its importance lies in the thing which made it shocking in 1900—the rejection of an opportunity for a moral directive, and the uncompromising treatment of its material. For it introduced a pretty woman who twice stooped to folly and did so almost casually and without punishment, a salesman who entered almost as casually into a liaison and also went unpunished, a stronger man who went down to beggary and death, and a part of the American scene appallingly imbued with materialism and impoverished in culture. Only the last of these things shocks a reader today. A half century ago, however, *Sister Carrie* was a kind of Kinsey report upon middle class morals, and the middle class was naturally scandalized.

Now heroines in American fiction from Charlotte Temple on had occasionally lost their virtue and been pitied if not forgiven. But Carrie Meeber was not the victim of an extenuating grand passion. Her loss of innocence was motivated by a longing to improve her lot and by animal provocation. It was almost pure will in Schopenhauer's meaning. To her a man was attractive if he wore good clothes and had smooth manners, spent money, and were not repulsive in appearance —an unromantic attitude toward love in 1900. More reprehensible was Carrie's profiting from her sins, and the fact that it was the man who, possessing a hunger for beauty, came thereby to moral disintegration and suicide while the woman remained unscathed.

Sister Carrie was not, it should be remembered, the first full-bodied naturalistic novel in our literature; the priority goes to Norris's *McTeague* (1899). But critics who followed the leadership of H. L. Mencken in the 1920's made so much of Dreiser as a symbol of revolt against gentility and the American way of life and of *Sister Carrie* as a courageous denial of the Victorian compromise that in the acclaim Norris's work was pushed into the background. *Sister Carrie* is praiseworthy because of its truth-telling about natural morality in clash with social morality. It is more praiseworthy because it holds abundantly a quality rare in American fiction—compassion, and this in spite of the unlovely set of characters that people it. Carrie Meeber is commonplace, inert, soft-hearted, amoral in her acceptance of comfort; she is unconventional yet quite colorless. Drouet is superficial, given thoughtlessly to the enjoyment of the moment. Hurstwood, seeking something of loveliness, is willing to rob his friend of a woman and his employer of money. Yet over them all Dreiser throws the mantle of his understanding and his pity, and Carrie's will to live becomes unintentionally the will to power and the novel becomes darkly but accidentally metaphysical. Not that Dreiser's determinism is accented in this story; it is brought out explicitly only in an allusion in the eighth chapter to a tiger's irresponsibility among "the forces of life." Rather that his representation of his creatures as groping for something in a moral twilight, as succumbing to "variability" because they cannot balance instinct with ideal, because they have not evolved far enough to have left the brute behind, is enriched by a fellow-feeling that is a triumph of the creative act. The moral sense in all three, he lets us realize, was blunted by their natural and social breeding, and for the moment we agree. Yet at this point Dreiser's commiseration outran his reasoning and he fell into a confusion of thought which permitted him to judge society as a whole by conventional standards while exculpating individuals on temperamental grounds. This is to forget that individuals, even when victimized, make up society and should be held responsible for what they make. Setting pity and self-pity upon a monument can only delay that social progress which Dreiser in 1900 hopefully envisioned.

One indispensable instrument in the struggle for power, the machine, was in 1900 and 1901 almost overlooked by American story-tellers and poets. The magazines here and abroad, especially the scientific ones, did report upon the inventions which had to do with the conquest of distance and might have to do with the defeat of man. Some examples of this reporting threw far-reaching shadows: M. L. Azoulay in the *Revue Scientifique* (9 June, 1900) predicted that the phonograph would work a revolution in all fields of human accomplishment; the *Scientific American* (11 August, 1900) described the trial of a "huge" Zeppelin in Germany; in the *London Graphic* (4 August, 1900) H. W. Wilson found that

France was leading in submarine construction; the first motor advertisements in *The Saturday Evening Post* appeared in 1900, the year in which 4,192 cars were manufactured in the United States; M. S. Geffrey in *La Science Illustrée* (11 May, 1901) told of a portable boat to be used by cavalry. On the nineteenth of November, 1901, Alberto Santos-Dumont won a $20,000 prize by circling the Eiffel Tower in a dirigible, and on the fourteenth of the following month Guglielmo Marconi announced that he had received a wireless message across the Atlantic. These machines were going to bring fuller life and quicker death to thousands of Americans, but creative writers for the time almost passed them by, William Vaughn Moody being exceptional by predicting in "The Brute" (*Atlantic Monthly*, January, 1901) that the machine, a beast of "iron hoof" bestowing "cynic favors" upon a few and taking joy from the humble, would in the future be man's slave, helping him erect a great civilization, leading the "tyrant weather," and receiving in the end a blessing from God.

Most inexplicable was the failure to write much about the locomotive, for the railroad has been of such importance in the economic history of the United States, has from the childhood of most Americans been associated with so much of glamor and play and ambition, that its neglect by romancers and realists alike has been one of the mysteries of American literature. It has, of course, been celebrated in songs and ballads, one of the most famous of the latter having been composed after John Luther (Casey) Jones on 30 April, 1900, drove an Illinois Central locomotive into a freight train. And at the turn of the century two minor writers of fiction, both experienced in railroading, were turning out stories about their past occupation. Cy Warman, who had been publishing since 1895, issued *Short Rails*, a collection of short stories often anecdotal in form, in 1900, and Frank H. Spearman published a novel, *The Nerve of Foley*, in 1900 and a book of tales, *Held for Orders*, in 1901. Both writers suffered from pedestrian style and sentimental approach but they deserve to be remembered as pioneers in a type and as capable historians and authors of non-fiction about railroads.

Better reading is found in the novels of a team composed of Samuel Merwin and Henry K. Webster, who collaborated upon *The Short Line War* (1899), which recounts a struggle for the control of a western railroad, and the more widely read *Calumet "K"* (1901). The latter, a panegyric on energy and the drive to success, is not strictly a railroad story for it revolves about the forced building of a grain elevator because of the attempt of a "Clique" to corner wheat, but the effort of the C. and S.C.R.R. to balk the undertaking makes up a dramatic part of the plot. The hero, Charlie Brannon, is worth noting: he said "ain't" and "damn" and "he don't" with equal readiness, but he worked sixteen hours on Christmas, eating only two sandwiches he had stowed in his pockets, he refused to accept a holiday even to go on his honeymoon, and he took a condescending attitude toward laborers and a truculent one toward unions. Better reading, too, is Vaughan Kester's *The Manager of the B. & A.* (1901), with railroad management, local politics, love, and a forest fire as framework.

"I never saw a farmer yet that wouldn't grab a chance to get even with a railroad," declared the hero of *Calumet "K"*, and the greatest railroad novel in American literature grew out of the hatred of farmers for a railroad.

It is possible that the ecstatic vision of Presley in the ingeniously constructed first chapter of *The Octopus* (1901) is autobiographical, for Frank Norris, who as a young man had written *Yvernelle*, must have warmed to the romance, especially to the feudal undertones, in California history, scenery, and living. California was a land of mingled cultures, where the memory of Spanish chivalry, liberality, and religious faith was still green, quickened by the presence of old Missions, of haciendas, of tales of the Conquistadores. It was a land of physical contrasts, of ocean, mountain, and hot valley, of ranch and harbor, of miles of flowers and of oblique cypress trees that had reminded Stevenson of ghosts fleeing before the wind, a land of fertility and barrenness. It was the fertility that awed Norris, the epical heave and swell and nourishment of the good earth that might easily be deified and worshiped, the earth that symbolized the force which seemed to be responsible for all being, the creative energy at the thought of which every nerve of Presley thrilled. Presley would indite the epic of this land, and there can be little doubt that Norris's desire was also to do just that, only to celebrate in the rites of prose the union of man with Dea whereby the human being joins his brawn and intelligence to the vital principle in the soil and produces life if granted sun and water.

Like the land itself, *The Octopus* is a sum of contradictions, added, one realizes upon careful reading, with much skill. The Spanish and American, the old and new, the romantic and realistic constantly interpenetrate the two chief plots with an effect that is at once, because of the use of sound and of organic structure and of incident, symphonic and epical, for Norris had an ear for words and long lyric lines, a fondness for themes repeated and built upon, and an admiration for the heroic. The Spanish theme is found in the place names, in allusions to the past grandeur of De La Cuesta, in the ruined Mission of San Juan, in the humane and wise Father Sarria. The old and the new confront Spanish with American ways, the Jeffersonian simplicity of an earlier American society with the ruthlessness and duplicity fostered by industrialism, the integrity of Magnus Derrick with the trickiness of his eldest son, the primitiveness of the shepherd Vanamee with the agricultural methods of Annixter, the dreamlike Angèle Varian with the robust Hilma Tree. And the romantic and realistic impulses in Norris's art play over this thematic material with shifting beauty. Vanamee, brooding and mystical, coming and going like the wind, possessing extra-sensory impressions and the telepathic power to summon others from a distance; Angèle, upon whom the author expends some of his most extravagant writing; the transformation of Annixter's character under the influence of love; settings of unsurpassed color

and perfume; the stand of the embattled farmers against the
Octopus; descriptive passages marked by a profusion of poetic
images—all these contribute to *The Octopus* those patches of
romance which Norris believed were indispensable to the true
representation of life. On the other hand realism is everywhere
mingled with this material: in the accounts of farming, in the
characterizations of most of the persons, some of whom Norris
must have known, in the use of history.

In a statement which Norris would have liked, *The
Octopus* has everything, and one can believe that brought to
the screen in technicolor it would make a superior movie. It
conjures up the spell of desert and of paradisiac seed ranch;
it has a pitched battle in which heroes die; it pictures a hair-
raising race between locomotives driven respectively by an
outlaw and by an agent of the law; it introduces a poet seeking
the soul of California, honorable men who descend to political
chicanery, immigrants wantonly impoverished by the railroad,
a corporation tyrant, a lovable priest, drunkards, gamblers, a
bad man intending to shoot up a barn dance, and one of the
unforgettable lovers in literature.

The two main plots intertwine at many points and are never
separate for long. Within the story of the love of Vanamee
for Angèle Varian Norris exercised an exuberant diction that
reminds one of the characteristic writing of Thomas Wolfe,
without, however, the mood of self-pity which the later novelist permitted himself. Norris's excess is that of a man confident
of an abundant talent aiming to present nature in such a pas-
toral manner as to heighten the mysticism which gives
meaning and weight to the whole book. Angèle and Vanamee
are constituents of this aspect of nature; their love is an un-
dying, haunting thing, "one of those legendary passions,"
Norris wrote, "that sometimes occur, idyllic, untouched by
civilization, spontaneous as the growth of trees, natural as
dew-fall, strong as the firm-seated mountains." To naturalize
the unearthly in this story Norris allots for the lovers a superb
setting of a unique and beautiful stretch of five hundred acres
of roses, violets, lilies, tulips, iris, carnations, tuberoses, pop-

pies, heliotrope—acres royal with vermilion, azure, yellow, and immensely fragrant. The flowers, to be sure, are more than setting for a romance. They are symbols of immortality in their death and re-birth; they give of their aroma and tints to the loveliness of the girl who lives among them; and they offer a promise that a terrible crime may eventually be covered by beauty that has little to do with resignation. Norris wrote the passages of floral description with joy, repeating them over and over with disregard for rhetorician's precepts, giving a fugue-like development to one of the movements of his prose symphony.

The story of Angèle and Vanamee has an isolation that is no part of the plot organization but is a thing of feeling and imagination, for it seems to be staged in a haunted glen and to move to the accompaniment of a hush apart from the passions of the San Joaquin Valley. The story has at once mysticism and mystery—mysticism in the agony of Vanamee's search for assurance that his beloved is not dead, mystery in the un-solved question as to who the Other was. This is the only such mystery in Norris's fiction, and he treated it so lightly as to suggest that it did not much interest him. He was concerned with the episode as contrast and as consolation: the rape occurs in a garden of tranquil beauty, and the dead girl re-appears later, a modern Proserpine, to teach Vanamee that nothing dies. Love produces life, the earth produces life, and love and earth are equated as forces that overcome death. Evil also can produce life as well as death, and so Angèle dies that a daughter may be born and farmers are killed in order that their cause may be lifted high.

As Norris writes of the far stretch of the wheat near the flowers his language becomes orgiastic, for as the flowers sym-bolize beauty and love and immortality, so does the grain. It is significant that on the same night of vigil Vanamee sees the sleep-walking younger Angèle whom his strange power has called to him, and Annixter discovers that his desire for Hilma is more than animal. Flower and wheat are made to grow side by side as Norris composes a new kind of Earth-song, with the would-be owners of love and land brought to grief.

In his rhapsodies about the fecund earth, about the force of the wheat for good and evil, about the almost sexual embrace of soil and plow, Norris introduces a major and dionysiac strain into his work, thematically repeated again and again. Thereby he develops the second principal plot, that of the struggle between the railroad, which his animism transforms into an octopus, and the sturdy but not always honest ranchers like Annixter and the Derricks. This, the larger, the more realistic, the epical part of the novel had its origin in an actual battle between the Southern Pacific Railroad and some of the settlers in the San Joaquin Valley. The railroad officials, who had agreed that they would sell lands granted along the right of way for $2.50 an acre later raised that figure to as much as $30 an acre, defending their change of mind with an argument that unintentionally supported one of Henry George's theses relative to the wrongs of landlordism. The enraged farmers formed leagues in their defense and took their case to the Federal Courts and to the Department of the Interior. When they lost their appeals and the S.P. began to dispossess them, the settlers of Mussel Slough arranged for an assembly of protest in a barbecue at Hanford on the eleventh of May, 1880. On the same day a U.S. marshal, his deputies, and a supposed agent of the railroad arrived to oust the farmers from their homes, and in the subsequent shooting five farmers and two officers were killed. Seventeen farmers went to prison, and the Southern Pacific won its fight. This affair supplied Norris with the climax of *The Octopus*, closely correlated with the tale of the resistance of the ex-engineer Dyke, probably suggested by the remarkable exploits of Christopher Evans, an alleged train-robber.[26]

In spite of—indeed, often because of—its repetitious de-

26. Not all histories of California or of western railroads mention the Mussel Slough skirmish. The above condensation is based upon Stewart H. Holbrook, *The Story of American Railroads*, New York, 1947, which also relates the adventures of Chris Evans, pp. 376-84.

scriptive passages, unrestrained vocabulary, headlong youth-fulness, and *tempo rubato*, *The Octopus* is Norris's supreme literary achievement. Up to the time of Presley's first leaving Los Muertos for San Francisco it is, if not the Great American Novel longed for at the opening of the century, then the closest thing to it written by Norris's generation; beside it *Sister Carrie* is lame in style, defeatist in effect, non-typical in incident, and haggard with sex. The art of *The Octopus* is marred, it is true, by Norris's confusion in dealing with sensual and supersensual forces. It is right that the wheat should be both beneficent and destructive, should bring prosperity to a section of California, should nourish man round the world, should at the same time bring retribution to S. Behrman and loss and death to the men who had worshiped it reverently and been slaughtered much as Vanamee's sheep were torn by the wheels of a freight train. But like so many Americans of his day, Norris admired the Strong Man, admired power for its own sake and no matter how it was employed. He felt that he must condemn a giant's strength when used in a giant's way, and he made the railroad the villain of the novel, yet near the end he puts into the mouth of Shelgrim, modelled upon Collis P. Huntington, an apologia for the Will to Power whose logic a child could demolish. For instead of accepting tycoons and their schemes and deeds as inevitable and possibly good phenomena in the economic evolution of the nation Norris relapsed into his mythopoeic mood and at that page thought of the railroad as having independent existence apart from the machinations of executives and the toil of laborers. In *Chapters in Erie and Other Essays* (1871) Charles Francis Adams, Jr., no mystic, had written of railroad empire-building as "a great, quiet natural force," and whether or not Norris had seen this opinion he toyed with the same idea. Shelgrim's defense is on a par with the judicial decision that a corporation, having no soul, cannot be sued. It was as though Norris were saying that dishonesty and cruelty are not words for human attributes but are realities that somehow get into steel and coal and iron and wood and produce wickedness. It was for this reason, as critics of Norris have shown, that Norris was willing to forgive Magnus Derrick for conniving at bribery; the unhappy old man, the author would have us believe, bowed before a disembodied force stronger than his will.

After Presley goes to San Francisco *The Octopus* falters, not only in the chopping of the story into unexpected fragments but also in the amateurish contrasts between dinner among the rich and the starving of Mrs. Hooven and the descent of the pretty Minna. Here Norris found himself caught in an artistic trap, sprung by his indecisive morality. Indubitably his sympathies were with the beaten ranchers, and Presley's denunciation of the "task-masters" is memorable because it articulates part of the novelist's feeling about the United States in 1900:

"We know them for what they are—ruffians in politics, ruffians in finance, ruffians in law, ruffians in trade, bribers, swindlers, and tricksters.... They swindle a nation of a hundred million and call it Financeering; they levy a blackmail and call it Commerce; they corrupt a legislature and call it Politics; they bribe a judge and call it Law; they hire blacklegs to carry out their plans and call it Organization; they prostitute the honor of a State and call it Competition." [27]

Yet at bottom it was the romance of battle that had appealed to Norris, the epical battle between foredoomed men and a monster, not the larger issue of social justice for all. He had little of the crusading zeal of David Graham Phillips or Upton Sinclair, and his theme is unlike that of *The Grapes of Wrath*, for Norris, impatient of the poor, was far from being a proletarian writer, and it is indicative that in his eloquent closing paragraphs it is the Wheat that remains unassailable, and that although he saw to it that good came out of evil in the Vanamee episode, no good compensated the ranch folk who were dispossessed, killed, and driven to hunger and prostitution.

27. *The Complete Works of Frank Norris*, Garden City (N.Y.), 1928, II, 261.

Norris told Howells that "The story of the Wheat was for him the allegory of the industrial and financial America which is the real America," and most contemporary reviewers while they objected to Zola's influence were quick to seize upon the allegorical intent.[28] Representative of those reviewers was Frederic Taber Cooper, who, with a flourish that mirrored some of Norris's zest, commented upon

... the spirit of the nation, typified in the wheat, unchanged, indomitable, rising, spreading, gathering force, rolling in a great golden wave from West to East, across the continent, across the ocean, and carrying with it health and hope and sustenance to other nations—emblem of the progressive, indomitable spirit of the American people.[29]

With so much said to and about the American people, *The Octopus* has nevertheless not been one of the popular novels. Nor is it an artistic masterpiece. But it has the abundance, the passion, the truth, the excitement, the breadth and depth of view, and the use of the heroic principle that make it a great novel, which is something artistic masterpieces rarely are.

As though to corroborate Frank Norris's testimony concerning the violence of the forces let loose in this country an anarchist shot the President of the United States in the Temple of Music at the Pan-American Exposition in Buffalo on the sixth of September, 1901, and when William McKinley died eight days later an angry populace cried out against tolerated radicalism and blamed Emma Goldman and Johann Most, even William Randolph Hearst, for the crime, since for years the last had carried on a campaign of abuse against the chief executive, a campaign in which Ambrose Bierce had a part. In the shock following McKinley's murder the president's failings were forgotten and a nation found unity in mourning a martyred man. Yet while black-draped photographs appeared in windows everywhere and congregations

28. For Norris's admission see William Dean Howells, "Frank Norris," *The North American Review*, CLIIV, 772.
29. "Frank Norris's 'The Octopus,'" *The Bookman*, XIII, 246.

gathered to sing the favorite "Lead, Kindly Light," Eugene V. Debs boldly asserted that although socialists were opposed to the shedding of blood they could not forget the innocent victims shot by militia in Buffalo a few years before and the miners riddled with bullets in Latimer in the name of law and order. "As long as society breeds misery," he is reported to have said, "misery will breed assassination." Theodore Roosevelt, taking the oath of office immediately after McKinley's death, promised that "it shall be my aim to continue absolutely unbroken the policy of President McKinley for the peace and prosperity of our beloved country."

II

Americanismus and Americanism

The young man who succeeded to the presidency of the United States for 1902, 1903, and 1904 was probably the only one in the country who could support the name of Theodore, wear a cord attached to his pince-nez, and at the same time project upon the screen of national consciousness the outline of a wholly virile Strong Man, but this is what Mr. Roosevelt did, and with such virtuosity that only persons who were in those years viewing the march of history can truly appreciate the performance of his rôle.[1] The effect that he produced upon a hero-worshiping generation, still addicted to torchlight parades and to awe of the silk hat, arose not merely from the contrast between his personality and that of his predecessor, though that was pronounced; even McKinley's friends had spoken of him as stolid and dull, whereas Roosevelt was dynamic, crusading, ebullient, with a natural affinity for headlines and the center of the stage, the first president to be photographed smiling, even laughing, the first one to have a child's toy named for him. He was also the first president since Abraham Lincoln to be called generally by an affectionate nickname, but for a different reason: Lincoln had presented a father image to the American people, but Roosevelt offered the image of the Rough Rider, the man of daring action, thereby incorporating within himself the American genius of the decade and giving hearty encouragement to it.

1. A certain Duffield Osborne did argue in *The Forum* for Feb., 1910, that Roosevelt had a feminine mind, but at the time the ex-president was hunting big game in Africa and Osborne was safe from reprisal.

Nor did the effect arise simply from the knowledge that a page of our national chronicles had been turned, that William McKinley was the last president who had been an officer in the War between the States and Mr. Roosevelt was the first one to have been an officer in the Spanish-American War, this fact highlighting the realization that a new era was opening.[2] It arose, rather, from the manner in which Roosevelt confronted the changing times, the way in which he denounced Americanismus, the money-madness which Europeans alleged was our national disease, and preached a counteracting Americanism which, it now appears, may have been his most substantial contribution to American life.

By 1902 Americans had come a long way from the philosophy of Poor Richard, and in the course of the journey had converted the Age of Business into the Age of Finance. The point of view of the man bent upon making big money, the man whose outlook was represented by the capitalists and politicians mentioned in the first chapter, had enlarged many times from that of a merchant in the days of Franklin and Jefferson; the Gilded Age had provided him with the materials and the opportunities for headlong exploitation of human and natural resources, and by virtue of the immunities afforded in that period he had often evolved an attitude of contempt for law, for government, and for the weak which he carried over into the twentieth century. Sometimes this attitude was cloaked in what was either rationalization or hypocrisy, as in George F. Baer's celebrated declaration in a letter to W. F. Clarke of Wilkesbarre in 1902 that "the rights and interests of the laboring man will be protected and cared for—not by the labor agitators, but by the Christian men to whom God in

2. The only American heroes of the Spanish-American War to remain public favorites for long were two Rough Riders, Roosevelt and Leonard Wood. George Dewey lost popularity by deeding to his wife a house which the nation had bought him; Richmond P. Hobson became a congressman and an agitator for local option; William T. Sampson and Winfield S. Schley gave offense with their rivalry and dropped from sight; Arthur MacArthur is remembered as the father of Douglas MacArthur; William R. Shafter was quickly forgotten.

His infinite wisdom has given the control of the property interests of the country"; sometimes it was stated more frankly,
as when President David M. Parry of the National Association
of Manufacturers in 1903 compared labor unionists to Huns,
Vandals, and savages; occasionally it was expressed with cal-
lous humor in such remarks as Joseph Cannon's upon becoming Speaker of the House of Representatives in 1903: "I am
goddamned tired of listening to all this babble for reform. . . .
America is a hell of a success."

The point of view of the American philistine was upheld
more ingratiatingly by George Horace Lorimer, editor of *The
Saturday Evening Post*, in one of the popular books of 1902,
Letters from a Self-Made Merchant to His Son.[3] The letters
are supposedly from John Graham, a pork packer whose
career is based loosely upon that of P. D. Armour, who with
disregard for gender but with recognition of his irascibility is
dubbed by his employees Old Gorgon. Graham is a bourgeois Polonius who despises the effete East, its manners, its
inhabitants, and its kind of schooling, and who reiterates advice
to his son to work hard, save money, give up frills, and outgrow
conceit—advice which brings to the son the desired business success and a good wife. The Old Gorgon spiced his letters with
anecdotes and apothegms almost worthy of inclusion in the
most famous of American almanacs:

The lady on the dollar is the only woman who hasn't any senti-
ment in her make-up. (p. 100)
Beauty is only skin deep, but that's deep enough to satisfy any
reasonable man. (p. 116)
You can trust a woman's taste on everything except men. (p. 119)
I might add that you can't trust a man's taste on women, either,

3. According to Alice Payne Hackett, *Fifty Years of Best Sellers,
1895-1945*, New York, 1945, p. 19, it reached eighth place among the ten
best sellers of 1903, a year after publication. However, the two comprehensive histories of popular literature in the United States (Frank Luther
Mott, *Golden Multitudes: The Story of Best Sellers in the United States*,
New York, 1947, and James D. Hart, *The Popular Book: A History of
America's Literary Taste*, New York, 1950) do not list Lorimer's volume
among the over-all better sellers.

and that's pretty lucky, too, because there are a good many old
maids in the world as it is. (p. 119)
It isn't what a man knows, but what he thinks he knows that he
brags about. Big talk means little knowledge. (p. 160)
Education will broaden a narrow mind, but there's no known cure
for a big head. (p. 161)
It's easy to stand hard times, because that's the only thing you can
do, but in good times the fool-killer has to do night work. (p. 161)
A tactful man can pull the stinger from a bee without getting
stung. (p. 163)
Appearances are deceitful, I know, but so long as they are, there's
nothing like having them deceive for us instead of against us.
(p. 178)

However formulated in written word or in thought,
Americanismus was responsible for continuing inequalities
and injustices throughout Roosevelt's first administration, and
critics of our society deplored the fact that combination, not
competition, was the rule of trade, that swollen trusts were
strangling the right of free men to rule themselves, robbing
them of a decent livelihood and degrading their humanity. It
was estimated that one per cent of the families of the United
States owned ninety-nine per cent of the wealth; that the cost
of living had risen forty per cent over that of July, 1897; that
twenty thousand little children, some five or six years old,
worked in southern mills; that some sixteen thousand children
under fourteen were employed in New York City; that many
coal miners earned less than $300 a year. The average work-
man put in ten to twelve hours for a daily wage of $1.25. The
public, as the muckrakers were going to demonstrate, ate food
and bought patent medicines poisoned for the sake of gain,
voted for officeholders who maintained an "unholy alliance"
with financiers, invested its small savings in fraudulent stocks
or rigged insurance policies, surrendered most of its earnings
to landlords and storekeepers, and read newspapers and magazines which largely defended the *status quo*.

This public could have learned in 1902 that the United
States Steel Corporation had an income of $84,779,298 for the

first nine months of that year, and, if it looked into *The World Almanac*, that there were 3,546 millionaires in the United States; in March of 1903 it might have noted the organization of the National Packing Company with a capital of $15,-000,000, and in June of the same year it could have reflected that the indifference of railroad management to passenger welfare was chiefly responsible for a total of 49,571 deaths and injuries in accidents during six months. The southern whites, vexed with problems essentially economic, continued to regard the Negro as an inferior; the intent of Thomas Dixon's sensational *The Leopard's Spots* (1902) was to uphold this prejudice; the appointment of a colored postmistress in Indianola, Mississippi in 1902 created a furor; and in May of that year there was a serious race riot in Atlanta. In 1904 Governor James K. Vardaman of Mississippi advocated illiteracy for blacks on the ground that education increased their criminality, and in the same year the reported number of lynchings for the whole country stood at 104. In 1903 it was observed that the national spendings for liquor per capita had almost doubled since 1880, that the number of murders had increased to 8,976 and of suicides to 8,597, and socialists were quick to insist that there was a coincidence between these statistics and the statistics of economic exploitation.

Now Theodore Roosevelt did not condemn wealth as such nor did he ever pretend to deprecate power wielded in the fashion he regarded as righteous. His assaults upon the trusts were motivated not by their bigness but by their disregard for law. He had no intention of allowing the authority of the government of the United States, or of a State, or of the presidency to be subverted by a financial oligarchy, and he saw that the time had come for at least a preliminary test of strength between the money power and the democracy. To make that test he urged corrective legislation upon the congress and he traveled up and down the land preaching, with gritted teeth and pounding fist, a gospel of Americanism suitable to the twentieth century, a gospel which might serve as a cure for Americanismus—the fever, as Henry James put it, to make so much money that one would not mind anything, the vitiating malady which the president diagnosed as a threat to the national tonus.

What Roosevelt meant by Americanism can be partly explained by reference to the most popular novel of 1902, Owen Wister's *The Virginian*, dedicated to the president and praised by him. The hero of this romance of Wyoming was not in all respects like the chief executive for he was only twenty-four, was tall and handsome, and had spells of protracted taciturnity, but he was like Roosevelt in his respect for physical fitness, in his talking softly but carrying a deadly revolver, in his chivalry without nonsense, in his love of western plains and mountains, in his hatred of lawlessness (although the heroine at first thought of the Virginian's execution of western law as lynching), in his belief that equality means being equal to one's job, with the chance for the best man to win that job, and in his fathering of "many children" after marriage. The novel appealed to Roosevelt not only because it proclaimed that "true democracy and true aristocracy are one and the same thing" but also because of its setting, its action, its blend of South and West, for his mother had been a southerner and he had, as all readers were aware, lived on a ranch in South Dakota and had written a history of the winning of the West; in fact, although politicians never forgot he was a New Yorker, he was so often caricatured as a cowboy that it was easy to think of the westerner as his Secret Sharer. His Americanism, like the Virginian's, was founded upon physical hardihood and fair play. He maintained a "tennis cabinet," he once discomfited desk officers of the War College by taking them for a hike along Rock Creek, he chose to present a picture of abundant vitality, he constantly exhorted young men, especially educated and privileged young men, to play the game hard and fair.

Above all, Roosevelt's Americanism was nationalistic, with militaristic undertones, for he declared that a man who did not love his own country better than any other was on a par with him who did not love his wife better than any other woman, and that it was a man's duty to be prepared and willing to fight just as it was a woman's to bear children; later in his life a song called "I Did Not Raise My Boy To Be a Soldier" provoked his wrath, and his upbraiding of "race suicide" was caused by his concern for the strength as well as the social health of the United States. He was no stickler for the rights of small nations or of peoples then regarded as backward or of the inept and the spineless; he had in the nineties been a leading imperialist, and he never, in spite of his shibboleth of fair play, abandoned a belief in the virtue of an aggressiveness based upon an expansive spirit and an expanding economy.

In judging this inconsistency it must be remembered that Roosevelt felt an obligation to solidify a nation which scarcely a generation before had been torn bloodily apart, and that like the English Winston Churchill he was the product of a century which did not prepare him for the radical changes of the twentieth and which had bequeathed him a quantity of moral contradictions. In 1902 he was, politically, not far from center. When asked if laboring men would be welcomed at the White House he replied that they would be, but no more so than business men, and this desire for a balance of power, this essential conservatism, was the very core of his Square Deal, the first of several Deals which have become partisan catchwords. This is why in spite of his noisy impeachments of "malefactors of great wealth" he did not seriously hamper the growth of trusts, why he kept Philander C. Knox as his Attorney-General, why he often infuriated both industrialists and socialists.[4] He admired and made incarnate the American Strong Man, but unlike a true Nietzschean he expected from that man a recognition of and action under social responsibility. On the other hand he had no esteem for weakness even if linked with justice, and one feels that he paid heed to labor unions not because they represented a submerged class but

4. See Frank Parsons, "The President and the Trusts," *The Arena*, XXVIII, 449-56.

because they had, under leaders like John Mitchell and Samuel Gompers, gathered strength unto themselves. Roosevelt was a young man of inherited wealth and patrician outlook who had for years dramatized the Will to Power, who at the age of forty-three had risen to one of the most eminent positions in the world, and he could not fairly be asked to carry reform very far, to have deep sympathy for the frustrations and despairs of the ineffective and inadequate or to assume a social point of view which his birth, his experience, and his temperament made improbable.

In seeking to set up and sustain a balance of power between capital and labor, between Wall Street and First Street, Roosevelt naturally antagonized extremists of both sides and also many liberals. When early in 1902 he ordered Mr. Knox to bring suit against the Northern Securities Company for violation of the Sherman Anti-Trust Act, and when in the summer of the same year he alluded in a speech at Providence to the possible control of trusts by the government, the unregenerate capitalist had excuse for seeing him as a fanatic intent upon destroying free enterprise and the foundations of the Republic, but when in the course of years the "trust-buster" had not stopped the spread of monopolies, liberals and socialists wondered if he were not a figure of sound and fury, and the more dissatisfied taunted him with charges of being a war-monger, of having been bloodthirsty in Cuba, of being a shrewd exploiter of political trends for his own advantage, of being emotionally unstable.

There was justification for diverse opinions. To the world Mr. Roosevelt gave the impression of having full self-confidence, energy, versatility, and integrity; he seemed to thrive under his burdens and to enjoy them to the limit, and while he bored Henry Adams and alarmed Mark Twain he delighted most of the public with his evident relish of youth and power.[5] But like all supermen Roosevelt fused a con-

5. "My neighbor, Roosevelt, is a terrible bore, owing to his absorption in cheap politics. He suffers from the insanity of the *idée fixe* to a degree hardly credible in a sane mind" (*Letters of Henry Adams, 1892-1918*, ed.

viction of superiority with a feeling of inferiority and was therefore at facile turnings a reformer or a demagogue. His consciously histrionic behavior, his stridency, his oddly melancholy cadences in the spoken sentence indicate within him the presence of psychic tensions then not guessed and probably never to be understood, though they may well have had their beginning in childhood liabilities.

Nevertheless it was fortunate for the United States that in a time of little-realized emergency it had for president a man who, whatever his shortcomings, apprehended as clearly as Woodrow Wilson did the reaction against democracy that had set in throughout the globe, who placed himself in opposition to this counter-revolution, and who, by affirming a vigorous, positive Americanism wholly in tune with the will of the majority in this nation rallied his countrymen to his side.[6] Western imperialism of the nineteenth century was about to reap the whirlwind in the twentieth century, about to bring the gravest perils to the safety of this country, and men like Roosevelt, Elihu Root, John Hay, and Henry Adams could read the portents, though they did not always agree upon interpretations. In his darker moments the president thought that the United States was engaged in a race between education and disaster, with only a fair chance of winning; Adams, as we shall note, foresaw the collapse of western civilization about 1917; all of these men divined that the Pacific would be the scene of future battles for world domination and all of them gave thought to preparation for them. As for domestic perplexities, principally those created by the high-handedness of monopolists who were truly bi-partisan,

Worthington C. Ford, Boston, 1938, p. 433). "Mr. Roosevelt is the most formidable disaster that has befallen the country since the Civil War—but the mass of the nation loves him ... even idolizes him" (*Mark Twain in Eruption*, ed. Bernard DeVoto, New York, 1940, p. 18). These are samples of many such gibes by these two men.

6. Meanwhile, Woodrow Wilson was elected president of Princeton University, 25 Oct., 1902. When he came out forcefully for the humanities, for a *studium generale*, the *Tiger* for March of the next year printed a cartoon showing him sitting alone on the campus.

and whose greatest wrong to democracy lay in spreading corruption and the desire for luxury, Roosevelt met them with a philosophy calculated to encourage both stability and change.

Reading the newspapers of 1902 gives one a sense of interruption in the international turmoil after passing the item telling of the Boer acceptance of surrender terms in May, and the columns given to the postponed coronation of Edward VII and to the accession of Alfonso XIII suggest that editors as well as subscribers were hoping for calmer days, though most of these persons were realistic enough to think Cecil Rhodes insane for dreaming of a world federation.[7] Yet apart from the headlines were the reports which revealed that the struggle for power had abated not at all, that political and economic tyrannies and ambitious foreign offices were still responsible for misery, violence, and diplomatic agreements which were so many dragon's teeth sown. At the opening of 1902 a revolution broke out in Venezuela, a republic which was to be at the boiling-point during Roosevelt's first term, and there were outbreaks in China in March, in Haiti in June, in Portuguese West Africa in July, in Macedonia in September; on the fifteenth of November an attempt was made to assassinate King Leopold of Belgium. A British-Japanese alliance to guarantee the integrity of China and Korea, signed 11 February, could easily be heard as a prelude to war on the Asiatic mainland, and the renewal of the Triple Alliance on the twenty-eighth of June moved the seesaw of power in Europe. The American public, half forgetful of the campaign to pacify the Philippines, was reminded of it by charges that our military were committing atrocities in Samar and by Secretary Root's announcement that operations there had cost us, by the middle of June, $170,326,586; the president's signing of the Isthmian Canal Bill and his promotion of a revolution in Panama in 1904

7. Mr. Rhodes died on 26 March of that year. Others who died in 1902: John P. Altgeld (12 March), Thomas Dunn English (1 April), Frank R. Stockton (20 April), Bret Harte (5 May), Edward Eggleston (2 Sept.), Émile Zola (29 Sept.), Frank Norris (25 Oct.), Elizabeth C. Stanton (26 Oct.), G. A. Henty (16 Nov.), Thomas Nast (7 Dec.), Mary H. Catherwood (26 Dec.).

served notice that the United States was frankly turning its face toward the great western ocean in the world-wide reach for economic and political mastery.

The ferment, continuing through 1903 and 1904, produced in the latter year one of the major wars of modern history. The year 1903 recorded a rebellion in Morocco in January, war between Brazil and Bolivia and an uprising in Honduras in February, fighting between Albanians and Turks in March, a horrifying massacre of Jews at Kishnieff in May, the crossing of Russian troops into Korea in the same month, and battles between French and Algerians in June; an attempt to assassinate Alfonso in Madrid in January and the murder of King Alexander and Queen Draga of Serbia in a palace revolt on the fourth of June testified to the precarious life of royalty in an atmosphere of anarchist and dynastic conspiracy, so that Italy joined Germany in asking that the United States help in breaking up the lawless underground which, they reminded us, had just been accountable for the death of one of our presidents. In 1904 the spotlight rested briefly upon the British who, having settled the conflict in South Africa, sent an expedition into Somaliland in January and another into Tibet in April, and in the latter month concurred with the French that Morocco should lie within Gallic influence while Egypt should fall to themselves. Meanwhile, without waiting for a declaration of hostilities, Japanese torpedo boats had attacked Russian warships in the harbors of Port Arthur and Chemulpo on the eighth of February, and the contest for possession of the peninsula "pointed like a dagger at the heart of Japan" and for control of Manchuria was on, with American sympathy at first given to the Japanese, principally because they appeared as underdogs but also because we actually had more ties with and better understanding of them.[8]

American fiction, drama, and poetry had almost nothing to say concerning all this convulsive shaping of the twentieth

8. Among war correspondents who tried vainly to report upon military engagements from near the front line were Jack London, Richard Harding Davis, and John Fox, Jr.

century outside world, an isolationist coloration taken on since the Civil War. Even the Graustarkian romances failed to provide their usual oblique comments. David Graham Phillips, whose efforts to earn a living with his pen meant that he wrote an occasional potboiler, began one of these confections as a parody of the type, but by the time he had completed telling of the love of the rich Frederick Grafton for the Duchess Erica of Zweitenbourg, with an accompanying duel and an escape by means of a spurious Velasquez, he had given up his original purpose and *Her Serene Highness* (1902) became one of the poorer specimens of this *genre*. George Barr McCutcheon's *Beverly of Graustark* (1904) deservedly had wider reading, for this brisk reversal of the plot of the author's biggest success brought together a Virginia girl and the Prince of Dawsbergen, unavoidably incognito, but it dealt with imaginary politics rather than real Balkan alignments. And Louis Joseph Vance's *The Romance of Terence O'Rourke* (1904), presenting a hot-headed, mildly philandering soldier of fortune adventuring from the Sahara to the non-existent duchy of Grandlieu, was equally silent about *realpolitik* and communicated only the slightest feeling for global tensions.

Nor did the historical novel which in Roosevelt's first administration could have been found in the hands of most American booklovers shed more than an indirect illumination upon the pressures, strains, and fissions of the day. In 1902 four of the ten best sellers were of this kind: Charles Major's *Dorothy Vernon of Haddon Hall*, Emerson Hough's *The Mississippi Bubble*, Mary Johnston's *Audrey*, and Booth Tarkington's *The Two Vanrevels*. In the first of these Major adapted a real love story of about 1560 involving a lovely spitfire as heroine, a swordsman hero, a regal Queen Elizabeth, and a Mary Stuart who is pictured as "a white snaky lady." Hough's romance followed the history of John Law with some closeness until he came to America, where he saw maize for the first time, visualized wealth in fields of grain, acquired a nobility not corroborated by fact, and went on to a happy ending. Miss Johnston's tragic tale had its setting in colonial

Williamsburg and its environs. Tarkington's shamelessly romantic novel was written as though its author had never heard of the expostulations and replies of Howells, or of the work of Crane, Norris, and Dreiser. The younger man made no secret of his conviction that the first purpose of fiction is to entertain, and in this narrative he sought to carry out that purpose by capitalizing upon the popularity of both the historical and the political novel. History, however, is but an afterthought. The war with Mexico is dragged in at the end, and politics is introduced chiefly to motivate a feud which has a deadly outcome. Most of *The Two Vanrevels* has to do with the ravishing Betty Carewe, beloved by all males young and old, and with the special and complicated rivalry between a charming scapegrace and his exceedingly unselfish friend. Indeed, the magnanimity of the hero might have brought a calamitous end for the heroine had not her irascible father, mistaking the identity of an evening caller, brought the tale to an almost credible and certainly satisfying last page. The next year Tarkington published an even more trifling romance in *Cherry*, whose horseplay has reference to the historical only in that the time is 1762 and that Nassau Hall appears in the background.

By 1903 the fad for the use of history had so tapered off that only John Fox's tale of a boy growing to manhood in the Civil War era, *The Little Shepherd of Kingdom Come*, made the list of best sellers, but in 1904 it revived with Winston Churchill's quasi-epic story of George Rogers Clark's march through the "drowned lands" to capture Vincennes, *The Crossing;* with Ellen Glasgow's notable portrait of a blind old Virginian lady who under a delusion preserves the ante-bellum spirit of the planter caste, *The Deliverance;* and with Mary Johnston's record of adventures in Elizabethan England, *Sir Mortimer*. It will be noted that in keeping with the bourgeoning of national self-consciousness and pride most of these novels given the laurel of public approval moved within the arena of American history, and this trend is even more apparent among the romances which did not sell in the highest brackets.[9] France, once a lodestone for entertainers who wished to drape their fabulae with the silks of kings and courtiers, came near being neglected in these years. Frederic S. Isham did use it for *Under the Rose* (1903), which, recounting the vicissitudes of a seeming jester and jestress at the palace and in the forests and fields of Francis I, was an almost perfect specimen of the use of simulacra stuffed with stock virtues, and Robert Neilson Stephens returned to it for *The Bright Face of Danger* (1904) in which, by sponsoring a son of the hero of his earlier *An Enemy to the King* (1897), he spun a tale as alluring as its title. But of foreign lands England fared better, even below the level of the best seller: Hallie Erminie Rives's floridly written *The Castaway* (1904) restored some interest in Lord Byron, and Gilbert Parker's *A Ladder of Swords* (1904), another return to the time of Elizabeth, made picturesque the island and inhabitants of Jersey. The Italian peoples had their turn also, for F. Marion Crawford's *Marietta: A Maid of Venice* (1902) told of a conspiracy against the Venetian Republic and of the glassworkers in the city on the Adriatic, and Edith Wharton's *The Valley of Decision* (1902) was laid in the invented duchy of Pianura at the end of the eighteenth century. Despite the fact that it had a limited reception *The Valley of Decision* is in many ways superior to the other historical novels so far mentioned in this chapter; its milieu, especially with respect to social stratification, is arranged with care, its contrast between Bourbonism and liberalism was capable of a contemporary interpretation, and its psychological crux, the temptation of Fulvia Vivaldi to become Odo Valsecca's duchess of the left hand in order to throw her influence behind the new ideas, is achieved with conviction and poignancy. A few historical novelists, aware that their ores were thinning, prospected for new lodes in faraway places. Ottilie Liljencrantz went to the Vikings and the discovery of America for *The Thrall of Leif the*

9. Unhappily, Paul Leicester Ford, shot and killed by a brother on 8 May, 1902, did not live to see his wish about the predominance of American historical fiction come true.

Lucky (1902) and to the Danish conquest of Britain for *The Ward of King Canute* (1903), but it must be said that the novelty of her folk and the attractive colored illustrations did not cover the hackneyed plots. More original stories are to be found in Nevill M. Meakin's account of the Third Crusade and those fanatical retainers of the Old Man of the Mountain who added a word to the English language (*The Assassins,* 1902) and in Elizabeth Miller's evocation of Hebrew persistence and Egyptian arrogance, of the trappings and sets of the period when Moses stood before Pharaoh (*The Yoke,* 1904).

Of the outpouring of novels inspired by American history a few require passing mention. Frank R. Stockton's *Kate Bonnet* (1902), a novel of the time of Blackbeard, took for heroine a daughter of Stede Bonnet, a real pirate, and Charles F. Pidgin made in *The Climax* (1902) his second attempt to vindicate the character of Aaron Burr.[10] For *The Maid-at-Arms* (1902) Robert W. Chambers again returned in fancy to pre-Revolutionary Tryon County, New York, with Walter Butler re-enacting his part as villain *par excellence*, with Jack Mount supplying local color in humor, and with the hoydenish but comely Dorothy Verick rescuing the hero from Indians in a scene exciting for action and for display of Indian lore. Gertrude Atherton's *The Conqueror* (1902), chosen by Van Wyck Brooks as "perhaps the best of all American historical novels of the decade 1895-1905," may be assigned to that category only because its writer was a novelist; actually the book was designed to tell not a story about Alexander Hamilton but the story of that statesman, an appropriate protagonist to make his bow to a generation that highly esteemed the Strong Man.[11] Almost a biography by reason of the research that went into it, and of the manner of presentation, *The Conqueror* is strongly biased in point of sight: Tom Paine is never named during the account of the

10. His first was *Blennerhasset* (1901).

11. Mr. Brooks's opinion is found in his *The Confident Years: 1885-1915,* New York, 1952, p. 214.

Revolution; Jefferson is drawn as a crabbed schemer and coward; Burr appears as a cunning lost soul; "one Freneau" is a traitorous scribbler; Hamilton's moral peccadillos are minimized, his vaulting ambition glorified. In no sense is this a good novel. The form is marred by arbitrary hiatuses and by unexpected insertions from memoirs, speeches, and letters; for long stretches it reads like a third-rate textbook of Washington's presidency. If it is to be applauded at all it must be for the investigations which bolstered the first two Books, for the filial characterization of the Father of his Country, and for its attempt to be a novel of ideas, something of a rarity in this school of writing. Upton Sinclair's *Manassas* (1904) came closer to re-creating an American crisis without factitious props and succeeded in making understandable the passions in north and south just preceding the War between the States and the conduct of many persons while the fighting was on.

Literary historians are inclined, if they allude to Gertrude Atherton at all, to write of her in terms suitable for another Marie Corelli, and Mrs. Atherton did share with the English author a tropical mood, a style whose fundamental principle Osric would have understood, a self-impressment that came near pretentiousness, and a desire to instruct that approximated condescension. In the days of the flowering of historical and sentimental romances this California novelist was openly aristocratic, openly for the Hamiltonian way of life as against the Jeffersonian, and openly scornful of American literature and the American reading public. In 1904 she was writing that

American literature today, taking it as a whole, taking no account of its strangely few exceptions, is the most timid, the most anemic, the most lacking in individualities, the most bourgeois, that any country has ever known.[12]

And in the same year she was maintaining that although American readers were losing their shallow optimism they

12. "Why Is American Literature Bourgeois?" *The North American Review*, CLXXVIII, 722.

still showed too little interest in life to be pessimistic.[13] It is therefore only just and understandable that in the three years now being considered she should have written the only novel dealing competently with *le haute politique*, the only one that made a sincere, informed, and remarkably prophetic effort to explain to American readers some of the intricacies and dangers of the global drive for power and to people its pages with "individualities"; understandable, too, that a public which was, at least in her opinion, complacent and timid should have turned from her uncomfortable *Rulers of Kings* (1904) and allowed it to be interred within the graves of books in second-hand stores. It should have a brief resurrection.

The rulers of kings, this amalgam of Graustarkian fantasy and historical romance presently tells us, are the international bankers who can support or overthrow thrones, and one of them is the American Fessenden Abbott, heir to a fortune of some four hundred million dollars. Although he has been given a Spartan education by his father, he has "read the romances of the day which dealt with the imaginary princesses of the imaginary modern kingdom," an indulgence which was to open the door to part of his fate. But this reading represents only a tiny segment of his acquaintance with books; his tutors have seen to it that he prepared himself for his responsibilities by a study of history, and we learn on the first page that "his ideals had soared in stellar spaces—ideals created by passionate brooding on the careers of Washington, Hamilton, Napoleon, Nelson, Cromwell, Kossuth, the great Hunyadis, Alexander, Caesar, Rudolph the First of Austria." His own career is related only in the large, but by thirty-one he is a superman, contemptuous of the problems of a decadent Europe. And he has met Kaiser Wilhelm II, a young, theatrical, audacious monarch, a kind of Teutonic Roosevelt, whose dream of Pan-Germanism shimmers before Abbott's eyes as it did before Mrs. Atherton's, and has grown to love him this side of idolatry, and from him derived confirmation of his

13. "Some Truths about American Readers," *The Bookman*, XVIII, 658-60.

own anti-democratic beliefs, for Fessenden Abbott defers only
to a Strong Man, and one of his ambitions is to unite the
South American republics under North American hegemony.

"Although [he says] I believe in permanent centralization, to the
extent of a ruler elected for life or good behavior—and I believe
this principle is growing in the minds of all thinking republicans
who are not only sick of corruption but of seeing a fine man in
the presidential chair the slave of politicians, and shelved coinci-
dently with the full development of his usefulness—still that ruler
must be the free and deliberate selection of a majority of the
people.... With democracy I have no more patience than with
the autocracy of Russia..." (p. 285)

In Austria-Hungary this embodiment of the reaction against
democracy meets the Archduchess Ranata, fictitious daughter
of Franz Joseph. Since she is dedicated to the freeing of
Hungary and since she knows that Wilhelm II is scheming to
seize the Empire when her father dies, she has set herself
ardently against the German *Drang nach Osten*, and this provides a test of loyalties for Abbott who, of course, falls deeply
in love with her, as she with him. Parental objection is another obstacle, but when Franz Joseph refuses to permit the
marriage of a daughter of the Hapsburgs to an American he is
threatened with two weapons newly developed in the West:
bombs that hurl dynamite and can kill ten thousand men at
one explosion, and steel fortresses that can move cross-
country. These will be given to Russia unless the Emperor
consents to the wedding. When he is reminded that

"The most malignant force in the world today is Russia....
Moreover, Russia is the one menace which prevents Europe and
England from enjoying a moment's security. She creeps and
creeps, and never retraces a step. In far-sightedness Russia is
the greatest genius among nations, and she is absolutely unscrupulous..." (p. 341)

he is brought to terms and the present-day reader is almost
persuaded he is reading contemporary newsprint. Mrs. Atherton's familiarity with Central European politics and labyrin-

thine intrigue was not profound, but her attempt to apprehend and publicize them, her feeling for Hungarian patriotism, her predictions of superbomb and tank partly atone for what is otherwise faded melodrama and make *Rulers of Kings* one of the more respectable artifacts of the decade.

The circulation figures that Harriet Monroe quoted in the issue of *The Critic* for February, 1904, to show that romantic novels of the kind just discussed were selling best in the opening years of the century are bulwarked by the monthly lists printed in *The Bookman*, by the statistics recently compiled by Frank Luther Mott and James D. Hart, by the dusty copies to be found in circulating libraries and second-hand bookstores of every American city, and by the theater programs of the days when *Richard Carvel* (1899) still sold best of all, for the star system, that reflection of the worship of the exceptional individual, and the drama had to accommodate themselves to the demand for sentimental and historical stories. In 1902 Minnie Maddern Fiske was playing in " Mary of Magdala," Eleanor Robson in "Audrey," James K. Hackett in "The Crisis," Viola Allen in "The Eternal City," and Robert Edeson in "Soldiers of Fortune," so that Mrs. Patrick Campbell and Eleanora Duse, on tour with standard repertories in this country, found themselves at a disadvantage. Mrs. Fiske turned in 1903 to "Hedda Gabler," but Forbes-Robertson brought "The Light that Failed" from England, the matinee idol Kyrle Bellew starred in "Raffles" to compete with William Gillette's perennial "Sherlock Holmes," Bertha Galland drew crowds to "Dorothy Vernon," and other crowds unaware that they were witnessing the genesis of a gigantic industry stared curiously at the first movie with a plot, "The Great American Train Robbery." In 1904 dramatic critics did report signs of a "classical" revival, for although Dustin Farnum established himself in the theater that year with "The Virginian," Ada Rehan and Otis Skinner appeared in "The School for Scandal" and "The Taming of the Shrew," Richard Mansfield triumphed over his strange pronunciations in "Ivan the Terrible," and E. H. Sothern and Julia Marlowe, for many years to be the favorite American Shakesperian team, produced "Romeo and Juliet."

As one consequence of the yielding to a taste satisfied with the non-intellectual and trivial, American magazines carried frequent complaints that the theater was losing its value as a cultural seminar, even as a playhouse, and its friends searched anxiously for the cause and cure of what they erroneously thought a decline. It is not surprising that several commentators should have blamed a theater trust, or that William Archer should have proposed in the July, 1902, number of *The Monthly Review* a National Theater which could be independent of the box-office, that David Belasco should in *Smart Set* for September, 1904, have pointed an accusing finger at the prevailing materialism of Broadway producers, for these censures were in keeping with the increasing willingness to decry the pursuit of big money. Nor is it any more surprising that E. H. Sothern should have reminded readers of *Good Housekeeping* for June, 1903, that women, who comprised most of the audience in a legitimate theater and who determined family approval or disapproval of performances there, were actually in control of the stage and responsible for its billings.

Another consequence of the inferior taste for drama, certainly no worse than when Edgar Poe fretted over its artificialities, was the lack of encouragement for any native talent that might have aspired to shock theater-goers out of their contentment with a routine of tears and laughter, with the love-is-enough theme, with the rusty machinery of footlight intrigue, with a complacence about life in general and American life in particular, or that might have attempted revolutionary changes in production. The theater-goers were satisfied with what they had, and willing to pay for it; the playwrights were satisfied to give them what was wished and be paid for it; and there is no record then of a young American dramatic genius who tried to bring to the proscenium innovations for which audiences were not prepared. In *Harper's Weekly* for 16 January, 1904, William Dean Howells correctly awarded the palm for young American dramatists to Clyde Fitch, and Fitch is a symbol of the young man of talent who can not break the conventional bonds of the medium in which he works and who leaves behind for his accounting a fraction instead of a whole number. In 1902 Clara Bloodgood made his "The Girl with the Green Eyes" one of the talked-of plays of the year; today it is not likely that this study of feminine jealousy would be included in an anthology of best American dramas for the half century, for Fitch's dramaturgy is now seen to be largely synthetic, his knowledge of psychology often as innocent as many medical diagnoses of the time, his readiness to deal in the material of popular melodrama too apparent. Whatever his intentions may have been at the outset of the writing of a play, he was almost sure to end with something calculated to fill the house. Talent in the early 1900's was no guarantee of immunization against Americanismus.

Among the many things in the new century which wearied Henry Adams, Theodore Roosevelt had a high priority. The elder man dreaded White House dinners with poor food, poor champagne, poor service, with the host monopolizing the talk, re-telling anecdotes of San Juan, and anxious to impress guests with the catholicity of his tastes and interests. Yet the spectacle of force at work always interested Adams, and in Roosevelt he observed a force not so primitive as that which drove Ulysses S. Grant, but more volcanic—an energy the very thought of which made Adams tired and led him to regard the president in a mood of exasperated affection. For Roosevelt was a spectacle to him, a one-man act so diverting as to conceal the stage upon which the comedy was played, an amusement and something of a horror to one who brooded happily over a civilization that was, he thought, tearing itself to pieces. "The twelfth century," Adams wrote, "still rages wildly here in the shape of a fiend with tusks and eye-glasses across the way. The Wild Boar of Cubia! I love him. He is almost sane beside his German and Russian cousins, but he is mad enough to suit me." [14]

Both attracted and repelled by the elemental in Roosevelt, Adams made it plain in his letters that when with the president he felt himself too much i' the sun and therefore put on as defense a mild raillery or mock humility. However, contrasted with William McKinley, Grover Cleveland, and Benjamin Harrison the incumbent in the White House in 1902 did exhibit a kind of Renaissance wholeness, or at least intellectual liveliness, and for the escape from dullness Adams was grateful, if dubious. Not until the Bull Moose campaign was he certain that "Theodorus I" was a maniac and that medical authority supported his opinion.[15]

As an energizing factor in American culture Theodore Roosevelt cannot be exaggerated. Nobody could have been blamed for thinking that Americanism demanded that the physical man be always in motion, always vocal. By train Roosevelt traveled throughout the nation, making countless speeches. He wrote more than 150,000 letters. He hunted game, he rode horses, he planned the stealing of newspaper headlines, he posed for so many photographs that he must have been one of the most valuable assets of the camera industry. The intellectual man was equally tireless. He wrote books, articles, and book reviews; he read widely and with relish; he championed simplified spelling; he denounced "mollycoddles" and praised athletes and sportsmen; he fought with the Congress and sometimes with his Cabinet and got his way in most matters; he challenged conservative business and radical socialism; he ranged foreign chancelleries against each other; he played politics for keeps; he preached and practiced the strenuous life so successfully as to increase the tempo of American life. To the crabbed Henry Adams he was exhilarating and appalling.

Of course Roosevelt was not alone responsible for the fact that much of American literature of his time went outdoors.

14. *Letters,* p. 445.
15. *Ibid.,* p. 605.

Back of him were such things as the incorrigible atavism of modern man and the examples of romantic writers from Rousseau to Whitman. But his reputation as an outdoor enthusiast was an encouragement to the nature writer and to the novelist of western spaces, and it is not merely coincidental that the number of such authors during his presidency was striking. John Muir and John Burroughs found his friendship advantageous, and although Jack London had begun his stories of Alaska before Roosevelt went to Washington, Rex Beach, Harold Bindloss, Oliver Curwood, Harold Bell Wright, Gene Stratton-Porter, and Zane Grey found a public readied by its fondness for Roosevelt to enjoy romances of northern forest and river or southwestern plain or limberlost or Ozark peak, and the verses of Joaquin Miller acquired a fresh reading for the same reason. Indeed, the return to nature, accompanied by the experiments of Luther Burbank and the back-to-the-farm movement begun by Professor L. H. Bailey of Cornell University, was so notable that the American Robert Bridges remarked in *Collier's Weekly* (12 March, 1904) that our fiction had entered upon a "vegetable era," what with the wheat of Frank Norris, the hemp of *The Reign of Law*, the cabbage in *Mrs. Wiggs*, and the tobacco in *The Deliverance*. To demonstrate that his relation to this kind of writing was not nebulous Roosevelt took time out from executive duties in 1907 to laud the prose of Stewart Edward White and John Burroughs but in the same essay in the June *Everybody's* to arraign William J. Long, Ernest Thompson Seton, Charles G. D. Roberts, and Jack London as nature fakers, climaxing his accusations by rating the chapter in London's *White Fang* (1906) which tells of a fight between a dog and a wolf as "the very sublimity of absurdity." When in the *New York Times* for the second of June the Rev. Mr. Long, who keenly realized that his career was imperilled, replied tartly that Roosevelt, being only a killer, knew very little of the habits of animals outside the chase, John Burroughs a week later came to the president's defense in the same daily

by doubting Long's qualifications as naturalist. To the delecta-
tion of the public Roosevelt prolonged the battle by another
assault upon Long in *Everybody's* for September, and having,
as so often, the last word forced his opponent to turn his pen
to another kind of writing.[16]

In many such ways Theodore Roosevelt's effect upon
American culture was something more than indirect. So many
Americans were like him in kind, or wished they were like
him, that he was a pier glass for national impulses, a mirror
that not only reflected the features of the nation but also threw
light upon them. For example, it was, perhaps, inevitable that
Indiana should have produced in those years a lengthy roll of
authors—James Whitcomb Riley, Charles Major, Booth Tarkington, George Ade, Mary H. Catherwood, George Barr
McCutcheon, Meredith Nicholson, Theodore Dreiser, Joaquin Miller, John Hay, Robert Underwood Johnson, William
Vaughn Moody, and David Graham Phillips were Hoosiers—
yet Roosevelt's advertisement of the West certainly did nothing to hinder their acceptance by the public. Likewise the
endeavor of Percy MacKaye, Cale Young Rice, Josephine
Preston Peabody, and Olive Tilford Dargan to revive poetic
drama owed more to the example of Stephen Phillips than to
the encouragement of the president, yet Roosevelt's personality
suffused his countrymen with a spirit that could best be expressed through the grandiose. Roosevelt may also be looked
upon as a proximate cause for the vogue of football fiction
purveyed by Ralph Paine, Jesse Lynch Williams, and Arthur
Stanwood Pier; he was one reason Bernarr Macfadden was
able to make *Physical Culture* pay (first issue, March, 1899).
His career heartened other writers who held or aspired to
hold public office: Tarkington served one term in the Indiana

16. The nature-faking controversy had its real beginning with two
essays by John Burroughs: "Current Misconceptions in Natural History,"
The Century Magazine, LXVII, 509-17, and "On Humanizing the Animals,"
The Century Magazine, LXVII, 773-80. At that time Roosevelt was of the
opinion that animals taught their young.

legislature, Jack London was a candidate for mayor of Oakland, Brand Whitlock was mayor of Toledo for four terms, Winston Churchill sat in the New Hampshire legislature and was the Progressive candidate for governor of that state, George W. Peck, author of the famous story of a bad boy, opposed the elder LaFollette for the governorship of Wisconsin, Upton Sinclair, a constant amateur in politics, tried to be governor of California, and Charles Edward Russell was the socialist candidate for governor of New York in 1910.

One evidence of Roosevelt's many-sidedness is found in the pleasure he took in reading poetry, for poetry is essentially the speech of evasion, the language of passion and reflection conveyed obliquely through comparisons and nuances, and the president disliked "weasel words." In 1902 he did not read Ernest Crosby's socialistic *Swords and Ploughshares*, and it is a pity that he did not then make the acquaintance of the best verse of the year, Edwin Arlington Robinson's *Captain Craig: A Book of Poems*, for the title poem is the most concentrated, the most tender, and the wisest an American had yet published. The captain, an old starving derelict, is rescued and pensioned by a group of young men who find consolation in his assertion that life is neither all black nor all white but something to be surmounted by the free man who has the courage to laugh at folly, sing to the sun, and love with understanding, this quality providing him with a shield against misfortune. Set down baldly the theme seems only a bit of homely stoicism, but Robinson delivered it in epigrammatic lines of great nobility and discernment and with a freshness as though it had never been said before, so that the whole becomes a paean to humanism. It must be admitted, however, that harmony and libretto are more precious than *motif*, for the last by itself cannot dispel the dread of man's futility. Advice that one should wish neither to be "cursed with happiness" nor to "feed his very soul on poison" but "to see the truth of things" and thus be strong to endure defeat menaces the ego, and was a denial of that Will to Power which might have made Robinson one of its victims had not Roosevelt rescued him in 1905 by praising (in *The Outlook* for 12 August) his *Children of the Night* (1897) and appointing him to a government position.

Even in those areas of creativity, knowledge, and experiment in which the president had no aptitude the Roosevelt myth and the Roosevelt actuality seemed to give off emanations that reacted mutually with the Zeitgeist. At no other time, perhaps, would Solon Borglum, the cowboy sculptor, have made a reputation so quickly; at no other time would the Commonwealth of Pennsylvania have erected so resplendent a Capitol with its majestic groups of statuary by George Gray Barnard, its murals by Edwin Abbey, its unfortunate record of jobbery; at no other time would the Gibson girl, whose pompadour and firm chin were burnt upon leather, printed on plates, and woven in silk handkerchiefs as well as preserved in hundreds of drawings, have captured so easily the vanity and the imitativeness of a generation.[17] For the first time an American operatic baritone could write that "it may fairly be said that America stands at the head of the nations in its appreciation of the Art of today," [18] for while Main Street and most of Broadway danced to ragtime, sang tunes from Victor Herbert's "Babes in Toyland," and paraded to Sousa's marches another part of Broadway sought to house the greatest opera company in the world, and to that end presented Enrico Caruso in "Rigoletto" on the twenty-third of November, 1903, and assembled a cast that could sing "Les Huguenots" on the third of February, 1904.[19] Richard Strauss and Pietro Mascagni were induced to conduct their own compositions in the metropolis; musical Americans flocked to assess the fame of Paderewski, the heroic Eugène Ysaÿe, the Viennese Fritz Kreisler, and, if fortunate, the sixty-year-old Adelina Patti on a farewell tour. The same Americans gave vent to national

17. John Singer Sargent, who painted the official portrait of Roosevelt, John Alexander, and William M. Chase were still pre-eminent as portraitists.

18. David Bispham, "Music as a Factor in National Life," *The North American Review*, DLIII, 796.

19. Principals in the cast for Meyerbeer's taxing opera were Sembrich, Nordica, Caruso, Plançon, Journet, Edyth Walker, Scotti.

pride by boasting of Horatio Parker and Edward McDowell, our foremost composers, and of Theodore Thomas, our first great conductor of an orchestra.

It is doubtful whether the people of the United States have ever been more cheerful, more self-assured, more light-hearted than they were in the years between 1901 and 1910, and this in the face of present and foreseen dangers. "Theodore helps us by his gaiety," Henry Adams wrote in January of 1902,[20] and the high spirits of the first Roosevelt persuaded a majority of his countrymen that though this might not be the best possible of worlds the nation in which they were living was the most exciting, the freest, and the strongest. They subscribed to humorous magazines unequalled at any other time in our history: *Puck* (founded 1877), *Judge* (1881), and *Life* (1883), the last of which broke many lances against social abuses. They chuckled over the stories, parodies, and newspaper columns of Gelett Burgess, Finley Peter Dunne, O. Henry, George Randolph Chester, George Ade, Oliver Herford, Charles B. Loomis, Will Irwin, Ellis Parker Butler, Irvin Cobb, Marshall P. Wilder, Simeon Ford, John Kendrick Bangs, and Carolyn Wells, a roster of humorous talent not to be matched elsewhere in our literature. They pondered the merits of yellow journalism, and on Sunday, probably against the cautions of their ministers, read the "funny papers"—colored comics, the most popular one at first being R. F. Outcalt's "Buster Brown." [21] They amused themselves with novels light as butterfly wings, novels gay in language and situation: could Monty Brewster in George Barr McCutcheon's *Brewster's Millions* (1902) spend a million dollars prudently within a year so that he might inherit seven million? Could Richard Comstalk of Harold MacGrath's *Hearts and Masks* (1905) extricate himself from a cellar in which he found a beautiful unknown who had also fled when a thief spoiled their evening

20. *Letters*, p. 364.
21. The most fanciful and best drawn of American comics also belongs to the Roosevelt era: Winsor McCay's "Little Nemo in Slumberland." The story was brought to the stage by Billy B. Van in 1908.

at a ball? Who was the wearer of the red tam in Meredith
Nicholson's *The House of a Thousand Candles* (1905), and
why was that Indiana mansion besieged? They frightened
themselves by hearing in imagination the baying of a gigantic
hound across the moors in Arthur Conan Doyle's *The Hound
of the Baskervilles* (1902), first detective novel to reach the
best seller list in the United States, by trying to explain the
strange movement of a plant in Mary Wilkins Freeman's *The
Wind in the Rose-Bush* (1903), by witnessing a murder in
Anna Katherine Green's *The Filigree Ball* (1903).[22] They
were a little uneasy over the *miles gloriosus* in Richard Harding Davis's *Captain Macklin* (1902), but they found Brand
Whitlock's *Her Infinite Variety* (1904), obviously written
with the gentle malice of a politically experienced man, a
palatable satire on the young statesman who takes himself too
seriously and on the young women campaigning for the vote.
And they made another best seller of Myrtle Reed's *Lavender
and Old Lace* (1902), a tale so milky that it must have been
in Agnes Repplier's mind when in *Harper's Bazaar* for April,
1904, she rejoiced in the decline of novels for women.

The older American novelists were unable to adjust themselves to a changed taste which some of them regretted; *The
British Weekly* for 7 July, 1904, reported that Henry van
Dyke had said in an address at Liverpool that his countrymen
suffered from "three mischievous and perilous tendencies:
idolatry of military and conquest, growing idolatry of wealth,
growing spirit of frivolity." In this atmosphere of "frivolity"
Mark Twain's gusty humor seemed to wear miner's boots in
a drawing-room, and his burlesque of Sherlock Holmes in
A Double Barrelled Detective Story (1902) failed as completely to amuse as his rebuke to General Funston in *The
North American Review* for February of the same year and

---

22. After Poe, detective fiction in our literature was kept alive chiefly
by Anna Katherine Green (Rohlfs) and Katherine Cecil Thurston. Mary
Roberts Rinehart was soon to join them. For a readable history of our
detective and mystery fiction see Howard Haycraft, *Murder for Pleasure:
The Life and Times of the Detective Story*, New York, 1941.

his diatribe against vivisection in *A Dog's Tale* (1904) failed to accomplish their purposes. Howells, paying a tribute to Zola in 1902 as "most terribly, most pitilessly moral," [23] proved his loyalty and proved also that he was still battling over "realism," while his sense of contemporary manners had so far drifted from actuality that he could introduce in *The Kentons* (1902) a heroine who took to bed with a crisis of the nerves after having been kissed without permission by a young man. In *The Son of Royal Langbrith* (1904) he assumed a practiced stance, for this story of a conscience which tortures Mrs. Langbrith into making a choice between disillusioning her son or of losing the love of Dr. Anther supplied the moral problem and the highminded persons which together always gave him his best fictional milieu. Hamlin Garland, continuing to approve Howells for "sanity in fiction," had done his lasting work in the preceding decade.[24] Frank Norris, dying in 1902 shortly after undertaking to write a column for *The Critic* and before he could complete the Epic of the Wheat, had never unbent to frivolity, and his essays in *The Responsibilities of the Novelist* (1903) showed how earnestly he had undertaken his craft and had hoped to be a spokesman for the new Americanism.

According to Norris a novelist's weightiest responsibility was to tell the truth, which was not to be mistaken for mere cataloging of facts, and to tell it purposefully, for the highest type of novel is that with a purpose, although this must not run away with the story as it frequently does in Tolstoi and George Eliot. To learn the truth the novelist must be in the midst of life, must be of the world of working men, and to tell the truth he must be not only a "realist" but also a "romanticist." Trying to define these vexing terms Norris wrote that "Romance . . . is the kind of fiction that takes cognizance of variations from the type of normal life. Realism is

23. William Dean Howells, "Émile Zola," *The North American Review*, CLXXV, 590.
24. See his "Sanity in Fiction," *The North American Review*, LLXXVI, 336-48.

the kind of fiction that confines itself strictly to the type of normal life." [25]

From these definitions it follows that "Zola... is the very head of the Romanticists" (p. 164) and that Howells, "as respectable as a church and proper as a deacon" (p. 164) was an example of a realist. Since life is a combination of usual and exceptionable the truth-telling novelist must be both romantic and realistic.

Then Norris went on to hand down some *obiter dicta* which leaned heavily upon the New Nationalism rather than upon old critical tenets with which he was probably not familiar. It will be remembered that Vanamee in *The Octopus* urged Presley not to publish his poem "The Toilers" in magazines, where it would be read only by the well-to-do, but in the daily papers, where it would reach the workers to whom its message was addressed. In *The Responsibilities* Norris reaffirmed this point, arguing that literature must be vulgarized (p. 211), must be couched in the language of the populace, who in the long run will fix its rank. With more enthusiasm than respect for history he wrote that "the fact is indisputable that no art that is not in the end understood by the People can live or ever did live a generation" (p. 6), and "In the last analysis the people are always right" (p. 222). Great literature, he argued, is moral, which is an acceptable truism, but he should not without clarification have added as a corollary that "The better the personal morality of the writer, the better his writings" (p. 213), and he showed ignorance of Tolstoi's biography by citing that Russian as proof of his contention. *The Responsibilities of the Novelist* has little worth for the logician, the semanticist, or the critic, but its honesty, its democratic outlook, its lack of concern for *la jeune fille*, its call for the writer to desert the cloister for the outdoors illuminate both Norris's character and the temper of the early 1900's.

25. *The Responsibilities of the Novelist, The Complete Works of Frank Norris*, Garden City, 1928, VII, 164. All page references to this volume will be to the same edition.

Of the older writers Henry James published in 1902, 1903, and 1904 novels so outstanding that they will be given separate treatment. His disciple Edith Wharton, demonstrating a more concentrative dramatic talent than her teacher, still did not at that time succeed in establishing herself either as public favorite or finished artist, though her *Sanctuary* (1903) united two of the noblest themes available to a writer, themes that she was to employ over and over: other times tragically bring other manners, and children suffer for the sins of their parents. Clemence Verney of the second part of this novelette represents the new American girl who would never have immolated herself for such a fantastic reason as Kate Peyton did in the first part, and who worships at the altar of Success; Mrs. Peyton hovers with complete devotion over a son who, she fears, may have inherited a weakness from his father; and thus the two women become the bad and the good angels respectively in a battle whose tactics are nearly concealed in a fog of cerebration. *Sanctuary* irritates because it does not stretch its author's ability far enough. Its style, dependent upon fresh and vivid images, glows with the cold light of Mrs. Wharton's intelligence, yet glimmers into sentimentality when it touches the mother-son relationship. Its characters, netted in painfully credible temptations, lose flesh and blood and float off into an ether of brainstuff. "You and I," Dick told his mother, "are rather complicated people," and the common reader will vote this an understatement while he frowns unbelievingly over the sensitivity and clairvoyance of the principal actors.

There were few complicated personalities in the stories of the far north with which Jack London was still regaling his following. London was himself more complex than his whites and Indians and Eskimos of the land of the midnight sun for they grew starkly out of his conviction that the world was a battleground in which individuals and races fought for power, wealth, and women, while he could not hide his admiration for the cruelty of the Nordic type at the very time he was preaching the brotherhood of man. He was not insincere, he was muddled. He admitted there was something demoniacal about what he called the "breed," the descendants of "Clive and Hastings, Drake and Raleigh, Hengist and Horsa," but he rejoiced in its efficient brutality, seemingly unaware that this belief in race superiority fed the imperialism he condemned as a spring may feed a river. After living like a castaway in the London slums he could tell in *People of the Abyss* (1903) pitiful records of the unemployed, the unemployable, and the beggarly, with some bitter asides for the Salvation Army, and he could declare in the same year that "deep down in the roots of the race is fear" and like Mrs. Atherton blame the bourgeoisie for the decline of fiction in the United States,[26] but he could also contend in *The Reader* for June of 1903 that albeit Kipling was under a temporary cloud he would regain favor because he "memorialized" the Anglo-Saxon.

This racism, not rare among Americans then and not absent from Roosevelt's Americanism, London flaunted in his *Children of the Frost*, a collection of ten short stories published in 1902. The white men, says Tyee in "The Sunlanders," have "an unrest in them, which is a devil, and they are flung out over the earth to toil and suffer and fight without end," and he therefore finds himself caught in a conflict with them which can end only in extermination for, as Imber remarks wonderingly in "The League of Old Men," the white men and women appear soft, yet are strong enough to take and rule all the land of the Whitefish. Sometimes, however, the natives win, as they do in "In the Forests of the North," and in "Li Wan, the Fair" the white girl is unable to escape from her Eskimo husband. Four of the stories exhibit a humor which occasionally catches the grimness of the settings. Nam-Bok, returning to his people after years among the whites, tells them of such marvels that they exile him; Lone Chief is restored to health by a blow on the head; Keesh carries out the quest demanded by his sweetheart and gives her the heads of her

26. "The Terrible and Tragic in Fiction," *The Critic*, XLII, 540.

father and her three brothers; the astute shaman Secundo solves the theft of a blanket in a tale which every London follower will like, "The Master of Mystery." This mixture of wryness and farce also appears in three magazine stories London printed between 1902 and 1904. "Moon-Face" (*The Argonaut*, 21 July, 1902) tells of a Poesque murder; "The Faith of Men" (*The Sunset Magazine*, June, 1903) of a misprint which ruins a man's life; "The Marriage of Lit-Lit" (*Frank Leslie's Popular Monthly*, September, 1903) in lighter vein of an Indian who tries to extort more for his daughter than he had agreed to accept.

But none of these narratives lodges so securely in the memory as does "The Law of Life" (*Children of the Frost*) for here London distilled with a detachment that was almost approval his appreciation of the nakedness of the struggle for survival. An old Eskimo, given a few sticks of wood to keep up a fire, is left behind by his tribe, including his son, and as they move on to the hunting-ground and while Koskoosh reviews his long past he apprehends Nature's will that man be born, grow to consummation, reproduce, and lay down his life for the good of his folk, and when he permits the ring of hungry moose to close about him he does so with the knowledge that the law assigns life to the young and strong. Because that was London's faith, too, he could make *The Call of the Wild* (1903) one of the few classics about a dog; millions of readers young and old have responded to "the dominant primordial beast" in Buck, thrilled at the regression to the primitive, and hung upon his deeds of loyalty and of savage pugnacity. How much this short novel owes to Alfred Ollivant's *Owd Bob*, issued in the United States in 1898 as *Bob, Son of Battle*, it is impossible to say. The plot of the English novel has more to do with human rivalries and hatreds, has no throw-back to the elemental, but like Jack London's story it has scenes in which clubs are used on dogs, in which dogs fight for mastery, and in which a pack tears one animal to pieces. Whatever the relationship, the American work is so superior in creating suspense, in suiting environment to action and theme, and in feeling for the untamed that its place in literature cannot be shaken.

Nor can *The Sea-Wolf* (1904) be forgotten as a monument to the fierceness and frankness of the Will to Power early in the twentieth century. The speeches of Wolf Larsen are those of Nietzsche minus the lyricism, and although the wolverine captain softens toward the end and speaks wistfully of "emotional delight" as apart from reason, he dies unconverted. London intended *The Sea-Wolf* to be a satire on the super-man, yet it is Larsen who lingers in the memory as a lesser Miltonic Satan, and the two lovers and their sentiment that are readily dismissed from mind. There can be no question of the author's sympathy for this character. He made Larsen in paralysis and death an heroic figure, the voice of a philosophy which pursued London as a hound of hell. "Might is right," the captain of the "Ghost" avowed, "and that is all there is to it. Weakness is wrong. . . . One cannot wrong another man. He can only wrong himself." London did not accept the first part of this creed but he did believe weakness was wrong. When he thought he had discovered the causes of weakness among men he became a socialist, but when he observed the feebleness of the disinherited he recoiled like a crab and exulted in strength. He never thought his way through this confusion.

All of the narrative elements mentioned above are combined in London's first novel, *A Daughter of the Snows* (1902), judged by reviewers the best novel written about Alaska. Its skein unwinds from two reels: London's confidence in Nordic supremacy, and his fondness for and skill in writing a story of the outdoors. In carving out an empire in the Yukon Jacob Welse, father of the heroine, has learned that competition is the secret of creation. "Battle was the law and the only way of progress. The world was made for the strong, and only the strong inherited it, and through it all there ran an eternal equity." Frona Welse is the true child of this Nietzschean. Today she would be an invaluable member of an Olympic team for she swings clubs, boxes, fences, swims, makes high dives, chins a bar a score of times, and walks on her hands. At twenty she is quite conscious that she articulates race and must embody its ideals, which differ no whit from those of Beowulf's thanes. Her sophomoric monologues defend these ideals and her conduct exemplifies them, for she braves the ascent of the Chilcoot, penetrates the Inside in search of her father, teases a man because she has to spend an innocent storm-swept night in his tent, bears her share of burden and danger, smashes with an oar the hand of a drowning Scotsman and sends him to his death, and accompanies one of her suitors to the gallows when his nerve fails him. She delights to look "upon the strong males of her kind, with bodies comely in the sight of God and muscles swelling with the promise of deeds and work. Man, to her, was preeminently a fighter."

For all her trust in "Anglo-Saxon supremacy" Frona is troubled when another of her suitors mentions the Slav, "the only stripling in this world of young men and graybeards," and we come upon another of the premonitions of the threat that Russia might be to Western leadership. But Frona is shaken only for a moment. "May not we," she asks Vance Corliss, "who are possessing ourselves of the world and its resources, and gathering to ourselves all the knowledge, may not we nip the Slav ere he grows a thatch to his lip?" London's doubts lasted longer, and his division of thought was revealed by Colonel Trethway's meditation: "It seems a new Christ must arise and preach a new salvation—economic or sociologic —in these latter days, it matters not, so long as it is preached." Despite immature thinking and highflown phrasing *A Daughter of the Snows* is better than its author thought it was. The flashlight pictures of hardships endured and of slow painful death, the feats of strength and boldness, the rude court of justice which brings the story to its end allow pardon for the stilted dialogue, the naïve reflections, the amateurishness of much of the plotting. London was learning to pass from the short story form to the novel form, learning fast and happily. Indeed, the years between 1900 and 1905 may have been his happiest as man and writer. Like one of his imagined adventurers he had through adverse circumstances fought his way to desired achievement; he had youth and health and friends; he was a writer, he was making money, he had a first taste of fame. In 1904 the future turned a smiling face in his direction.

Frank Norris would have called London's version of the New Woman romantic and by the same token would have named David Graham Phillips's *A Woman Ventures* (1902) realistic, for Emily Bromfield of the latter novel was more representative of the pioneering undertaken by American girls in what she terms "this practical age" than was Frona Welse. On the other hand, her likeness to Meredith's Diana Warwick and Olive Schreiner's Lyndall prevents her from being purely an American phenomenon and gives her the outline of the typical rebellious young woman of the western world at the turn of the century. She is determined, that is, that she will not "settle down," that in marriage she will not be a chattel, that she will have an independent career and as much freedom as is feasible, and that in sexual behavior there shall be a single standard. Like Diana she loves more than once—a husband who divorces her, a married doctor who tempts her, and at last the man who meets her test. Unlike Diana and Lyndall she surveys her fellows with a cynicism which is partly innate, partly absorbed from her newspaper experience, and which is important not only because it catches a persisting mood in Phillips but also because it mirrors a widening reaction to the Age of Finance. "Who doesn't live lies," Emily asks a minister who confesses he doesn't believe what he preaches, "cheating himself and others?" Later she decides that friendship "means the opportunities for petty treachery, and the chance to assassinate in a crisis" and that "The difference between the mob and the intelligent few is that the mob is hypocritical and timid, while intelligent people frankly reach out for what they want." This toughmindedness, however, is largely on the surface. Emily is at heart something of both prig and prude, and her value as an early career woman in our fiction does not redeem a novel whose plot is melodramatic, whose characters paradoxically lack tension, and whose style is pedestrian. As social history it is pallid when contrasted with Gertrude Stein's tale of three lesbians written in 1903 as "Quod Erat Demonstrandum" but published in 1951 with the title *Things As They Are*.

Emily Bromfield's first important assignment as a newspaper woman was to help cover a strike near Pittsburgh, and there as she watched militia shoot down men and women and listened to the curses of a colleague she learned some of the facts of industrial life in the United States. By 1904 almost two million members of labor unions had learned how valuable a weapon the strike was in the struggle for power and had used it so freely and sometimes so violently that Clarence Darrow, counsel for the United Mine Workers, recommended in a speech at Chicago in 1903 that workers turn their attention to political rather than to direct action. The most severe strike in Roosevelt's first administration was that of the Pennsylvania coal miners in 1902, ultimately settled by the intervention of the president, but the same year saw also a strike against the American Woolen Company in February and riots by teamsters in Chicago in June; in 1903 there were strikes among textile workers, subway workers, trackworkers, teamsters, carpenters, even grave-diggers; in 1904 a strike in the Chicago packing industry, another among 30,000 mill workers in Fall River, with rioting as sympathetic strikes spread, and the "most dastardly" of all, a strike among hearse and carriage drivers in Chicago. To Theodore Roosevelt, to most of the muckrakers, to the novelists and playwrights who were going to make use of them, and to the general consumer strikes were sporadic intervals of recrimination and violence in which, the principle of collective bargaining not yet accepted, workers tried to wrest from their employers more money, better working conditions, a better living generally. To Thorstein Veblen in *The Theory of Business Enterprise* (1904) they were proof of the breakdown of a culture based upon the romantic postulate of natural rights and the rise of one whose aspects were determined by the machine. Veblen went further than this in his indictment of a "protracted predatory culture." After again blaming the financial bourgeoisie for waste, ostentation, and snobbery he accused business of being more interested in cut-throat competition than in production for use, of encouraging overproduction, of achieving prosperity only through an arms economy or some extraneous or fortuitous series of events, and of propagating points of view so specialized that capital-ists and workers could not understand the needs and aspirations of each other and hence lived in mutual suspicion and dislike. As personal, as heavily phrased, and as loose-jointed as *The Theory of the Leisure Class* (1899), this new volume like the earlier one was an ammunition depot for socialists, who shrewdly made use of its doctrine that an economic system, not individuals, was responsible for social ills and who ex-pressed sympathy for the very rich as victims rather than carriers of Americanismus.

This scientific approach did not satisfy the moralists who, without raising the issue of free will, found it necessary or practical to fix upon unrighteous men the blame for economic dislocations and malpractices and who, in line with President Roosevelt, set out to denounce by name the financiers, politi-cians, and corporations which brazenly violated or by-passed federal and state laws. For a few years the most prominent and certainly the most sensational of these commentators was a group of journalists, held together only by an honest desire for reform, who were presently and for a curious reason stig-matized by the president as muckrakers. Their motives and their methods in criticizing public men were almost as old as American writing, but muckraking as a movement in our literature may be said to have begun in October of 1902 when *McClure's Magazine* printed "Tweed Days in St. Louis," jointly authored by Lincoln Steffens and Claude H. Wet-more.[27] This ten-page article, devoted largely to the account of Joseph W. Folk's courageous campaign to clean up corrup-

27. For histories of the muckraking movement see in the bibliography Louis Filler and Cornelius C. Regier.

tion in the Missouri city, set the pattern for so many succeeding exposures of bribery and profit-sharing, of the non-partisan alliances among city officials, contractors, and heads of utility companies that a steady magazine reader might have been convinced that American politics was honeycombed with graft, especially when he noted in 1904 that for the first time in our history a United States Senator was sentenced to prison for malfeasance in office. More rousing in the long run than Steffens's essay was Ida Tarbell's *History of the Standard Oil Company*, printed as a serial in *McClure's* from November, 1902, through October, 1904, and published in the latter year, for it is one of the most comprehensive and accurate chronicles of the rise of a big industry ever attempted, devoid of sensationalism, yet frank in its revelations of corporate intrigue and personal ruthlessness. With page after page of unassailable facts Miss Tarbell showed how a monopoly had been established chiefly through rebates from greedy railroads and through other Machiavellian tactics of a gifted man whose sincere religious faith and business behavior were as disparate as though he had lived in Italy during the Renaissance. No document did more to make John D. Rockefeller the symbol of finance Caesarism, to make him also the most execrated American of the Roosevelt period. The *History of the Standard Oil Company*, a pat economic education in 1904, remains an invaluable record of the development of our industrialism.

In May of 1903 the muckrakers were given additional incentive by Dr. Harvey Wiley's announcement of the poisonous content of several vendible drugs, and the next year the *Ladies' Home Journal* warned its readers against dangerous patent medicines. In September of 1904 *Leslie's Monthly Magazine* began a fight against railroad accidents; in the same month Thomas W. Lawson, soon to be a storm center in the agitations of the era, contributed to *Everybody's* an article on the administration of some insurance companies, an attack followed up by an article in *The Arena* for November. By 1905 muckraking had become a lucrative occupation pursued by writers whose intentions and characters were rarely open to question and whose findings, eventually so vexing to Theodore Roosevelt, must be related to the growing number of novels dedicated to a serious interpretation of the life of the time.

"The romance of labor, of traffic, of politics," wrote Bliss Perry in the last chapter of *A Study of Prose Fiction* (1902), "in our strangely composite civilization, has been perceived by a few writers; but how much is still to be told!" But Anthony Hope was of the opinion that our writers were turning out the novel of trade and commerce, of competition and commerce, with zest and had found a welcoming audience, and in this instance the English visitor had the better discernment. For American novelists between 1902 and 1905 were aware of the fictional values of Americanismus, aware, too, of a duty to inform their readers of its threat to national health, and whatever they lacked in artistic skill they made up in a courage and veracity which command respect today because they produced a lasting picture of the Strong Man in his environment, of the Will to Power driving nakedly through the markets and senates of those years. Even if the formal histories of Roosevelt's first administration were to be destroyed we should have in the work of Frank Norris, David Graham Phillips, Robert Herrick, and lesser penmen a reliable report upon the spirit which prompted too many citizens to disregard laws and morality and human sympathies in order to accumulate fortunes which later rested heavily upon their consciences, for just as Andrew Carnegie in April of 1903 gave a million and a half to the Peace Palace in The Hague, and John D. Rockefeller in the same year donated millions to the University of Chicago and to medical research, so did the self-made rich heroes of the novels frequently end in some kind of repentance.

Repentance does not come to William Thorndike, the industrial tyrant of George Kibbe Turner's *The Taskmasters* (1902), because he is murdered by an unfairly treated worker, but John Mayhew, the idealistic lawyer who is the hero of the tale, acquires wisdom through the realization that both political parties are corrupt, that there is justice on the side of the employer as well as of the laborer, and that industrial and financial evolution, bringing incidental barbarities, will end in something good and great. This impartiality is not entirely the author's, for Turner believed that a manufacturing aristocracy would undermine a republic, and in his final chapter while scorning the Utopian proposals of Henry George he put brave words into the mouths of the "weary figures" before his mind's eye:

"All we ask for is our show. And we are going to have it. Sometime, some way, sooner or later, we shall have our privileges and our honest rights; and all your tricking and cheating and class legislation and juggling will not avail you. We are the strongest in the end; the great tendency of men's affairs swings toward us."

The Taskmasters is not a good novel. It fumbles in a technique that would later have been labelled "Our-Town," and its characters and incidents soon slip from memory, yet its echoes of social attitudes and changes preserve it from failure. Superficially less serious was I. K. Friedman's *The Autobiography of a Beggar* (1902), but the drollery of this book is based upon an understanding of human nature and of the time, and when Mollbuzzer proclaims that his motto is "ef ye can't git what yer want, don't sit down and cry, but jist go and grab it" we hear an authentic voice. No humor is to be found in Harry Leon Wilson's *The Spenders* (1902), which tells how a third generation by means of waste and gambling dissipates an inherited fortune. Brand Whitlock's first novel, *The Thirteenth District* (1902), told how Jerry Garwood, likable though he had an underdeveloped sense of honor, was nominated for congressional office by a machine and thereafter became a creature of its boss.

In 1903 Alfred Henry Lewis testified to the crookedness of municipal politics in *The Boss*, Meredith Nicholson touched gingerly upon sharp business *pratique* in *The Main Chance*, David Graham Phillips gave what he meant to be a frightening history of a multimillionaire in *The Master Rogue*, and Frank

Norris transported his wheat from the fields of California to the Chicago Grain Exchange in *The Pit*, with an exciting description of stock manipulation and of battle between operators. Of these four novels, each of which treats of the symptoms and progress of Americanismus, the first is the gloomiest, for making use of the career of Richard Croker it presents our largest city under the heel of a man who is a complex of sternness, treachery, cunning, cynicism, lawlessness, and introspection—a metropolis in which the organisms of self-government have broken down, where "morals and truth as questions will ever depend for their answer upon environment and point of view" and where "one will be wise, who regards generosity as a disease, and sets to cure it with every sullen, cruel drug the case demands." The phrasing is blurred, but Lewis's disenchantment was genuine enough to forward a conviction that there is no real cry for reform from the voters, that reformers are therefore futile, that politicians are animals at the trough, that democracy has been degraded to the point where shame is useless. Beside the Boss, Nicholson's Timothy Margrave of *The Main Chance* is, in spite of his use of blackmail, physical violence, and assorted chicaneries, a tepid figure, and the Indianian's novel remains more a love story that an indictment of big business.

David Graham Phillips's sardonic characterization of a very rich man in *The Master Rogue* is neither quite interesting as fiction nor convincing as social documentation. The novel purports to be the autobiography of a financier as he awaits with a mixture of dread and defiance the cerebral stroke which will bring an end to a career that had begun with a bold theft, had made him enormously wealthy, had seen him crush the will of any opponent, and had left him in the end hated, despised, and alone save for a daughter. The Rogue reveals himself a monster, unfeeling, arrogant, conscienceless, utterly without belief in anyone or anything save himself, exulting in his scheming brain, contemptuous of wife and children except for a respect for his youngest child, Helen, who is very much like himself, only strictly honest. There is material here for verbal sculpture such as Dreiser was going to exhibit in his carving of Frank Cowperwood, but Phillips worked hastily; his method was principally to have the Rogue condemn himself by writing almost invariably the opposite of the truth which the reader could perceive—a method taken over by Sinclair Lewis—and in the end this resulted in thinness and monotony. The business transactions are only sketched, the persons around the Rogue are dangled in puppetry, the Rogue himself is allowed too few gradations in personality. Only in the Faustian ending when the solitary old man, tempted to regret his past and to recant the rationale by which he has lived, faces death with courage and resignation does the reader get a true catharsis. Otherwise the novel is a hard-to-believe calendar of selfish acts, with Phillips as unrelenting as his protagonist, and with Helen, the one intuitively drawn character, receiving too little care. When she says in the last sentence that her father was "one of the noblest men who ever lived— and nobody understood him but me" she was inviting the author to rewrite his book with a meticulous examination of the relationship between parent and daughter and with more sympathy for the man. And in that sentence Phillips confessed *sotto voce* that there was in the fierce Will to Power of Master Rogues, in their terrible creativeness, a blending of baseness, grandeur, and the pitiful. *The Master Rogue* falls short as fiction and as satire, and is instead an angry sermon on the text that it profits nothing to gain the world and lose one's soul.

Frank Norris's *The Pit*, read with such approval that it became a best seller in the year of its publication, is also disappointing. It is common to say that this continuation of the Epic of the Wheat pales in contrast with *The Octopus*, and much as one hesitates to repeat the critical cliché there is no candid alternative. Perhaps Norris found the Board of Trade such a subject as made it difficult for him to fuse "romance" and "realism" according to his prescription; perhaps the character of Curtis Jadwin, the Strong Man who plays the market not to gain power but because he succumbs to the gambling fever, was antipathetic to him; perhaps he felt the love story sinking into a parlor *amusette*.[28] At any rate, Norris allots most space to the story of Laura Jadwin, one of the earlier heroines in American fiction to be neglected by a husband absorbed in business. Laura bears a resemblance to the more famous Carol Kennicott: she longs for culture, she admires her husband's strength, she is sensitive to the temptation of an artist, she finally cleaves to her husband, though for a reason much more romantic than Carol's. Norris obviously sought to mold a complex woman in this instance, for two sides of Laura raise a major issue. She craves refinement, yet is fascinated by the battle of the Street simply because it is a battle. She makes wan progress through a wan mid-western cultivation, going from Verdi to Wagner to Berlioz, from Romantics to Victorians in poetry, from Bougereau to the Impressionists.[29] Yet the instinctive woman shrinks from all this at last and responds to the heroism in a man who fights to the death, a man who is bored by literature and the other arts. Laura is more strongly realized than Jadwin, who is caught, as he says, between two sets of circumstances and who does not keep his promise to stop speculating because his will abdicates in the presence of an impersonal force. The obsession with gambling is a Zolaesque touch, but the novel contains more fatalism than sociological determinism, and Curtis Jadwin is punished for his sins, though not so harshly as Behrman is in *The Octopus*. Again the wheat proved unconquerable, thus supporting the thesis and the mysticism with which Norris began the unfinished trilogy.

The Pit owed its popularity to the increasing number of "office wives" in this nation and to readers who found excite-

28. According to Franklin Walker, *Frank Norris: A Biography*, New York, 1932, pp. 8-15, Jadwin's mannerisms, tastes, appearance, and background are those of Norris's father. Jadwin's attempted *coup* was based on Joseph Leiter's corner in wheat in 1897.

29. In 1908 in Ye Liberty Theatre of Oakland, Cal., the performance of "The Pit" began with the playing of a Victor recording of the Quartet from "Rigoletto" made by Caruso, Bessie Abbot, Louise Homer, Antonio Scotti.

ment in the fight that Jadwin put up for fortune and wife. Two novels of 1904 told more of the ravages of Americanismus, more of the corruption slowly creeping through all levels of our society, undermining family, weakening professional integrity, menacing all the old principles. The architect Jackson Hart of Robert Herrick's *The Common Lot* hears from a friend that "What man respects in this town is money—first, last, and all the time," and further on he agrees that "the supreme prize of man's life today" is "a little pot of gold." The desire for wealth poisons not only the man whom Pauline Gardiner marries in David Graham Phillips's *The Cost* but even prompts the heroine to ask: "But shouldn't you like to be rich and famous and—all that?" In both novels retribution overtakes the men who sell their souls for money: John Dumont of *The Cost* triumphs over the financial wolves who seek to ruin him, then dies suddenly "in the heaps and coils of ticker-tape," and the hero of *The Common Lot* recovers his manhood and his family only by confessing his share of guilt in the erection of a firetrap, risking a jail sentence, and returning in poverty to his first job.[30] Neither of these somber novels gives countenance to the struggle for worldly success, "that beast-struggle," as Herrick called it, "to snatch a dollar that some other man wants to get from you," but *The Cost*, one of whose two protagonists is a young, honest politician with a distant likeness to Albert J. Beveridge, breathes more of the Rooseveltian confidence in a strenuous Americanism. Francis Lynde's almost forgotten *The Grafters* (1904), a fair novel about an unworthy governor and a gallant hero who saved a railroad, is also hopeful about the America of the future.

The deaths of Pope Leo XIII (20 July) and Herbert Spencer (8 December) in 1903, and the celebration of the Emerson centenary in the same year inevitably raised the question of what the Christian churches and what philosophy

---

30. *The Common Lot* spells out on p. 319 the words "son of a bitch." This is the earliest such instance I have noted in American fiction.

could or would do to halt the corrosions of mammonism, materialism, skepticism, even the kind of altruism Spencer taught.[31] The question was a perturbing one, especially for all true churchmen. Francis Marion Crawford was probably correct when in the *New York Journal* for 29 December he asserted that scientific atheism was on the decline, but it was all too apparent that the industrial proletariat, telling over its grievances, was losing interest in church doctrines and services and that this interest would not return until the church could restore a design to the somewhat chipped mosaic of American society. One of the more useful men in labor relations, the Rev. Charles Stelzle, recommended that ministers sermonize less about Hittites, Levites, Perizzites, Jebusites, and consider more fully the problems of Pittsburghites and Chicagoites. Other clergymen had other policies: John A. Dowie founded Zion City on the shores of Lake Michigan in 1901; Newell Dwight Hillis in *Everybody's* for April, 1904, proposed a church unity to parallel the organization of a trust; Bishop Henry C. Potter dedicated a saloon, the Subway Tavern of New York City, in August of 1904; Thomas C. Hall of the Union Theological Seminary warned in the *North American Review*, for June, 1904, that socialism was Christianity's strongest rival, a belief that was to get into print often during the decade. Woodrow Wilson in a pamphlet called *The Young People and the Church* (1904) emphasized the value of a good example in the home and the teaching of love as a motive for conduct. Sir Oliver Lodge affirmed in the first issue of *The Hibbert Journal* (October, 1902) that the highest science and the truest theology must be mutually consistent, but William James, writing with some wistfulness of the psychological side of religion in *The Varieties of Religious Experience* (1902) stated that he took religion pragmatically, that he could not accept Christianity or theology, and that he regarded immortality as unproved.

31. Others dying in 1903: Julian Ralph (20 Jan.), Charles G. Leland (20 March), Richard H. Stoddard (12 May), William E. Henley (11 June), George Gissing (28 Dec.).

The restless mind of Henry Adams, despairing of any successful harmonizing of twentieth-century ethics with the teachings of Jesus, offered solace to a few of his friends in *Mont-Saint-Michel and Chartres*, which he printed in a small private edition in 1904 because he did not believe there were in the United States a hundred persons able to read it. Adams' books were in their final casting meant to be helps to teachers of history, and this volume, concerned with an interpretation of the past in such a way as to achieve within itself a unity in multiplicity as well as to indicate the occurrence of this phenomenon in historical events, scaled its purpose by becoming a masterpiece of impressionism through which the author taught that the highest intensity of vital human energy is stated in two terms, religion and art. Spurning modern history, Adams went back, as all his readers know, to the Middle Ages, specifically to the hundred years from 1150 to 1250, to find a faith which permeated and directed man's activity, which inspired architects, painters, musicians, poets, soldiers, lovers, kings and queens, theologians, the ignorant peasants and stonemasons who lovingly gave of time and body to erect memorials to the Queen of Heaven. Chapter by chapter what Adams had to say about cathedrals, about medieval architecture, about the four queens, about Abélard and St. Thomas Aquinas, about the Virgin herself may not satisfy the experts, but the total effect of these chapters communicates to any reader a feeling for medieval Europe, a nostalgia for order consummated in belief, that can scarcely be matched elsewhere. Adams, who called himself a Conservative Christian Anarchist, and who wrote to Charles Gaskell in 1904 that "The Virgin and St. Thomas are my vehicles of anarchism," [32] put so much of himself into this volume that it becomes a touching as well as an anti-materialistic reaction to the McKinley-Roosevelt Period. For there we find his contempt for the run of his fellows, the denial of his own time, the search for a Golden Age in which "progress" stood still, his interest in old manu-

32. *Letters*, p. 452.

scripts, his awe for the construction as well as for the spirit of the Merveille, the enthusiasm for stained glass which John La Farge had inculcated, the idealization of his dead wife transferred into reverence for the Mother of God, the passion for color and form and non-puritanic sex which had been balked in his own country—all adding up to an undogmatic adoration of the Virgin Mary as the fount of harmony and beauty, the force, too, through which the weak civilization of western Europe had come to strength by virtue of a common worship. To the cynical old man the Virgin incarnated all that was powerful through purity and loveliness; she was indeed so real, so present to him that he could think of her as supervising the building of the edifices in her honor, encouraging, planning, playing with the stones as toys, and thoughts of her could ever associate themselves with his perception of anything beautiful. "No one," he wrote in 1902, "ever loved the dog-wood and Judas tree as I have done, and it is my one crown of life to be sure that I am going to take them with me to heaven to enjoy real happiness with the Virgin and them. She will so delight in the color, though it would be quite off Chartres!" [33]

Adams judged *Mont-Saint-Michel and Chartres* to be his masterwork. In 1910 he was willing to avow that "The only book I ever wrote that was worth writing was the first volume of the series—Mont-Saint-Michel" and in the same letter he dismissed the *Education* as "drivel." [34] It is therefore pleasant to note that his poor opinion of the intelligence of his fellow-citizens was not wholly justified; by 1913 requests for a larger edition of his confession of faith were so insistent that he consented to a republication. Although it never attained as *The Education* did the distinction of better seller, and although it may be praised for its estheticism rather than for its scholarship, *Mont-Saint-Michel and Chartres* will remain a favorite with readers who wish to reach the heart of one of the most talented and most unhappy men of his generation and who

33. *Ibid.,* p. 387.
34. *Ibid.,* p. 540.

can rejoice in the brilliant interpretation of a century which he did much to make valid to Americans.

Before 1904 Henry Adams had concluded that the dynamo was to the twentieth century what the Virgin had been to the twelfth. Few Americans in that year would have followed his reasoning; few had the sense, as they read in magazines of the research, the inventions, and the discoveries which could render their lives more comfortable, that the machine was to become in their span of time the fateful instrument of vast forces organized for conquest. The flight of Alberto Santos-Dumont's dirigible at Monte Carlo on the twenty-eighth of January, 1902, and of Wilbur and Orville Wright's heavier-than-air plane at Kitty Hawk on the seventeenth of December, 1903, provided topics for conversation but promoted no apprehension. Even reputable scientists doubted that Guglielmo Marconi's wireless telegraph would work, and the Italian's message across the Atlantic just before Christmas in 1902 was not believed decisive. But the man in the street was interested in the automobile, though not to the point where he would spend more than $80,000,000 on all the roads of the United States in 1904. The *Philadelphia Record* complained in 1902 that some autos were being driven forty or fifty miles an hour; *Medical News* (2 January, 1904) protested that automobile driving increased nervous diseases; neither of these objections hindered general fascination with the "red devils" on the highways or speculation as to when these carriages might supplant the horse instead of merely being playthings of the wealthy. For the first time a novel about a machine achieved popularity in the United States. This was *The Lightning Conductor* (1903) of C. N. and A. M. Williamson, a writing team, half American, that invented a successful formula for fiction which it used over and over: that of an impersonation which should have deceived nobody, carried on during a motor tour through scenic, historic parts of Europe, and ending with the winning of a beauteous girl who is either on a walking trip or is a passenger in a Mercedes. It was a feeble stereotype, but for at least seven years it did not fail to please.

The most amateurish oracle could have foretold the result of the presidential campaign of 1904. Some disgruntled Republican leaders had talked of replacing Roosevelt with Mark Hanna, but Hanna died on the fifteenth of February in that year, and this event, coupled with the president's undoubted standing with the public, made a re-nomination inevitable.[35] To persuade the disaffected that Roosevelt was after all "safe and sane" Joseph G. Cannon was chosen to make the notification speech at Sagamore Hill on 27 July, after which the nominee withdrew in dignity and made no tour of speechmaking. The Democrats by-passed the twice-defeated Bryan, turned down William Randolph Hearst, and picked as candidates Alton B. Parker and Henry G. Davis. The socialists again named Eugene V. Debs, with Charles H. Corregan as running-mate.[36] Roosevelt's opponents accused him of irresponsibility, of having dictatorial ambitions, of militarism, of having fomented a revolution in Panama in 1903 so as to secure from an independent government the right to a canal zone across the isthmus. In an undistinguished election the most

35. Others dying in 1904: Parke Godwin (7 Jan.), Edwin Arnold (24 March), Samuel Smiles (16 April), Anton Dvorak (1 May), Henry M. Stanley (10 May), Matthew S. Quay (28 May), Anton Chekhov (2 July), Samuel M. (Golden Rule) Jones (12 July), Paul Kruger (14 July), Lafcadio Hearn (26 Sept.), Frederic A. Bartholdi (4 Oct.), Trumbull Stickney (11 Oct.).

36. Theodore Roosevelt, stockier than most photographs suggest, punctuated his spoken sentences with his teeth in an effort to make his words distinct; his voice was not strong; his gestures were those of a fighter or of a one-armed woodchopper. Bryan, solid, serious, had an unrivalled resonance of tone. Debs, tall, gaunt, bending from the waist with arms extended, palms up, seemed to invite his hearers into a conversation. The present writer, who heard all three in addresses, remembers J. Frank Hanly, Republican governor of Indiana in 1904, Prohibition candidate for president in 1916, as the most moving speechmaker of the day. Woodrow Wilson at his best was an incomparable public speaker and the most practiced orator who ever sat in the White House.

caustic notes came from Alfred Henry Lewis, who heard the rattling of dead men's bones; in the October *Book News* he wrote scathingly of all campaign literature, quoting Horace Walpole's remark that he might love his country if it were not for his countrymen, and he published *The President*, a novel which stressed the economic motive as the most active one back of political ambitions. After Roosevelt renounced the idea of a third term, after the torches sputtered out, the hustings closed, and the votes were counted it was found that the Republican candidate had a popular plurality of 2,549,331. Strenuous Americanism was vindicated.

III

Henry James and the Direct Impression

The literary Great Awakening which in the past several years has elevated Henry James to an exalted place in the pantheon of American writers is a phenomenon to challenge at least brief attention. It cannot be dismissed as only an episode in the evangelism of critics and biographers, for the sale of books about James and of reprints of his fiction suggests that it represents a conversion of an impressive segment of the literate public, though to be sure, books purchased are not always read. But everything associated with the revival indicates that James is being read with great respect, if not always with great enthusiasm, and the desire to know why becomes irresistible. Hollywood has done something to make James's name a familiar one for its adaptations of his stories have generally been intelligent and well acted, and the Broadway stage has done equally well for smaller audiences; even television and radio have helped to spread James's reputation. College courses have listed James as required reading for thousands of students; off the campus his work has had a snob appeal which may not be discounted. A few critics may have turned to him in the wish to exploit something new to the present generation, and it may be hopefully proposed that the wish to return to excellence at a time when our writing too seldom rises above shoddiness, and the longing to find creative formalism in a world grown suddenly chaotic, have had not a little to do with the vogue of the Master. Two World Wars in the past forty years, with millions of Americans obliged to live abroad, induced us to realize certain contrasts between

American and European ways of living and of looking at life, a subject which inevitably occupied James's mind and informed his art, though some close students of his tales choose to argue that the international angle of vision was for him a fairly unimportant one. Finally, it may well be that a host of booklovers has found, not quite spontaneously, that Henry James has everything or almost everything to meet its demands for novels of a high standard, and that it has derived a rare pleasure from stories of which ambiguous reports had been current.

Only two of these causes were operating in the early 1900's. It was thought then that a well-read person should be acquainted with James, that there was a certified distinction about so doing. And thus some persons came to like James as they may have developed a taste for artichokes. He was, it is well to remember, the most discussed American novelist of the decade, with criticism assuming a configuration which has been changed only by the addition of Freudian and Marxian embroideries. But criticism of James immediately after 1900 was often fault-finding, if not hostile; the bits of it which are quoted from time to time in this volume reveal an attitude ranging from the querulous to the scandalized. Most of the complaints at the opening of the century are echoed today. For example, Charles B. Loomis, after drawing up parallel paragraphs by James and by himself as explaining what James was trying to say, went on to allege that

It is for the complex souls that he weaves the involutions, purposely misplaces words, and in a way to gratify their sense of immeasurable leisure takes his tortuous way along to an ending that is no end of a delight to him and to them, but is no end at all to the common reader.[1]

The sentence makes a three-pronged attack, for it charges James with deliberate obscurantism, with intentionally catering to an élite, and with involved processes of characterization,

1. Charles Battell Loomis, "An Attempt to Translate Henry James," *The Bookman*, XXI, 464.

with putting his victims on the rack, as James Lane Allen
had phrased it twenty years before, and bending over them
to catch the last gasp of an expiring consciousness. One former
accusation against James, however, is not likely to be heard
today. Frank Moore Colby, also contributing to *The
Bookman*, declared that

> Never did so much vice go with so much vagueness.... His love
> affairs, illicit though they be, are so stripped to their motives that
> they seem no more enticing than a diagram.... Six phantoms meet
> and dine, three male, three female, with two thoughts apiece, and
> after elaborate geometry of the heart, adultery follows like a
> Q.E.D. Shocking it ought to be, but yet it is not.... No flesh, no
> frailty; that may be why our sternest moralists have licensed
> Henry James to write his wickedest.[2]

In this instance the puritanic demur so outspeaks the dissatisfaction with James's evocation of character as to leave the
secondary impeachment almost unnoticed.

Before we smile too broadly over the arraignment of James
as wicked we should in all fairness admit that there were in
1902 more grounds for this view than critics in recent times
have taken the opportunity to point out. Almost from the
beginning of his career James had been questioning the
rationality of the sentimental, the romantic idealization of
love, had been exhibiting it as a baneful emotion, a kind of
madness descending upon men and women of the nineteenth
century. And by 1900 he was, in his coveting of the larger
existence, of the truly good and free life for his personae,
willing to have them defy what was to him a cheap concept
of love and sometimes willing to defy the Victorian conventions which buttressed it. The genteel reviewer could not but
be offended by this approach and he could not overlook the
adultery which appeared in *The Wings of the Dove* (1902),
The Ambassadors (1903), and *The Golden Bowl* (1904);
hardly could he forgive the fact that in the second of these

2. Frank Moore Colby, "The Queerness of Henry James," *The Bookman*,
XV, 397.

the author condoned the crime, even seemed to recommend it under conditions which in his eyes produced a richer, more perceptive living for one or both of the participants. This was not morality in the days of Roosceveltian Americanism, nor had it ever been in any considerable part of our nation. More-over, relieved of all their artistic virtues these novels had a superficial vulgarity, not invisible to a later reader. In the first an English girl, pitilessly conspiratorial behind her brain and her exquisite sensibilities, spends a night with an Englishman so as to persuade him to marry an American heiress and commit what would have been legal embezzlement; in the second an American learns from his Parisian mistress how to outgrow the parochial limitations of Massachusetts, how to fit into an environment of good taste and art and thought, only at the end to wish to discard her and pass on to fresh experience; in the third James employed a basic plot that might have been concocted by the shabbiest of writers for the subway trade, for it deals with high life and with a quadrilateral of adulterous intrigue in Europe. Even the names of his characters over the years had given off a faint odor of vulgarity: Joscelind Bernardstone, Barbarina Canterville, Marcellus Cockerel, Florimond Daintry, Greville Fane, George Gravener, Reginald Langstaff, Mora Montravers, Hyacinth Robinson, Leolin Stormer, Fleda Vetch, Frederic Winterbourne, and many others that sounded as though they might have been at home in the narratives of Mrs. E. D. E. N. Southworth. Today, the Genteel Tradition having been given its quietus, and the reader inured to scenes of turpitude and lawbreaking, James's situations no longer administer a shock, and as for the names of his characters, they are seen to represent the same play of association that James Joyce utilized in his later experiments.

In the book reviews and in chapters on James in the opening years of the century he was praised, if at all, for the same merits attributed to him today. He was called a painstaking and fine-fingered analyst of character, a master of the "psychological" novel. He was recognized as an expert technician, equipped with extraordinary skill in the assembling of the elements which make a whole story. He was admired for the quality of his realism in small matters, and he was admitted to be so conscientious a craftsman as to have produced the most precise writing in the history of the novel in English. With these concessions and tributes, however, the praise ended; only Howells among outstanding American critics was ready to call James a great novelist. Today there is little argument about James's pre-eminence, and commentators attend to the business of eulogy and explication. Nevertheless the question of Henry James remains, for it would be premature to assume that future generations will be as reverential toward him as we are. And that question reduced to its simplest terms is two-fold: what did James conceive a novel to be, and what do his clients wish it to be?

It is sometimes forgotten that James believed a novel was neither more nor less than a story, that its components of plot, characterization, setting, action, dialogue, style, and form could not be developed and contained separately but must be blended into and read as a unit. "I cannot see," he wrote in "The Art of Fiction," "what is meant by talking as if there were a part of a novel which is the story and part of it which for mystical reasons is not,"[3] and in the same essay he was of the opinion that "The only obligation to which in advance we may hold a novel, without incurring the accusation of being arbitrary, is that it be interesting" (p. 384). Up to that point there is likely to be nearly complete agreement between James and his client, although there can never be unanimity with respect to what is interesting. But James went on to say that his intention was to create "a direct impression of life" (p. 384) and that "The novel seems to me the most magnificent form of art" (p. 402), and it may not be taken for granted that the client will approve the intent, concur in the verdict, or agree that James's novels between 1902 and 1905 were magnificent works of art. Some novel readers prefer not to come upon what is drafted as a direct impression of life;

3. Henry James, "The Art of Fiction," *Partial Portraits*, London, 1888, p. 399.

almost all of them are willing to make a detour now and then; and the status of the novel as art raises problems as insoluble as those of sin and politics. The corpus of recent criticism amply demonstrates that the question of Henry James is sufficiently complex, but if we accept his quoted dicta as fundamental, though early, and hypothesize his client as mature and critically-minded, then the question can be re-stated with some assurance: did James write interesting stories which gave a direct impression of life and do they qualify as works of art?

In *The Wings of the Dove, The Ambassadors,* and *The Golden Bowl* James did have interesting stories to tell, stories which, viewed with detachment, are essentially those of intrigue and suspense. This is especially true of the first and the last in which we have, respectively, an attempt by an English couple to take money from an American girl so that they may marry after the latter's death, and an undertaking by an Italian prince to deceive his wife with her stepmother and still preserve the amenities of an unusual ménage; *The Ambassadors* lets the client wonder whether Lambert Strether will adopt a Latin attitude toward the relation of the sexes or will remain puritanic either from conviction or expediency. All three, told with verve, with clarity and simplicity and against a verifiable background, might well have struck the fancy of the public. However, *The Ambassadors* was the only one to be well received, and it did not approach the best-seller list. Yet *The Wings of the Dove* is one of the tenderest love stories ever penned, and *The Golden Bowl,* the consummation of James's skills and the final enunciation of his view of life, is a massive and high-embowed cathedral of narrative. Our hypothesized reader will agree to these judgments, but he may do so with serious, if timid, reservations; he may, indeed, find that two of the three novels are interesting only in parts, and this not because he is looking for a story that can be a substitute for a summer game of tennis but because certain things in the telling weaken his attention and give him pause.

The first complaint, one need hardly repeat, is against the style of these novels of "the major phase," a style so loquacious, so clause-bound, and in the instance of *The Golden Bowl* so frequently Olympian and flatulent at once that the client feels that James was putting language protectively between himself and the world. There had long been objection to James's idiom and it is probable that there always will be; he had for years been accused of applying too much power to achieve his ends, of using a spray gun to paint a small canvas, of sending a giant to do a boy's work. The unkindest cut had appeared in H. G. Wells's *Boon* (1915), with the Englishman likening James to a hippopotamus trying to pick up a pea which had rolled into a corner of its cage; later William James humorously suggested that Henry had changed his stenographer and that the habit of dictating had damaged the manner of writing. An anthology of the reviews of James's fiction would print hundreds of remonstrances on this score, remonstrances that would often be warranted, for James was not one to throw a phrase over his shoulder and let it lie—he had to tease it, worry it, walk round and round it, and finally elongate it, so that presently the reader, discovering he needs mental seven-league boots to follow in the author's tracks, speculates upon the possibility that James compensated himself for being out-talked as a child by opening the dikes of the dictionary when he became a man. The fault is most marked in *The Wings of the Dove* and *The Golden Bowl*, where what has been noted as the increasing feminization of James's mind seems to have been responsible for the prodigalities in exactitude, the anxious concentration upon the shade of meaning, the unwillingness to let go, the poetic opacity.

It is not alone the proliferation of words which becomes troublesome, it is also the order in which the sentences are constructed with a multiplication of parts that often leaves clauses wandering in search of antecedents and that breeds a confusion ending in fatigue for the reader. Inevitably, as James should have known, this mismanagement had its effect not only upon the client's pleasure in the flow of the story but also upon his response to the characterization. For example, the opening of Book Third of *The Wings of the Dove*, in which Milly Theale's nature is to be revealed by the fact that she sits alone above an Alpine prospect, could have been moving and beautiful; the imaginative idea, the emotion are there, but they are bound by ropes of phrases, clauses, parentheses without punctuation until the whole of the chapter becomes a mass of verbal freight. Worse still, as the story continues, is the unexpected tendency to write alliteratively, an effort to give vitality to a corpulent body from which the springing step is gone, a striving for a dignity which, lacking litheness, invites amused wonderment. Now and then, it is true, one finds a figure sharply realized, a flash of genuine humor, but not until Book Ninth, wherein James dissects Merton Densher's reasons for letting things drift, does the reader get his head above the flood of words which too often submerged the dialogue, and not until he comes upon the fencing between Densher and Kate Croy does he know that here is a superb story superbly told from that point on. Nothing, James admitted, was more exciting to him than a psychological reason, and in detailing the struggle, often inarticulate, always temperamental, between the Englishman and his sweetheart he contrived to triumph over his defects and communicate that excitement to a high degree.

But the defects of style, the wordiness, the involvement of modifier and appositive, the devious approach to the object, the occasional elephantine tramp of paragraph are very much a part of the question which is Henry James of his last period, as a few specimens must make clear. There is, for one, the passage in which we are to sight Milly through the appraisal of one of the bystanders:

Mrs. Stringham was never to forget—for the moment had not faded, nor the infinitely fine vibration it set up in any degree ceased—her own first sight of the striking apparition, then unheralded and unexplained: the slim, constantly pale, delicately haggard, anomalously, agreeably angular young person, of not more than two and twenty summers, in spite of her marks, whose hair was somehow exceptionally red even for the real thing, which it innocently confessed to being, and whose clothes were remarkably black even for robes of mourning, which was the meaning they expressed.[4]

Or the sentences in which James discusses the relations of leading persons in the same novel as affected by their acquaintance with Densher:

These things, however, came and went, and it set itself up between the companions, for the occasion, in the oddest way, both that their happening all to know Mr. Densher—except, indeed, that Susie didn't, but probably would—was a fact attached, in a world of rushing about, to one of the common orders of chance; and yet further that it was amusing—oh awfully amusing!—to be able fondly to hope that there was "something *in*" its having been left to crop up with such suddenness. There was somehow a possibility that the ground or, as it were, the air might in a manner have undergone some pleasing preparation; though the question of this possibility would probably, after all, have taken some threshing out. The truth, moreover—and there they were, already, our pair, talking about it, the "truth"!—hadn't in fact cropped out. This, obviously, in view of Mrs. Lowder's request to her old friend.[5]

This is, to put it honestly and bluntly, bad writing, and one can only marvel that James, after some thirty years of practice with his pen, could even with the taste which his generation permitted him have composed in such a ritualistic fashion.

The Golden Bowl has also its murkiness:

Treated on such occasions as at best a pair of dangling and merely nominal court-functionaries, picturesque hereditary triflers entitled to the *petites entrées* but quite external to the State, which began and ended with the Nursery, they could only retire, in quickened sociability, to what was left them of the Palace, there to digest their gilded insignificance and cultivate, in regard to the

---

4. *The Wings of the Dove*, New York, 1909 (New York Edition), I, 105. All page references to James's novels will be to this edition, in which revisions often entailed the use of more words than had been in the original publications. These revisions, however, usually do render the object or the feeling more tellingly to a patient reader.

5. *Ibid.*, p. 189.

true Executive, such snuff-taking ironies as might belong to
rococo chamberlains moving among china lap-dogs.[6]

This becomes intelligible only when it is explained that
James, with a heavy humor but slightly assisted by a buried
allusion to Louis XIV, was describing the reign of a baby
heir in an Italian household. Even with the explanation the
sentence remains labored and pompous, and sometimes lengthy
sections of the novel—notably most of Chapter VI of Book
Second—produce the same impression. In *The Ambassadors*,
however, the stylistic offenses, much less annoying, do not
retard the momentum of a narrative which gets under way
more quickly than in the other two novels. One must read
carefully, to be sure, and one must sometimes re-read. When
Strether asks Bilham "For what do you suggest that I suppose
her to take you?" or when he says to Miss Gostrey: "And
yet Mrs. Newsome—it's a thing to remember—*has* imagined,
did, that is, imagine, and apparently still does, horrors about
what I should have found," the reader who is trying to understand each sentence comes to an abrupt halt. But the exposition
is comparatively simple, and so is the direct narration, rarely
offering more difficulty than the following:

Waymarsh had been for a quarter of an hour exceptionally mute
and distant, and something, or other—Strether was never to make
out exactly what—proved, as it were, too much for him after his
comrades had stood for three minutes taking in, while they leaned
on an old balustrade that guarded the edge of the Row, a particularly crooked and huddled street view.[7]

And it must be set down as testimony to James's great strength
that the second volumes of both *The Wings of the Dove* and
The Golden Bowl absorb the reader in spite of the culmina-
tion of stilted Edwardian writing. In fact, there are at times
passages in which an afflatus is unmistakable:

She had got up with these last words; she stood there before
him with that particular suggestion in her aspect to which even

6. *The Golden Bowl*, I, 202.
7. *The Ambassadors*, I, 42.

the long habit of their life together hadn't closed his sense, kept sharp, year after year, by the collation of types and signs, the comparison of fine object with fine object, of one degree of finish, of one form of the exquisite with another—the appearance of some slight draped "antique" of Vatican or Capitoline halls, late and refined, rare as a note and immortal as a link, set in motion by the miraculous infusion of a modern impulse and yet, for all the sudden freedom of folds and footsteps forsaken after centuries by their pedestal, keeping still the quality, the perfect felicity of the statue, the blurred absent eyes, the smoothed elegant nameless head, the impersonal flit of a creature lost in an alien age and passing as an image in worn relief round and round a precious vase.[8]

Frank Norris would certainly not have assigned immortality to such writing, and its fashion is not to be recommended to the neophyte in composition. But studied carefully, this too-long sentence is seen to have been built toward a climax in sound and in emotion, the words having been chosen for color, for suggestion, and for tone, so that the whole has eventually a dithyrambic quality.

It has been urged that much of the apparent clumsiness of James's writing in his latter years dissolves once it is realized that he was counterfeiting the accent of human speech. This is an argument that cannot be entirely controverted. Yet few novels are intended to be read aloud, and it will probably be admitted that the speech in the novels under consideration could have been only that of James, who did, it is reported, talk in the way he wrote. Unfortunately, this style is also fitted upon all his characters; they, too, speak as James did, and the author made little endeavor to distinguish sex or age or degree of education or nationality by differentation in dialogue. All his actors, young and old, male and female, English and American and Italian, have the tongue of Henry James, committing only his errors in grammar, making no descent into small talk, and betraying no foreign origin. They converse with grace,

8. *The Golden Bowl*, I, 187.

wit, solemnity, sententiousness, almost never like the persons we daily meet, almost never with playfulness or relaxation.

They behave like James, too, with poise, polish, impeccable attention to the expected, with rarely shaken self-control, and with small likelihood of laughing at themselves. If they sin they do so with a *bel air* and with an excruciating self-realization. They are miraculously perceptive, aware of every vibration of an idea, divining the most hidden feelings of someone else, suspecting their suspicions, back-tracking in word, act, and thought lest they go too far ahead, trembling at every breath that disturbs the psychic balance. Only Americans seem to be surrounded by a non-conducting atmosphere, though even they may at last break through this ring and learn to touch with their minds instead of their fingers; after his stay in Paris Strether can tell by the tilt of a pink parasol what the relation is between Mme. de Vionnet and Chad Newsome.

Now the letters, diaries, memoirs, and histories of the class about which James was writing prove that members of this stratum not infrequently stamped their feet, cursed, got drunk, indulged in fisticuffs, took mean advantage of others, beat their wives, told off-color jokes, seduced downstairs maids, hunted with the hounds, and generally behaved like average human beings with more money and leisure than the average. The upper middle class in James's world does not do these things. Turn the bright light of verifiable fact upon James's characters and too many of them become incredible, while the novel in consequence falls into a certain shallowness. William James complained of them that they had too little blood, and it is doubtful if they would have bled much if cut. They do not have what Emily Dickinson called the look of agony. They may come close to humanity, as the Assinghams do; they may be marmoreal carvings, as Morton Densher is; they may be ectoplasmic, like Milly, who is as diaphanous as the gown of a nymph, who leaves her story as imperceptibly as she entered it; they may be wholly unbelievable, as Adam Verver is; but whatever their effect and their nature the client is seldom inspired to suffer with them, to long to comfort them or to intervene in their behalf. He is, instead, fascinated with the thing they represent in action, with the ideas and the manipulation behind them, so that ultimately they become not heart-warming fellow-creatures such as he finds in Dickens, or bemused living beings like those in the dramas of the contemporary John Galsworthy, but costumed and trained performers in a ballet. This is especially true of *The Golden Bowl*, which might well inspire ballet music and dances.

Essentially these characters and the situations they manufacture are timeless, and of interest to James chiefly because they were material to be woven. Even when he was idealizing his cousin Minnie Temple, as he was in *The Wings* and *The Golden Bowl*, he felt his persons less as folk than as the threads of his warp, and it is impossible to fancy him laughing and crying over his pages of manuscript as Dickens did, of being thus moved by their doings and their fates. His refusal to become involved, to beat his breast or shed a tear, was a sign of his remoteness from Victorian romanticism and simplification; his attitude toward his characters was strictly creative and proprietary, not redemptive, and when they had served their uses, when they had become a part of his complicated spinning, he dismissed them from his hand and, if the use of the metaphor may be prolonged, sent them forth into the markets of the mind. Talking with James about *The Ambassadors*, Agnes Whitney Cromwell was asked whether she knew what had happened to Strether, to Chad, to Miss Gostrey after the book ended. When she answered in the negative he confessed that he did not know, either.[9] The confession is not so cavalier as it sounds for it was consistent with James's beliefs, but many a reader must have wished to know more about Miss Gostrey from first to last and beyond. As to the situations, the narrative crises, they might have been found duplicated in practically any generation of mankind; they have, that is, a universality with no particular relation to the events of their years or to that Will to Power which made

9. Agnes Whitney Cromwell, "Innocent Among the Lions," *Vogue*, 15 Nov., 1951, p. 158.

portentous the decade in which James was publishing. None of the three novels bears upon international diplomacy or war, none deals with British politics, and none with the scandals, the cultural renaissance, the industrial growth, the vast energies and resources of his native land.

Our hypothesized reader of James has some right, therefore, to wonder whether James gave a direct impression of life at all, whether he did not instead give a direct and emphatic impression of form in his chosen art. Form, an indispensable servant of the plot, binds each part and particle of the subject within a preconceived picture fusing the primary and secondary material, and it is this arbitrary arrangement of the substance of his novels that no reader can miss and that some readers may find disconcerting. Melville warned us in *Billy Budd* that "truth uncompromisingly told will always have its ragged edges," by which he meant truth to the facts of particular or general experience. Life as most of us know it is irregular, extravagant, and perhaps chaotic at bottom; individuals wander into our ken and wander out, leaving little trace and having had little significance for ourselves; most acts have small meanings; most spoken words have too little coherence and but little thought; the purpose and values of human behavior are not easy to find, and if there is an over-all pattern it is discoverable only by philosophers with a mystical turn of mind. But in James, who was not a mystic in the ordinary sense, there are few ragged edges; all the things just mentioned are organized with the utmost care, all is formalized, all is pattern; act and word and thought are meticulously chosen and shaped to a given end. The figure in the carpet is woven with intense concentration and with such skill that often the one who handles the product does not weigh the stuff or note the texture, for he allows his eye to be held by and his judgment to be overawed by the intricate design. To find James interesting the reader, like him, must admit that at bottom the most alluring thing is "difficulty"— the task, that is, of setting in motion certain telepathic characters before the backdrop of a stylized society, endowing them with intellectualized speech and antique manners, and trapping them in crucial situations wherein they must expose their hearts and make their comments on existence correspond to their creator's.

Yet it would be an error to conclude that because his devotion to form rose above his sentiments about his personae, that because they were so exceptional as to violate some of the modesty of history, that because he did not select for development such topics as the muckrakers and naturalists brought close to a reading public James did not on the literal level contribute with any directness an impression of life. His wish that the volumes of the New York Edition should have photographic frontispieces is proof that his world was not altogether self-begotten, and there is further proof in his close examination and rendering of the details of palace and drawing-room, of garden and tea-party, of costume and face, of doorway and shop window, of *objet d'art* and street and bridge. Here his genius as the observer, the bystander with an eye for the dramatic, had full play in a sharp-sighted and unimpeachable realism; James's word pictures of places and persons are as reliable a social chronicle as the drawings of Charles Dana Gibson. But there is less kindness in James than in the cartoonist, and less sunniness. James saw and left the record of a society in which few favors were extended without the expectation of an equivalent return, in which the rule was *quid pro quo*, and in which as strenuously as in any American novels of the day sex and the love of money were the forces which drove men and women to deny their better natures. Beneath the proud phrase, beneath the deceptive surface flow of *The Wings of the Dove*, *The Ambassadors*, and *The Golden Bowl* is a recognition as keen as can be found in any naturalistic writing that intelligence too often surrenders to will, that honesty succumbs to greed and purity to desire. The language which the characters in these novels use is the language of James, and the idiom through which they move and have their being is his, but once the rich hangings of his style are brushed aside one can discover the fundamental human motives as completely realized and as nakedly exposed as can be wished.

This is tantamount to saying that James is most successful on the liminal level, on that threshold to realism where known and imagined meet, where the reader confronts truth wearing a robe that must be lifted. James's direct impression of life is to the untutored eye indirect, poetic and rapt in both conception and expression. From figurative title to the names of the characters to the last paragraph of the last chapter the three big novels employ one dominant image each to help communicate that impression; in *The Wings of the Dove* it is, of course, the gentle bird to which Milly is compared; in *The Ambassadors* it is Paris, the City of Light, the potentate to which come American envoys who leave with contradictory messages; in *The Golden Bowl*, in which symbolism is most frequent and apparent, it is the imperfect gift which lends its name to the story.[10] Through these and other symbols James returned to the mythopoeic tradition in American literature which he had inherited from Hawthorne and Melville and Poe and sought to give by way of ambiguities a direct impression of life, only his allegories had for hero not the pilgrim soul but the pilgrim conscience.

For as Theodora Bosanquet has pointed out, James saw life as an eternal warfare between the creatures of light and the powers of darkness, with victory going most often to the depraved ones who were not inhibited by grace or selflessness. Or better, as far as these three novels are concerned, it should be said that the victory of the wicked is only apparent, as it is in Conrad, who also celebrated the noble legion of the

10. In this connection it should be noted that James was one of the first important novelists to make good use of the figurative title. It has been suggested that the golden bowl symbolizes, among other things, the quality of European culture, but this raises the question of why Charlotte Stant, quite at home in that culture, did not remark the crack in the bowl. . . . Two of the most poetic titles of the decade were given by Louis Tracy to moderately popular novels: *The Wings of the Morning* (1903) and *The Pillar of Light* (1904). The first employed the well-worn plot involving the castaway pair, the second was more original in confining all its action within a lighthouse.

conquered. This was in James a profoundly Christian rather than a Zoroastrian dualism and therefore not so innocent as it might seem, for it recognized the existential reality of evil, saw this world as the domain of the Prince of Darkness, and provided for the elect. Milly Theale's death is hastened and made certain through her discovery of the treachery of the man she loved and the woman she trusted, but Milly's deeply generous love wins in the end, though in a manner she had not foreseen; Lambert Strether for a reason that would seem to many persons quixotic renounces a possible bride, her money, and his position, but he wins thereby freedom and understanding; Maggie Verver learns in the greatest of James's novels that her love and her father's devotion have been abused, but she perseveres in working out a *modus vivendi* which provides, with all the beauty of a miracle, the means of preserving what is most precious to her. In these novels, then, we are allowed to see the conscience of humanity in an unending quest for moral equilibrium and, in *The Golden Bowl*, finding its Grail. But only after pain and misadventure. For James, the disenchanted man who at sixty-seven discussed suicide with his brother, was no facile optimist. He knew that the tender, the truly intelligent, the beautiful were in this world usually at the mercy of the rough, the stupid, and the ugly, but he also knew that even if crushed they gave off a perfume which like a mercy covered sin and blotted out some of the universal stench. They were the ones who understood that the moral equilibrium, the golden bowl, can be grasped and held only when persons, refusing the romantic inclination toward a full release of individuality, act with the most vigilant tact, with a boundless consideration of others, with the willingness and courage to abandon self in those minute relationships which are the atoms of which the crystal cup is made, atoms which, invisible to the coarse, sensual eye, are discerned through the eyes of loving wisdom.

So much has been so well written of James the artist that any discussion of that distinction here is almost supererogatory. But because *The Wings of the Dove, The Ambassadors,* and

The Golden Bowl are capstones of his writing career, and because the question of Henry James as phrased earlier includes the matter of his artistry, a few further comments with particular reference to the three novels may not be altogether superfluous. Art is the structuralizing of material in such a way as to externalize an experience that has taken place in the imagination, in reflection, in action, or, as may be, in several or all of these media. Through it a novelist selects and discards material, draws the blueprint which is the plot and which is largely concerned with action, chooses a fundamental image, sets the key, determines the form, picks the point of view, adapts his style to his purpose and his substance, attends to the details of characterization, description, explanation, tempo, and speech, and brings all these things together into a symmetrical whole.

That James comprehended the need to do all these things to the top of his bent, and that he tried so to do them, can never be doubted. The Prefaces to the volumes of the New York Edition, written with wonderful authority and understanding, the long synopses which he prepared before embarking upon the final drafts, and the novels themselves demonstrate a rare consecration to the art of literature. No writer was ever more conscious of what he was doing and why he was doing it. This implacable supervision of a story in the making is at the same time one of his glories and one of his liabilities, for it meant that the tale would have unreservedly the attributes of his own mind. The deepest quality of a work of art, he believed, would always be the quality of the mind of the producer; if that intelligence were fine then the novel would partake of beauty and truth. This dictum is both correct and touching, for the quality and rhythm of James's mind can be welcomed only by minds that approach his in depth, in range, in excitement, in movement, and the full beauty and truth of his novels can be apparent to, can be interesting to, such intelligences alone. James had learned this painfully, and it is a measure of his heroism and integrity that in these late novels he should have made no concessions to inferior mentalities.

But a sensitive awareness of what one is doing, a devotion to art, and a fine intelligence are not of themselves guarantees that one is an artist. The proof lies, of course, in the work produced, and at this point the client has the right to decide that James did not, any more than his colleagues, turn out flawless syntheses of the various parts of a novel. We have already noted objections that may be made to his style, his habits of characterization, and his dialogue, objections arising from the fact that the technical gifts of the author sometimes overrode his subjective, his creative side. James wrote with astonishing prodigality in these years, yet never gave the effect of writing with haste or even with spontaneity, of letting the emotion or the story escape the tyranny of his skill. The consequence is an unavoidable athermancy. And because his patience and fascination with method were inexhaustible *The Wings of the Dove* and *The Golden Bowl* are, like many accepted musical and literary masterpieces, too long, *The Ambassadors* again being the exception to a stricture. James confessed that there was an excess of inert material in the first volume of *The Wings*—though we should regret losing the tantalizing unfinished miniature of Kate Croy's father—and most readers of *The Golden Bowl* would probably accept some condensation. Form in these three novels also suffers from an appreciable rigidity, a mechanical principle which, no matter how perfectly carried out, impairs credulity in the story. F. O. Matthiessen has reminded us of the care with which *The Ambassadors* was organized: twelve Books to be accommodated to the twelve installments in *The North American Review*, delayed entrances of the characters so as to heighten suspense, dramatically timed climaxes, a complicated point of view, and other devices whereby the tale was poured into the preconceived mold. Furthermore, traces of James's experiments in dramaturgy are to be found in *The Wings of the Dove* and *The Golden Bowl*, with their reliance upon fixed dialogue instead of a use of general conversation or of natural incoherence and confusion in speech, with a curtain at the end of each scene, with punch lines, even, it is possible to feel, with an actor playing the part of Densher or of Amerigo instead of the person himself appearing. In the latter of these novels James's preoccupation with the symbol, intended to contribute to firmness of texture and to suggestion, was responsible for so liberal a repetition of "golden" and of synonyms or other words hinting at the color and durability of the metal that the artfulness became too obvious.

On the other hand, James's very deliberate and evident shaping of his material accounts for his excellences, major and minor. Rather than let his personae and perhaps the story itself get out of control, with all the ramblings and unstudied realism which might result, he chose to make his plots precisely and helplessly the adjuncts to his art, and the newcomer to James is always surprised to find that these plots, reduced to skeletonic outline, are so full of exciting action that they make, as has been indicated, good scenarios and stage plays. For all his meanderings in the pursuit of motive James is so expert a planner of complications, of small and great climaxes, of the proper denouement, and so expert in the timing for these features, that they usually succeed even when plainly contrived. For example, the scene in *The Bowl* in which the prince and Charlotte are startled to discover that the keeper of the curio shop speaks Italian—a scene which wisely does not end at that incident—is startling also to the reader, for it provides not merely the surprise of the moment but also the speculation as to far-reaching consequences, and thus prolongs a thrill like a musical vibration in the air. And for an example of an even more triumphantly designed event we have the placing of Milly's death in *The Wings of the Dove* in the solemn Christmas season of vicarious expiation, one of the supreme strokes in imaginative literature. Because James felt that "art is nothing if not exemplary, care nothing if not active" he relished the "difficulty" inherent in the blocking out of these plots; to give direction and commentary to them he invented his celebrated point of view, illustrated nicely in *The Ambassadors* and given variations in *The Golden Bowl*, where the matter of the first volume is present to the consciousness of the prince and that of the second to the awareness of the princess, and in the contrapuntal composition of both *The Wings of the Dove* and *The Golden Bowl*.

With most novelists the experience and the philosophy which underlie a narrative are antecedent to the art performance. With James they were a part of it. London, Paris, Venice were experiences to him, but not as they were experiences to George Gissing, Zola, and F. Marion Crawford respectively. They were for James scarcely the haunts of men, scarcely places that exuded the ecstasies of suffering or religious aspiration or romantic self-denials of success, places in which the raw stuff of human behavior was displayed to the observant. He scanned them with an eye single to their representational values for his art; he saw those details which would interpret the city only in so far as it served as the backdrop for his story, formed in his mind before the setting was adopted. The provocative experience, the "wind-blown grain of sand," was likely to be an anecdote, a wistful sentence reportedly spoken by Howells, the memory of a young girl eager for life but condemned to early death, a reflection in his study. It cannot be true that he listened only to conversation that might bring him these incentive moments, but that is the implication found in many of the Prefaces, and it is permitted to believe that he heard only such things as might awaken his imagination and have worth as potential fiction. And these things were, especially in the last years, essentially transcendental, things that existed as ethical problems in and for themselves and having little contiguity with the streets of a capital city. By "direct impression" James did not mean the photographic plate of the naturalist; by "life" he did not mean the *halles* of Paris. By these terms he meant a collocation of what was seen and what was believed to be the highest beauty and truth. The experience, the imagination which captured its significance, the moral issue—these were not for James the tools for shaping a work of art, they were themselves contained in art. He gathered them in affectionately, broodingly, convinced that art was more than life, equating his moral imperatives with his artistic directives, teaching that living itself must be an art if it is to succeed. In this wise did Henry James give a direct impression of life, a kind of life known only to a gifted few from whom the remainder of us must learn.

IV

The Man of the Hour

In *The Dial* for 16 February, 1905, Charles L. Moore asserted that although our literature had deteriorated, owing largely to the infection of commercialism, Americans were twenty times as appreciative of the things of the mind as they had been fifty years before. This might be dismissed as transparent chauvinism if it were not for the fact that in the same year James Bryce, revisiting the United States after a long absence, reported great progress in the arts and sciences, in the sympathy of the richer classes for the poor, in education, and a "prodigious material development." [1]

There is, of course, no way of establishing the accuracy of Mr. Moore's ratio, but in clear retrospect Lord Bryce's finding seems amply supported. The American scene had acquired an animation unknown to the nineteenth century. Life in this country throughout the four years of Theodore Roosevelt's second administration was still real and earnest for the mass, but much of the grimness of the prior three centuries was disappearing. By itself the president's strenuous Americanism was paradoxically relaxing for it emphasized duty less and zest for the game, for achievement in the eyes of the world more, and with the ensuing transformation of the older puritanism the ego was released from a confinement which had too often made Americans rigid and bigoted. The result was a new buoyancy, felt in the air—a buoyancy arising not from a moral source, as had often been true in our past, but from a glimpse

1. "America Revisited: The Changes of a Quarter-Century," *The Outlook*, LXXIX, 733-40, 846-55.

of a material prospect, from a renewed conviction that life was an occasion for living. It was still a Golden Day for the bourgeoisie. In 1906 *Bradstreet's* announced that business was up 10% to 12% over 1905; national wealth was increasing enormously; science was prolonging life and making it more comfortable; production was increasing at a rate which brought more and more desired commodities to American homes; and the stock market crash with the attendant financial upheaval and unemployment in 1907 was significantly called a "panic," not a "depression." Even the underpaid worker caught some of the contagion of "fling and swing." In 1906 he read in his daily newspaper that the cost of living was the highest in sixteen years, and he grumbled and perhaps voted in 1908 for Eugene V. Debs, but he also perceived dimly that the Industrial Revolution was slowly and painfully adapting itself to the American Revolution and he knew that his dinner pail was rarely empty, that his union was stronger than ever, and that a strike had a chance to win his demands. Nor did he ever lose pride in his citizenship. He was likely to trust the president, to boast of the repute of our navy, to feel satisfaction in the invitation for our government to participate in the Algeciras Conference in 1906. Whatever his resentments, he was aware that his fatherland had become a world power and that this inevitably meant a better life for his children, if not for himself, since they would share a security, a prosperity which had never been his.

This *élan* naturally infused our literature and the other agents of what is in a restricted and popular sense thought of as culture. Museums, art galleries, churches, libraries, theaters, magazines, colleges and universities multiplied. Successful writers and painters earned more money than ever before; dancers like Isadora Duncan and Ruth St. Denis attracted large audiences in 1906; the best actors and actresses toured the land, playing in one-night stands; five cents would gain admission to a Theatorium where "Faust" or "Carmen" might be shown on the screen; the Victor phonograph brought good music into the homes of the millions; Paderewski and a Russian boy of seventeen, Mischa Elman, charmed music-lovers of even third-class cities; the Metropolitan Life Building rose to forty-eight stories in 1907; schoolteachers spent two-month vacations in Europe for $250. Bryce did not observe all these manifestations of a cultural effervescence but he was experienced enough and perceptive enough to detect a changing America.

The change was undeniably promising. But although the cultural pattern had brightened it had not essentially altered; old confusions and contradictions and limitations persisted, less alarming but unresolved. For one, the level of popular taste was not high. In music the public was satisfied with the latest ragtime hit and vaudeville ditty, and even the more sophisticated listeners in Oscar Hammerstein's Manhattan Opera House puzzled over the perfect opera, "Pelléas and Mélisande," in 1908. In art, the well-to-do hoped to hire John Singer Sargent and John Alexander to paint portraits and vied in purchasing seascapes by Winslow Homer, and the appreciative began to praise the work of Childe Hassam, but in the lower middle class artistic standards were likely to be fixed by prints of "The Horse Fair" and "The Stag at Bay" and the faery world of Maxfield Parrish, by calendar pictures, and by the book illustrations of Howard Chandler Christy, Charles Dana Gibson, James Montgomery Flagg, Howard Pyle, Harrison Fisher, and lesser brushmen. The most quoted poets were the English and American Victorians; after them the people reached for the homely verses of James Whitcomb Riley, the newspaper jingles of Edgar Guest (who began to win favor in 1906), and *The Spell of the Yukon* (1907) of Robert Service rather than the lyrics of Richard Hovey, Louise Imogene Guiney, Bliss Carman, and Lizette Woodworth Reese, who were selected in 1905 by critics as the more talented of the new singers.

To scan the lists of best sellers for the years from 1905 through 1908 is to see that most readers preferred fiction and that this fiction reflected the prevailing sentimentalism of a feminine public. The majority of the novels were love stories, pure and rather simple, replete with what was thought to be idealism and with a lightheartedness which testified to woman's expanding freedom—novels centering upon conflicts which arose within the hearts of the protagonists and were but little affected by time and place and social factors. Most of them gave such a distorted view of human motives and such a false picture of the attraction between the sexes that one cannot but wonder why they were read—was it because they allowed the unhappy to absent themselves from infelicity awhile, because they asked little mental collaboration, because they might rightly shape the morals of the young, because they exorcised a guilty conscience? There is, of course, no way of being sure of the answer, nor is it possible to know how much disappointment they may have provoked when their readers discovered the differences between literary courtship and actual marriage. Common sense, however, may assume that these tales, and others which had to do with adventure and with the detection of criminals, were read for their faculty to amuse, to provide shade in the heat of the day, and that only adolescents took them seriously. Surely no one over twenty believed that George Barr McCutcheon, publishing an annual best seller during these four years, was giving a transcript of life in the United States or even on a tropical island, where he might lay his scene.[2]

Of the forty novels on the lists, only a few have acknowledged literary values. *The Garden of Allah* (1905) by the English Robert Hichens is still one of the best attempts to imprison the genius of a place, and *The House of Mirth* (1905), *Coniston* (1906), *The Jungle* (1906), *The Awakening of Helena Richie* (1906), and *Mr. Crewe's Career* (1908) will occupy niches in almost any history of American literature, while some others, like *The Trail of the Lonesome Pine* (1908), will hold ambiguous positions. Most of the remain-

2. Twice McCutcheon did aim at seriousness. His *The Sherrods* (1903) is a sympathetic if superficial study of a bigamist, and *The Hollow of Her Hand* (1912) is a provocative story of a crime whose psychological motivation the author was not fully able to explore.

ing books can be found among the dog-eared collections of second-hand shops but are otherwise lost in a limbo to which the critics of their day consigned them, and in which posterity is content to let them rest. "There is no other kind of literary work, at least in prose, in which the level of performance is so low" as in the novel, wrote Herbert W. Horwill in *The Forum* for August, 1905, and although this decision was reversed promptly by Brander Matthews in *The North American Review* and by Henry Mills Alden in the "Editor's Study" of *Harper's* it was reaffirmed by Julian Hawthorne in 1906 and by John Cosgrove in 1908, the former making the familiar charge (in the February *Critic*) that journalism was destroying literature, and the latter (in the September *New England Magazine*) that our short story writers were more profound than our novelists, a preference that *The Bookman* seemed to have in mind when in the same year it lauded O. Henry as "a consummate artist." [3] Henry Holt gave a plausible explanation for both inferior reading taste and inferior publications when (in *The Atlantic Monthly*, November, 1905) he accused authors and publishers of fixing their eyes upon the main chance.

But the mentioned books deserve discussion, as do many others of the quadrennium even when they did not get a wide reading but when they nevertheless maintained tendencies or types already noted, when they gave a more representative version of life than did the popular works, or when they were the productions of significant writers. The historical novel obviously lost some of its appeal in a four-year interval loud with criticism of the contemporary event, and Charles Major was unable to hold his following with a story of Hapsburgs and Burgundians united by the marriage of hero and heroine, *Yolanda* (1905). In the same year Robert W. Chambers' *The Reckoning*, another romance of up-state New York, of Walter Butler and his secret wife, of Carus Renault and George Washington, proved that the Revolutionary War could scarcely fail to gain readers, and Thomas Dixon's *The*

3. "Chronicle and Comment," *The Bookman*, XXVII, 436.

Clansman, second of his trilogy dealing with Reconstruction in the South, roused such reactions on each side of the Mason-Dixon Line that it became a best seller.[4] The only other novel of the kind to reach a best seller standing was Mary Johnston's *Lewis Rand* (1908), which made good use of the Magnolia Tradition, of the hero whose ambition was too vaulting, of the passionate hatred between partisans of Burr and of Jefferson, of a melancholy ending. Alfred Henry Lewis's *The Patrician* (1908), also introducing Burr, failed to rival Miss Johnston's story; S. Weir Mitchell's *The Red City* (1908) dealt with the second administration of Washington but did not in any way equal the author's earlier writing; and Vaughan Kester's *John o' Jamestown* promised well but added little to the legend of John Smith.

Vendors of the Graustarkian novel also found themselves offering their wares in a diminishing market. Yet some of the best specimens of the saber-and-dolman school appeared at this time, notably Percy Brebner's *Vayenne* (1907), turned with the same gravity of style, thought, and inevitable denouement as Anthony Hope's more famous duo, and C. N. and A. M. Williamson's sprightly *The Princess Virginia* (1907), wherein the Emperor of Rhaetia makes the mistake of proposing a marriage of the left hand to a princess incognito. John Reed Scott was sufficiently encouraged by the reception of his *The Colonel of the Red Huzzars* (1905) to continue the record of the struggle for the throne of Valeria and for the hand of its fair daughter into *The Princess Dehra* (1908) and then into *The Last Try* (1912), when the American Armand Dahlberg finally triumphs over the Duke of Lotzen. However, three tales signalized the approaching end of a fad. The banality of William T. Eldridge's *The Princess Hilma* (1907) made it plain that the old formula could not be employed indefinitely; Harold MacGrath's rollicking *The Princess*

4. This novel was adapted in David W. Griffith's "The Birth of a Nation," first great American motion picture. *The Traitor* (1907) is the third in Dixon's trilogy. Chambers' *The Little Red Foot* (1913) is the fourth of his novels about colonial New York.

Elopes (1905) came near being a parody of the type; and George Ade laughed at the whole fashion by displaying in *The Slim Princess* (1907) a heroine whose lack of avoirdupois made her ineligible in Morovenia until an American came along. Clearly not even the current enchantment lent by "The Merry Widow" (1907) was going to endow a mythical Balkan principality with much glamor while Theodore Roosevelt was preaching the gospel of masculine Americanism, while muckrakers and other critics were with compelling sincerity and fact pointing attention to socio-economic illness, and while *The Jungle* rasped the nerves of a nation and made the summer novel seem frivolous.

By the turn of the century the momentum of the local color movement had well-nigh come to a stop, but the lessons it had taught were not to be forgotten; attention to the habits, speech, and setting of a peculiar people in a more or less isolated section was to help secure a hearing for many a novel basically a romance of sentiment or adventure or even of moral problem, this last being well illustrated by Margaret Deland's *The Awakening of Helena Richie*, where the environmental idiosyncracies of Dr. Lavendar's flock in western Pennsylvania have a bearing upon the case of the heroine. And Harold Bell Wright appropriated the local color technique so freely in *The Shepherd of the Hills* (1907) that it is inseparable from the redemption theme of this much-abused fiction. The status of Mr. Wright, one of the most read and most ridiculed writers of his generation, could be determined only by an extended investigation of the values of popular literature, but it may be said here that there is no way of proving that one book is better than another and that criticism is ultimately no more than the attempt of a professional to enlarge the understanding and better the taste of an amateur. The professional who was contemporary with Wright deplored that writer's omnipresent morality as naïve, suspected his motives for publishing, and laughed at his view of life. Mr. Wright's advocate might rejoin that there is nothing absurd about trying to raise the standards of human thought and behavior, that nobody

knows exactly why an author writes, that nobody compre-
hends the meaning and purpose of life, and that novelists like
Wright and Gene Stratton-Porter were in all likelihood good
for their special readers.

But if the hostile critic skirts the matters of morality in
literature and of the author's intent and concentrates instead
upon the item of craft he has the strongest charge to make
against Wright. For the author of *The Shepherd of the Hills*
saw the object only in relation to a dubious Wordsworthian
motif: nature cleanses and heals, the city corrupts. To Wright
a person, a mountain, an animal, the sky existed not in themselves but as notations on this text, and they were in this
example spread upon the pages of a story so immature and
unoriginal that it suggests the first attempt of a high school
senior. There are the betrayal of the innocent mountain girl,
her death after giving birth to a boy who grows up to be
slightly fey, the return and death of the remorseful betrayer,
the purifying effect of the Ozarks upon him and his once
aristocratic father, who had become the Shepherd. All this is
maneuvered in accordance with a transparent plan and told
in language so deficient in wit, sharpness of observation, or
novelty or distinction of any kind that the total effect upon
the professional man was of sweetness and dishonesty. In fiction, falsification of life has justification when, as in the
Graustarkian novel, it is the result of a tacit bargain between
writer and reader, but no such book can have stature in the
eyes of one who asks that literature essay a reading of man's
nature and destiny. *The Shepherd of the Hills* did not make
this attempt. Whatever inspiration to courage and decency it
gave to its admirers is certainly not to be discounted, but
American literature of the decade would have been a sorry
thing had it not gone further than this in achieving a knowl-
edgeable presentation of human personality, a freshness and
skill in the invention of plot, a feeling for the sense of words.

In *The Trail of the Lonesome Pine* John Fox, Jr., exploited
local color in a romance that shaded into realism, for he built
upon actual events in which he had sometimes been an actor.

This very successful story of the mountains of southeastern Kentucky, reaching the stage, the screen, and Tin Pan Alley, helped to establish a lasting vogue for hillbilly literature through an artful assembling of old elements: the pretty highland girl, the engineer from the outside (the lowlander), the contrast between two civilizations, the dangerous local suitor, the Appalachian scenery, and one of the most exciting clashes in the fiction of 1908, that between the law and the Tollivers. In 1907 Meredith Nicholson tried without the assistance of costume and faraway land to bring high adventure to the hills of Virginia in *The Port of Missing Men*, but this tale of Hapsburg intrigue and of a hero who turned out to be an Austrian nobleman did not hit public fancy so winningly as did two romances of rough-and-tumble existence for whites, half-breeds, and Indians in the frozen north, Rex Beach's *The Spoilers* (1906) and *The Barrier* (1908).

The master of the redblooded tale of outdoor incident was still Jack London, writing with a rapidity which was to drain his reservoir of material and his nervous reserves. Three books bear his name for 1905, and he was in addition to this output contributing steadily to magazines. Most of *The Game* is a reporting of a prizefight between Joe Fleming and John Ponta, with the former's sweetheart watching through a peephole. The subject gave London an opportunity to be lyrical about clean male strength and responsive and clean womanhood, and to exalt boxing as a sport which appeals not to the most brutal but to the most honestly competitive instinct, not to the desire for money or the urge to inflict suffering but to the manly will to win in fair fight. Unfortunately, the hero is killed in the match, and the story degenerates into a potboiler with only a simmering humor and pathos. Turning to his youth, London recalled in *Tales of the Fish Patrol* some of his experiences when at the age of sixteen he joined an unconventional crew engaged in hunting down oyster pirates in and near San Francisco Harbor, and in these unaffected, lusty narratives of the duels with Big Alec and his kind gave us proof of his love for the sea and of his leadership in the

"raw meat" school.[5] In *The Faith of Men* he reprinted magazine stories of his most successful type, that which transported
readers to a glittering unfamiliar world of sensation; his "Love
of Life," appearing in *McClure's Magazine* for December, is
a compressed statement of life as red in tooth and claw and a
masterpiece in the maintenance of suspense.[6]

Before Adam (1906) confirmed London's continuing allegiance to Darwinism; it also revealed what was to become his
scramble for material, for it seems too much like a resurrection
of Stanley Waterloo's *Story of Ab* (1897). Meant for not too
intellectual adults, this narrative has for hero a man whose
dreams are memories of his prehistoric struggle for survival,
of a time when only the strong, the cunning, and the swift
could live long in a jungle of snakes, wild pigs, wild dogs,
lions, and forest, and with such formidable enemies as Sabre-
Tooth, the apelike Folk, the Tree People, the Fire-Men, and
Red-Eye. Inevitably London had to theorize about the evolution of language, weapons, and the canoe, and to create the
Swift One with whom the hero falls in love in a manner more
chivalric than Darwinian. *Before Adam* can be quickly dis-
carded in favor of *White Fang* of the same year, another
story about a dog, but this time a dog that unlike Buck is
reclaimed by the affection of human beings.

As a socialist Jack London believed that capitalists would
not surrender the rewards of the profit system without bloodshed, and so his *The Iron Heel* (1907) told of an abortive
revolt of the Chicago proletariat against their "masters." The
uprising was quelled in a holocaust of fire and death, partly
because the workers had inferior organization and equipment,
partly because they did not receive expected help from other
cities. Socialistic novels need not end in either Utopias or

5. London's *The Mutiny of the Elsinore* (1914) is one of the best sea
stories in our literature.

6. London admitted that in writing this classic story he had used not
only his own knowledge of the far North but also Augustus Bridle and
J. K. MacDonald's *Lost in the Land of the Midnight Sun* and Adolphus
Greely's accounts of his polar expedition. See London's letter to *The
Bookman*, XXIII, 369-71.

defeats—several of the 1930's closed with the sound of march-
ing feet—and the ultimate hopelessness of *The Iron Heel* may
not be dissociated from the history of London's skepticism,
a progress which sent him off on a voyage to the South Seas
in 1908 at about the time when Robert E. Peary, embarking
for the North Pole in the "Roosevelt," reminded Americans
that the love of excitement whether in books or in action is
one of the most widely distributed of human cravings.

Booth Tarkington's *The Beautiful Lady* (1905), laying its
scene in Paris and Italy, was not of the vintage; David Graham
Phillips's *The Social Secretary* (1905) was a trifle told from
the point of view of a fetching young woman who made a
good catch with love included; and the common reader properly put them aside for more tasty fare such as he could find
in Mary Roberts Rinehart's *The Circular Staircase* (1908), an
exercise in mystification so ingenious that it was the first
American novel of its *genre* to reach the best-selling list and
has afforded many a *frisson* to successive generations who
have stood with Liddy Allen and her mistress on the stairs of
the Armstrong house when the lights went out, and in
O. Henry's *The Four Million* (1906) and *The Trimmed
Lamp* (1907).[7]

Recent criticism has tended to revise downward the esti-
mates made by O. Henry's delighted first readers. It has suspected him of writing for money, of being too servile before
editor and public. It accuses him of sacrificing characterization
and setting and faithful dialogue to a formula which called
for grotesquerie in person and place and for such speech as
had never been heard on land or sea, of throwing overboard
his consignment of rightful materials and relying chiefly upon
the contraband of unexpected climax, so that he became a
smuggler in literary wares, a literary Punchinello, too, and
therefore something of a fraud.

There is enough truth in these accusations to keep William

7. Mrs. Rinehart's latest mystery novel, *The Swimming Pool* (1952)
records one interesting cultural change in the United States: both sexes use
profanity, smoke, and drink cocktails quite casually.

Sydney Porter from ranking among the great practitioners of the short story. No one should refer to the O. Henry *conte* if he wishes to learn the exact appearances of New York City in the Roosevelt era. Yet he was more than a clown of the *feuilleton,* and the many who read him pleasurably in his lifetime were wiser than some of his later critics. For one thing, O. Henry was often a careful craftsman who had absorbed from Maupassant the lesson of compact and dramatic form and from Kipling the uses of contemporaneity and breezy vulgarity. For another thing, the duality of the man, seen in his artistic as well as in his private life, permitted him to catch in the same net the tension and the contradictory nonchalance of the American character; something, too, of its melancholy, shown in the strain for comic effect. There was much that was unreal, much that was grotesque in the bigness and strength of the metropolis that stood as a symbol for the grotesquerie of our whole striving civilization, and this he managed to convey to men and women who were like motes in this unreality. From our western humorists he had inherited slang, exaggeration, understatement, irreverence, puns, and burlesque, but he invested the inheritance in Bagdad-on-the-Subway and he dispersed his profits in coin of the realm. To change the figure, he heard the *timbre* of the Roosevelt period and he spoke with its accent, though not with its voice. He knew that the things most feverishly sought were money and caste and that in the seeking the small and weak were trampled underfoot: his sympathy was for them, for the shopgirls and the clerks who scrimped and loved and renounced and smiled through tears, and while he never tipped his hand at this point his interest in these little people was an indirect and often unnoticed index to a social critique which set an example for Damon Runyon, who likewise wrote with a blend of fun and affection, and for Ring Lardner, who wrote with a despair too deep for indifference. O. Henry's very title, *The Four Million,* was a gauntlet thrown down before the Four Hundred, a gauntlet covered by the velvet of comedy. But the steel was there. "The Gift of the Magi," "The Cop and the

Anthem," "An Unfinished Story" are not mere indulgences in sentimentality or mild farce; they are also comments upon poverty and oppression and ideals pitifully kept or lost. The persons who read those stories in 1906 relished their humor, relished too the parodies in "Memoirs of a Yellow Dog" and "Elsie in New York," relished the sly satire on the go-getter in "Shoes" and the runaway slang in most of the pages, but they were not so trusting as to believe that if they sat on benches in Madison Square or entered a haberdashery on Broadway or walked through the Bowery they would find literally what O. Henry planted there.[8] What they did recognize more or less consciously, and what gives Porter his lasting value, was a kindly interpretation of the American dream, a distillation of essence from appearance. O. Henry did not wear the whole mantle of artist, but he bore at least one of the sleeves.

Besides a moderately low taste politely overlooked by James Bryce certain other strains which left an impress upon our culture must be noted, among them a nationalism which kept pace with the kindred spirit in politics. Sometimes it inflated the reputation of a meager talent, always it led to a demand that Americans have an opportunity to see and hear and own the best. It came so near liquidating the provincialism of the nineteenth century that all but five of the forty best sellers in the years under study were written by our own citizens, and it gave liberal financial and critical bounties to the authors. It set up a cry for the Great American Novel which should make our country and our genius known forever to the world; it regarded James G. Huneker's enthusiasm for Shaw, Ibsen, Strindberg, Becque, Maeterlinck, and Hauptmann in *Iconoclasts* (1905) as outlandish in a double sense. When Theodore Thomas died on the fourth of January, 1905, this national feeling publicized a regret that we did so little to encourage American conductors, composers, and singers and urged that we provide musical aspirants with such

8. "Shoes" is in O. Henry's *Cabbages and Kings* (1904).

training here that they would not be obliged to study abroad, and it asked again why operas should not be sung in English in the United States.[9] It gave tribute to Henry K. Hadley as a coming composer; it saw to it that we had Arturo Toscanini and Gustav Mahler to conduct at the Metropolitan in November of 1908; it cheered the début of Geraldine Farrar as Juliette in November of 1906 and watched with pride as she became the indispensable prima donna opposite Caruso and the outstanding soprano for ambitious American girls to emulate.[10]

Another of these stresses was a residual puritanism evident in blue laws, in an anxiety for self-cultivation, in an almost morbid habit of self-examination, in the success of itinerant evangelists, in the accepted definition of refinement, in a censorship established by an equivocal attitude toward sex, publicly arraigned in spite of its private fascinations. In many states it was illegal to give a theatrical performance or to play baseball on Sunday. Lowell, Whittier, and General William T. Sherman were admitted to the Hall of Fame in 1905, but Edgar Poe was barred; Ralph Bergengren in *The Atlantic Monthly* for August, 1906, protested against the barbaric humor of comic supplements but in the same year and in the years immediately following newspapers printed highly lurid accounts of the murder of Stanford White and of the subsequent trials. In 1906 Maxim Gorki fell foul of public opinion by visiting us with an unconventional companion. In that year the Brooklyn Public Library withheld *Tom Sawyer* and *Huckleberry Finn* from children and Anthony Comstock wrote in *Leslie's Weekly* (30 August) that "the nude, as uncovered by so-called art, is a web which has enmeshed many a youth to his or her ruin," yet in 1907 the first Ziegfeld

9. Also dying in 1905: Lew Wallace (15 Feb.), Jules Verne (24 March), Maurice Barrymore (26 March), Joseph Jefferson (23 April), Albion Tourgée (21 May), John Hay (1 July), Mary Mapes Dodge (21 Aug.), Henry Irving (13 Oct.).

10. Other American women to sing at the Metropolitan included Minnie Hauk, Emma Eames, Lillian Nordica, Marie Rappold, Sybil Sanderson, Bessie Abbot.

Follies was produced and Elinor Glynn's *Three Weeks* was read *sub rosa*. In 1906 William Winter denounced the "putrescent plays" of Ibsen, Wilde, Tolstoi, and Shaw in the *New York Tribune* (19 September), but that did not prevent Alla Nazimova from filling theaters by her acting in the Norwegian's dramas. Performances of "Salomé" were stopped at the Metropolitan in January of 1907; elsewhere scores of thousands of persons "hit the sawdust trail" under Billy Sunday's exhortations. In 1908 President Roosevelt ordered the removal of "In God We Trust" from ten-dollar gold pieces on the ground that the motto was a mockery in our materialistic civilization, only to have the words restored by a dissenting congress. And the socialists, the liberals, the president, the pessimistic Mark Twain and Henry Adams, were reminders that the puritan conscience was still a quick one in our country.

Another factor to be weighed in relation to what James Bryce thought of as an intellectual renaissance was the increased heed Americans gave to that journalism which informed them as to the place of the United States in the world-wide struggle for power. By the end of 1905 their partiality for the Japanese had lessened. Taking Port Arthur in January, winning the Battle of Mukden in March, and destroying the Czar's fleet in May, the soldiers and sailors of Nippon had covered themselves with martial glory but had also aroused color consciousness abroad and uneasiness lest the Yellow Peril become an actuality instead of a scarehead.[11] There was a feeling of relief, therefore, when at the insistence of President Roosevelt a Peace Conference opened in Portsmouth, New Hampshire, in August and closed with a treaty a month later. But our intervention irked the militarists of the island empire, and when California proceeded to exclude Japanese immigrants we discovered that we had provoked a hostility so bitter as to strain relations between the two gov-

11. An absorbing account of the Battle of the Sea of Japan is to be found in Frank Thiess, "Tsushima," *Men at War* (ed. Ernest Hemingway), New York, 1942, pp. 309-39.

ernments; talk of possible fighting was common, and the Count von Reventlow's *World Peace or World War* (1907) predicted that the next armed conflict would be between the United States and Japan.

The Japanese victory made inevitable a race in naval construction, with England, Germany, the United States and Japan competing in the building of Dreadnoughts, the first of them being launched by the British in 1906. In that year Congressman Richmond P. Hobson bespoke for us a two-billion-dollar navy powerful enough to defeat anything afloat, and Roosevelt flouted precedent by leaving the homeland in order to speed work on the Panama Canal; in 1907 against the advice of experts he made the sensational gesture of sending the Great White Fleet on a trip around the globe, with, of course, a stop in Japanese harbors. The newspaper readers approved the secession of Norway from Sweden in June of 1905, were indifferent to mutinies and uprisings in Russia after its humiliation, and did not guess the significance of the forming of the Triple Entente in 1907, but approximately one hundred thousand of them lined the shore to greet our returning ships in April of 1908. Six months later we launched our first Dreadnought, the "North Dakota," and in November opened the War College.

The year 1908 brought crisis in the Balkans, with Pan-Slavism, Pan-Germanism, and Pan-Serbism in open collision and with Bulgaria proclaiming its independence from Turkey in October; farther south the Young Turks forced a constitution upon their sultan. In the autumn few Englishmen gave ear to Lord Roberts's warning that a million soldiers would be needed to repel a German invasion; it was as difficult for them as it was for Americans to realize that the Japanese success had helped set in motion a deep and potent groundswell of nationalistic feeling, of confidence on the part of the colored man that he could hold his own with the white, of determination of the have-nots that they must have, and that the armament rivalries, the forming of alliances, the revolts in Poland, the Balkans, and Turkey, the riots in Russia, the American advance in the Pacific were heralds of a new spirit and of mighty upheavals to come. The Russian disorders promoted violence elsewhere in 1908: the king and the crown prince of Portugal were assassinated in February, a little later a bomb was thrown at the president of Argentina and two were hurled at the Shah of Persia, the Chicago chief of police was shot by an anarchist in March, a Swede shot at the king of Norway a few days later, and at the end of the month a bomb exploded in Union Square. In line with anarchist aggressiveness Alexander Berkman and Emma Goldman published in the United States in 1908 a magazine called *Mother Earth*.

If not many Americans caught the implications of the moves in power politics and of the continued unrest among submerged classes, most of them had for various reasons interest in the new machines which might be major instruments in either peace or war. The automobile, as the only one they could likely own, interested them most, and they followed the returns of the Glidden races in 1905 and probably agreed in 1906 that 200,000 autos made an "alarming" number. The horseless carriage was proving its usefulness in fiction as well as on the road, and *The Princess Passes* (1905) by C. N. and A. M. Williamson was the most popular novel written with an automobile as the fulcrum of the plot. In the same year this pair turned out another of the type in *My Friend the Chauffeur* and Lloyd Osbourne published a collection of short stories called *The Motor-Maniacs*. The Williamsons repeated with *The Car of Destiny* (1907), and Richard Harding Davis's *The Scarlet Car* (1907) in three frothy novelettes told how an auto was the means by which Beatrice Forbes became better acquainted with its owner, Billy Winthrop, and disenchanted with her fiancé, Ernest Peabody. Compared with these tales of the new vehicle Cy Warman's *The Last Spike and Other Railroad Stories* (1906) seemed to speak for an age already passing.

Only a small minority of Americans had then seen an airship; to the majority this machine was as much a matter for speculation as the space ship was to be a half century later—

would it work, and to what fruitful use might it be put? There was disagreement as to whether the heavier-than-air or the lighter-than-air type would be more practicable, and in 1908 Simon Newcomb expressed in the September *Nineteenth Century* his doubt as to whether aviation would have any practical value. But two years earlier the *Technical World* had described the experiments of the Wright brothers; in April of 1907 Alexander Graham Bell predicted that the United States would use in warfare airships with a speed of 200 miles an hour; on 29 June, 1908, a balloon, the "Cognac," flew over the Alps; on 10 September Orville Wright remained aloft for over an hour above Fort Meyer; two days later a German dirigible flew for over thirteen hours; and daring aviators in Europe, seeking records for speed and endurance, made it clear that the plane was not a diverting toy but a contrivance to be reckoned with in military calculations. Hudson Maxim's invention of a noiseless rifle in 1908 had an undeniable relevance to the struggle for power, but this was not immediately apparent with respect to Elmer Sperry's invention of the gyroscope in 1905 or Lee De Forest's invention of the oscillating audion in 1906, and British illustrations of a caterpillar tractor in *The Graphic* (25 April, 1908) and the breaking of Atlantic records by the "Lusitania" in July of 1909 threw but dim shadows upon the walls of newsrooms.

When in his congratulatory essay in *The Outlook* James Bryce wrote of "a development of the higher education in the United States without a parallel in the world" he was especially struck with the excellence of our universities, comparing favorably with those of Europe, and especially pleased to find in our curricula a counterpoise to our passion for material progress. Elective and preceptorial systems encouraged independence among undergraduates; graduate schools had improved remarkably in the quality of their research; and while campus life in the United States seemed carefree to an outsider, seemed a mélange of horseplay, football, and serenading, it was actually far from resembling the comedy of George Ade's "The College Widow" (1905), which set the fashion for a score of college dramas and scenarios.[12] There was much truth then in the saying that a college student was a "picked" individual; public education had extended laterally to the point where the young of middle class families in towns and cities could take graduation from high school as probable, but only a few of those graduates went to college, and so many of the leading universities of the Atlantic seaboard excluded women that a girl with a college degree was almost as rare in the flesh as she was in the novels of the day. Indeed, there is pertinent social comment in the fact that the schooling of a fictional heroine was seldom mentioned.

Had Lord Bryce written his article a few years later he could have bolstered his opinion of our educational advance by reference to four published works which testified to the intellectual stimuli that might be encountered in American lecture halls. One of them was a poetically written view of the good life; the other three have attained the magnitude of classics, with one of them astonishingly setting a sort of record in sales.

George Santayana's *The Life of Reason, or the Phases of Human Progress* (1905-06) ran to five volumes. In the first, *Reason in Common Sense*, the author traced the evolution of the mind, which he regarded as a non-material agency promoting physical and spiritual growth but which he also conceived of as part of a mechanical universe, so that it in turn depended upon the body for protection. Reason, of course, had evolved with the growth of the mind. The second volume, *Reason in Society*, carried Santayana's rejection of both aristocracy and democracy, the latter being objectionable because, as he phrased it in the last book of the series, it bowed to the will of "majorities made by a system of bribes offered to the more barren interests of men and to their more blatant prejudices."[13] His preference was for a timoc-

12. In 1906 President Roosevelt ventured into the field of education by ordering the public printer to use thenceforth "reformed spelling" for 300 words. Four months later congress invalidated the order.
13. George Santayana, *Reason in Science*, New York, 1906, p. 255.

racy in the Platonic rather than the Aristotelian meaning, a society in which all would be born equal but would develop unequally as their potentialities were realized, and in which men of the highest merit would be recognized as rulers. He also found modern love less natural, less animalistic than it should be, he deprecated the worship of bigness and quantity, he condemned war and suggested rational substitutes for it, he admitted the need for patriotism but preferred a universal good will arising from the exercise of reason. *Reason in Religion* cast off supernaturalism and approved of religion as poetry and ethics; it also refused to accept the Christian idea of immortality but found compensation in the belief that a man of reason "not only vanquishes time by his own rationality, living now in the eternal, but he continually lives again in all rational beings."

In what is the most satisfying volume, *Reason in Art*, Santayana divided his subject into two kinds, the mechanical and the liberal. Both produced happiness, the one by its utility, never to be despised; the other by its beauty, which "gives men the best hint of the ultimate good which their experience as yet can offer." Since all art springs from the deepest impulses in human nature and is in its creativity related to the divine, Santayana concluded that "Of all reason's attributes art is therefore the most splendid and complete." Because *Reason in Science*, the last volume in the set, is a philosophical treatise on history, "mechanism," psychology, and dialectic related to ethics instead of what its title might suggest, and because it lacks concreteness and authority, it is less successful. Science is defined as "a myth conscious of its essential ideality, reduced to its fighting weight and valued only for its significance," and Santayana praised it because it destroys the feeble popular mythology and follows its subject matter with the purpose of knowing and of systematizing what it knows. "To live by science," he concluded, "requires intelligence and faith, but not to live by it is folly." Throughout the five volumes the philosopher characteristically attempted to harmonize his idealism with his awareness of what naturally exists, his

Platonism with his shrewd Latin insights, his never-lost Catholicism with an instinctive paganism. What he had to say in *The Life of Reason* may strike few of his colleagues as final —Santayana conceded that he had nothing final to propose— but he said it in a gravely beautiful prose whose style, learned partially from Plato and from Emerson, gives delight to the expert as well as to the thoughtful layman and goes far to persuade readers of the justice and nobility which give focus to Santayana's point of view.

In *Folkways* (1906) William G. Sumner, who though influenced by Darwin and Spencer was practically the father of American sociology, taught that the habits of the folk, almost instinctive with primitive people, passed on into tradition and custom and eventually became the doctrines of welfare, the *mores*, for the in-group. It followed that customs were right or wrong if they suited or did not suit a given time and place, and that cultural patterns originated in the adaptations of peoples to the conditions under which they lived. It followed, too, that Sumner could with some show of logic assume the reactionary point of view which manages his book, undisturbed by certain self-contradictions. "No systematic enterprise to enlighten the masses," he was sure, "can ever be carried out," [14] and "the great mass of any society lives a purely instinctive life just like animals" (p. 45). And later: "... changes which run with the mores are easily brought about" (p. 94). "That is why the agitator, reformer, prophet, reorganizer of society, who has found out 'the truth' and wants to 'get a law passed' to realize it right away, is only a mischief-maker" (p. 113). "Nothing but might has ever made right" (p. 65). "At every turn we find new evidence that the mores can make anything right" (p. 521).

Yet he granted that "Education in the critical faculty is the only education of which it can be truly said that it makes good citizens" (p. 633). In all likelihood Sumner intended this sentence to have a personal and aristocratic slant and was

14. William G. Sumner, *Folkways*, Boston, 1906, p. 51. All subsequent page references are to this edition.

scornful of that kind of education, implicit in muckraking journalism, which was enlightening the citizenry and giving it a critical faculty such as he did not have in mind. His advocacy of laissez-faire led him into the error of believing that whatever was, was right, of unwillingness to concede that the folk might decree changes in the economic system and that these changes would therefore also be right. He betrayed another weakness in his thesis by showing his anxiety over a moral dilemma buried in the heart of American society. "We live in a war of two antagonistic ethical philosophies: the ethical policy taught in the books and the schools, and the success policy" (p. 33), and "Amongst ourselves now, in politics, finance, and industry, we see the man-who-can-do-things elevated to a social hero whose success overrides all other considerations. . . . The antagonism between a virtue policy and a success policy is a constant ethical problem" (pp. 652-53). This was a correct if not profound observation which hardly jibes with his dicta previously quoted. The importance of *Folkways*, it is agreed, lies in its historic position, its priority. Phrased with measured arrogance, reading for lengthy spaces like Spencer's *The Principles of Sociology*, and now outdated, it did bring home to readers the question of the relativity of right and wrong and it did help to convert American sociology from a vaguely outlined and loosely taught subject to one with scientific pretensions.

If *Folkways* demonstrated that the age was turning sharply from "romanticism," William James's *Pragmatism: A New Name for Old Ways of Thinking* (1907) was a corroboration in as much as it showed a son rejecting a father's transcendentalism. For pragmatism spurned merely verbal solutions to the eternal problems and sought to take the black magic out of philosophy. It was a revolt against philosophers who held that truth could be found in the juxtaposition of ideas, in toying with paradoxes and metaphysical abstractions. It turned its back upon the obscurantism of professors who boasted that in three sentences they could lose the less trained hearer or reader. What is the worth, James asked in effect, of a philosophy which only the few can understand? Should not the test of the validity of ideas be, do they work? An affirmative answer to the latter question would, it is true, involve the recognition of a constant flux of values and an encouragement to materialism, but James accepted these hazards and wrote that truth became a classname for all sorts of working-values in experience. By emphasizing the practical results of ideas he expressed the activism of Roosevelt's Americanism and like the president wished to release us from what James called tender thinking; by stressing the place of things in relation to ideas and by speaking of the "cash values" of those ideas he may have helped to produce Babbitt. James's title confesses to a want of originality at the core of his thought, and he acknowledged a special debt to Charles Peirce. But because he was one of the few Americans born in the nineteenth century who managed to cut the leading-strings of European philosophical systems and because he set forth with clarity and persuasiveness the vision of the New World, of a people hard-headed, impatient of abstractions, yet altruistic, he made Pragmatism our chief contribution to world thought.

Santayana and James were professors at Harvard and Sumner was a professor at Yale when, in 1906, Henry Adams (who had been a teacher at Harvard) privately printed *The Education of Henry Adams*. This unique autobiography is in our literature the classic testament of frustration, the apologia of a proud, disappointed intellectual who saw himself as a runaway star in a multiverse he would never have made. At bottom it was an attempt to explain and minimize an inertia which troubled his New England conscience, a "Hamlet" substituting the second law of thermodynamics for a father's ghost. More matter-of-factly, it was a sequel to *Mont-Saint-Michel and Chartres*, an effort to provide a philosophy of history for students and teachers who had appropriated too much time to the investigation of what had happened without giving enough thought to why it had happened or to what data or reasoning would allow the historian to theorize safely about the future.

Since, according to Adams, history was the record of the play of forces, since it could be studied wisely only in connection with man, who tended to assimilate other forces much in the manner that he did food, thus acquiring the will to power, it was necessary to fix upon a period or upon periods in man's existence when the concentration of forces might be most closely observed. He found two such periods, and two symbols for them. The first period, as he had described it nostalgically in his preceding book, was the hundred years between 1150 and 1250 when Mariology was the controlling factor in man's functioning, when the Virgin stood for sex and faith, for eternal womanhood and religion, when there was multiplicity in unity. But the inventions of the compass and of gunpowder subtracted from the force of religion and threw the trend of man's living toward science and mechanics, so that in Francis Bacon's time force was expressed more and more through science in the modern understanding of that word and less and less through piety and its works. In the nineteenth century mechanical forces had doubled themselves every ten years; then suddenly in 1900 a new supersensual force that had little to do with the old mechanics appeared, and force again became concentrated in a new image, the dynamo. And now the new forces, accelerating at dreadful speed with man powerless to stop or retard them, with man, indeed, absorbed by them, were hastening from unity to disintegration, from a universe to a multiverse, with society racing at a speed which meant that like a wheel turning too fast it would fly apart, thus bringing an inevitable Götterdämmerung, a destruction of man's civilization.

This prophecy of a supreme disaster compelled by the dynamic acceleration of centrifugal force constitutes the climax of a volume which is throughout most of its bulk the autobiography of a man in search of an education, of the means, that is to say, of reconciling instinct or intuition with the social milieu. It was in the quest of that reconciliation that Adams came to his Gethsemane for, as most of the chapters of *The Education* tell us, the pressures upon him from childhood had been to make him a public figure, a lawyer or a politician or at least a productive member of the Harvard staff. His ancestry, his father's example, his training in foreign capitals pointed him toward statesmanship, toward a career of action, and his affection for John Hay was a response to this imperative. But Adams was by nature a man of thought rather than of action; his autobiography is wholly intellectualized and so aloof that it is written in the third person. That is why much of its smoldering irony sifts upon himself as well as upon the world exterior to him: he understood in his soul that he was the man born to the study, the anonymity in the arena, an alias for a senator, a writer-about, not a doer. Because he could not extinguish the feeling that he should have been, perhaps could have been, a president or ambassador or congressman, because he was that far in bondage to an education that divided his will, he looked about for someone or something to blame for his failure to live up to family traditions and to his rightful ambitions. He found them in Ulysses S. Grant and in the dynamo, both of them having disordered the world into which he had been born. That is why he abhorred the very memory of the elemental force in Grant—why he also disparaged and envied Theodore Roosevelt—why he stood in awe before the dynamo, why he took a cold satisfaction in contemplating the future collapse of an industrialized, faithless western world.

All this is not to say that Adams' Dynamic Theory of History may be summarily dismissed as the vagary of a history professor who chose to relax on the sidelines. Too much that has happened since 1914 would seem to give authority to his prognostication. But an attempt to understand the man's personality and a reading of his letters, which are full of direful predictions that never came true, take some of the edge off his forecast. "Thank God," he wrote in 1914, "I was never cheerful. I come from the happy stock of the Mathers, who, as you remember, passed sweet mornings reflecting on the goodness of God and the damnation of infants." [15]

15. *Letters*, p. 628.

This is, to be sure, a playful confession, but the twisted smile does not abrogate the essential truth. Four years earlier he had written to his brother Brooks:

The whole fabric of our society will go to wreck if we really lay hands of reform on our rotten institutions. All you can do is to vapor like Theodore about honesty!—Damn your honesty!—And law!—Damn your law! And decency!—Damn your decency! From top to bottom the whole system is a fraud,—and all of us know it, laborers and capitalists alike,—and all of us are consenting parties to it.[16]

This jeremiad, differing in tone from *The Education*, is nevertheless akin to it in the measure of its hopelessness. It was penned by a man who liked to think of himself as a friendless, lonely, nervous invalid, a man who was really a patrician afflicted with chronic ennui and who with an epical exasperation called upon the science of physics to underline his conviction that civilization was crumbling. Civilization has not broken down, and it may be that man will adjust himself to the acceleration that frightened Adams just as he has been able against many warnings and predictions to fly a machine at supersonic speed.

The Education attests the mobility of Henry Adams' mind, but it also suggests that he lacked greatness, lacked, that is, constancy and magnanimity and identification with a purpose greater than himself. He did not lack brilliance. *The Education* is for most of its length and within its chosen limits a remarkable piece of self-revelation, thrifty, urbane, lighted with pictures of men and places and events, served by a wit that is always fastidious. It has neither the spaciousness nor the beauty of *Mont-Saint-Michel and Chartres* but it has the sad wisdom, the steady march of apparent proof, the doubtful conclusion from correct premises which suited the depressed mood of America immediately after 1918, when it was given a larger publication. Its disillusioned key rather than its logic, its challenge rather than its evidence have kept it among the better

16. *Ibid.*, p. 549.

selling books of the decade. If history has any absolutes, it did not reveal them to Henry Adams.

Although the popular reading taste was not high it would be a mistake to assume that nearly all booklovers from 1905 to 1909 were content with the vapid novels of a George Barr McCutcheon or a Harold MacGrath and that the list of best sellers boxed in the greater part of American writing talent. Some of those best sellers, as earlier indicated, are assured of a long critical esteem, and furthermore there was in that interval a surprising boom for Henry James and an equally surprising growth of a serious theater. These items must be entered on the credit side of the cultural ledger together with a notation consisting of a fair number of volumes which, attaining no wide sales, are nevertheless assets in the shape of art or of social history.

Several of these better novels had to do with the place of the New Woman in the new century, specifically with changing attitudes toward marriage, the home, and divorce. The death of Susan B. Anthony on the thirteenth of March, 1906, provoked consideration of the progress made by the sex since the birth of that feminist in 1820.[17] The progress was so marked, both here and in Europe, that in 1952 Bertrand Russell wrote reminiscently: "Perhaps the most notable and surprising of social changes has been the emancipation of women." [18] In the United States the clinging vine was dying at the roots while women entered business and professional careers, thronged the mills of New England and the Middle Atlantic states, and attempted to solve unhappy wedlock more frequently by separation and divorce. As their economic dependence upon the male lessened, their threat to his supremacy increased, and antagonism between the sexes sharpened, with,

17. Others who died in 1906: Paul L. Dunbar (9 Feb.), Richard Garnett (13 April), Carl Schurz (14 May), Paul Cézanne (23 Oct.), Henry Harland (20 Dec.).

18. Bertrand Russell, "The Next Eighty Years," *The Saturday Review,* XXXV, 8.

however, a curious and complex resurgence of a new kind of chivalry—not unconnected with business enterprise—manifested in the glorification of the American girl, no longer bridling, blushing, and languishing, but healthy and sure of herself. The middle-aged woman had her clubs, her charities, her projects of reform, perhaps her job; the face of the young one appeared in the output of the illustrators already mentioned, on calendars, on candy boxes, and in Gift Books, while Florenz Ziegfeld and the moving picture industry publicized her charms. The chaperone was disappearing; young ladies in *Smart Set* and in the privacy of their rooms smoked cigarettes and sipped cocktails; sometimes they innocently visited a bachelor's apartment, though this was still a risky step. Older women might campaign for the vote and did cherish Henry James's comment in 1905 that American women were of finer texture than the men; younger ones made it their business to display more frankness in showing their choice of a mate.

It was noted, however, that as woman's liberty broadened her psychic pitfalls deepened; her open competition for a husband in a society which gave great respect to wealth and position sharpened her claws and her selfishness; comforts and services provided her a leisure which often guaranteed boredom; her restlessness increased as she found herself a neglected possession instead of a helpmeet. Men grew restless, too, when they learned that the exhausting struggle for power on the street was to be carried over into a battle for social leadership, when they discovered that their value came chiefly to be that of the provider, and when they saw their monopoly upon politics threatened. Still not liking to think of women as their equals, they fought back in various ways. Grover Cleveland, for example, explained in the *Ladies' Home Journal* for October, 1905, why suffrage should be withheld from women; the comic magazines, especially *Life*, made constant fun of the willowy, cigarette-smoking, cocktail-drinking girl of the country club set; two of the most acrimonious novels ever to deal with the American female came out in 1908. In one respect, however, male resistance slackened: it no longer tried to block woman's rights in property. Beyond that, woman's bid for equality, plus the eternal stringencies between the sexes, supplied discerning writers with material they dared not ignore.

Edith Wharton's *The House of Mirth* (1905), the first of her novels to reach a best-seller status, drew with almost mathematical precision and objectivity the diagram of a feminine problem which was not new but which had acquired fresh angles in a society where social climbing and greed for money could be juxtaposed against a group of the bourgeoisie which had some of the gloss of an American élite. Lily Bart's problem was that of the dependent marriageable female without money enough to attract an ambitious husband, without talent enough to support herself, and without character enough to snap the golden chain which bound her to relatives and friends who supplied her with the luxuries in setting and clothing she craved. The public had been prepared for this kind of story by reading Thackeray and Hardy and Zola; there is here a kind of *Vanity Fair* in the incisive satire upon a shallow regiment of parasites and a heroine trying to live without an income, a kind of *Tess of the D'Urbervilles* in the portrait of a pure woman betrayed not by a seducer but by her "friends" and in desperation brought to work in a shop as Tess went to toil in the fields, and a likeness to several of Zola's characters in the steady degeneration of Lily's personality, in the development of a drug habit, in the remorseless descent to the grievous end. There is even a kind of *East Lynne*, certainly a mid-Victorian, aura about the scene in which Lily pays a farewell visit to Selden, magnificent though that scene is in its restraint. Some of the readers of *The House of Mirth* must also have liked the novel because it offered compensation to those among them who could not live in Newport or take a trip abroad but could now read that one of the persons who did these things was none the less very unhappy—the book was, that is to say, a remotely muckraking one, though Mrs. Wharton could have had no intention of making it so. Finally, *The House of Mirth* sold because it was an excellent novel in which one could almost, as Lily put it, hear the sound of the furies' wings.

It is not intended to suggest that *The House of Mirth* was pastiche, but rather that Mrs. Wharton ascribed to her heroine frailties long common to humanity and put her at the mercy of persons and conventions about which there was nothing new save what the period enjoined. That she could have made something fresh and poignant out of the focal situation, that she could have made Lily as touching a figure as the literature of the decade contains, is proof of the author's command of the story-teller's art. The triumph is all the more remarkable since we are never sure that Mrs. Wharton liked Lily; she wrote of her often as "Miss Bart," and although this formality had some excuse in the manners of the time it is clear that the creator was aloof from her handiwork, aloof and dispassionate and judicial. Yet few novels of the time are more likely to evoke tears, and this is because Lily Bart is wholly lifelike and therefore wholly pitiable in her downfall. Her image is so large that almost any feminine reader can lose herself in it, so attractive that the male reader feels compassion even when he cannot gauge the nature of Lily's listlessness. She is beautiful, of course, or she would not have had a welcome in the fringe of the gilded class, and she is also high-minded, loyal, brave, and sweet. But, as in a Rougon-Macquart novel, heredity and environment are responsible for flaws in character: Lily is indecisive, covetous of ease, unable to steer safely past temptations. Reluctant to marry without money, she is also unwilling to marry without love, and her ensuing series of flirtations brings with it loneliness, emptiness, heartbreak, gossip, ostracism. Lily vacillates between choices, thinks to relieve ennui with card-playing and drink, makes two pathetic attempts to earn a living, finds surcease in chloral. Without being frivolous she ends the victim of a frivolous society.

She comes near being tragic in the classical meaning because though not of heroic proportions she is in her most exigent crises dignified, courageous, and honest. At the opening of the story she is twenty-nine, so that, unmarried as she is, the whole history is one of crisis, and Mrs. Wharton compels us to feel with Lily the strain of having reached that age without a husband, of having to listen to proposals of divergent kinds and be tempted. The first chapter adroitly registers the temperature of the prolonged crisis. Lily, we find, is a bit snobbish, is gay about her age, is in need of money, is a little free in her association with men, is a poor liar, is fearful of ugliness. The succeeding pages chart the progress of the fever, with Mrs. Wharton laying no cool hand of sympathy upon the heroine's forehead. But she does permit Lily to rally in rejecting the overtures of Rosedale and Trenor, in facing down her dismissal from the Dorset yacht, in accepting a degree of poverty and in meeting a forewoman's criticism, in paying a debt in her last moments, and above all, in fronting the discovery that a love once dead is never revived. In these scenes Lily sheds her irresolution and takes on the stature of all who suffer, justly or no, without whimper, whose heads are bloody and perhaps bowed but not laid in the dust.

In *The House of Mirth* Mrs. Wharton brought unity to her art and her experience. Writing from within the social caste which gives pungency to the ironic title of the novel, she revealed a class of idle men and women to whom money was if not everything, at least the summum bonum. To her satiric eye those persons neither possessed nor inspired mirth. Without resources of intellect or character they played the game according to the rule of dog eat dog, and in their weariness of spirit took to mildly illicit pleasures which were always slightly stupid. As in her other better novels Edith Wharton contrasted old manners with new, and with an authority that allowed small compassion showed how non-conformity to the etiquette of the day incurred penalty. Since she was so familiar with her material she could guide with a sure hand the direction of her satire, and her unlikable rich people are never monstrous, never allegorical figures, but breathing men and women whose natures were shaped by the walls of the House within which they live and from which they have neither the wish nor the will to escape. Brought up to rise above "dinginess," but without the means to do so unless she use her beauty as a decoy, Lily Bart was never quite within this House, never strong enough to walk away from it. But her innocence, her genuineness sharpen the point of Mrs. Wharton's pen even while they make her an inevitable sacrifice on the altar of the House. Lily was not black, nor was she white, but against the society painted in this novel she glowed in primary color.

In 1907 Mrs. Wharton returned to the Jamesian manner with *Mme. de Treymes*, in which a French lady, herself heartsick, baffled an American by preventing his marrying into her family even while she extended to him the chance to do so, and in which we learn again that the courteous member of the Gallic noblesse is deadlier than the forthright American. In spite of compactness of plot and of diction this novelette has an odor of staleness as though of a drawing-room closed for years.

The Fruit of the Tree, also published in 1907, is another of Edith Wharton's less satisfying fictions. Unexpectedly, it begins as a novel about labor, with John Amherst fighting for better working and living conditions for the employees at the mills where he is assistant manager. But three-fourths of the novel takes up the problem of a wife in relation to a dedicated man, and the plot through which this is done is so patently a contrived one as to eliminate that art which conceals art. Amherst marries the heiress of the mills; he is opposed by her father, who sees the workers as "low mongrelly socialist millhands," and by the icy Snedegar, who speaks for the *status quo*. Justine is made a nurse and a schoolgirl friend of Bessy so that she may be subjected to a terrifying temptation; a doctor suitor is rejected so that he may fit into a melodramatic turn of narrative; a dangerous horse is introduced so as to rid Amherst of the chief obstacle to a second marriage. A worldly wise matron gives advice to all concerned; a child leads to a moderately happy solution of an acute dilemma—all of these twists excusing the reader who murmurs "Of course." Despite pages of Jamesian dialogue, therefore, and of flashes of insight into character *The Fruit of the Tree* is one of Edith Wharton's failures, for the clichés of personality and of incident and the inhuman philanthropy of Amherst repel while little in the story attracts. The only moving and real person in the novel turns out to be—and it is unlikely Mrs. Wharton intended this—the young wife who tried to make her marriage work without having the intelligence required to do so.

Like Edith Wharton, though, it would seem, independent of her, Robert W. Chambers left the historical romance in 1906 and wrote three novels about a society much like hers, differing in having less pedigree but similar in that it worshiped money, that it did not know how to employ leisure in self-improvement, and that it was for women a Pandora's box. To add to the difficulties of his heroines, brought up and maintained in a hothouse atmosphere, Chambers toyed with theories that are not widely credited today. *The Fighting Chance* (1906) displays the intrigues and immoralities of the idle and the working rich in and near New York, with topical references to Theodore Roosevelt and insurance scandals and with a financial battle as background for a love story in which Stephen Siward, believing himself an alcoholic by inheritance, and Sylvia Landis, convinced that her female ancestors have passed on to her a tendency to "go wrong," finally take their fighting chance and oppose their fates together. *The Younger Set* (1907) presents in Eileen Erroll and Philip Selwyn as prepossessing a couple as the fiction of the decade can show. They are, however, kept apart by Selwyn's chivalry, for his divorced wife has married a bounder and under various stresses is losing her mind; he feels he is obliged to remain single and to await her inevitable need for him. The novel ends happily, but not before Chambers has agreed with other novelists then that divorce is a plaything for a flashy and irresponsible fraction of the well-to-do, and that man cannot really put asunder what God has joined. In *The Firing Line* (1908) Chambers again wrote of social climbers, blasé matrons, financial deals, and this time of a winning heroine who impetuously and for an absurd reason marries when too young. She falls in love, to be sure, with another of Chambers' self-denying heroes and is further impaled upon the fact that her husband is not too unworthy. No reader is surprised when all ends well.

Chambers wrote sprightly dialogue and invented likable if

idealized characters for his romantic leads. More importantly he saw with clearness some changes in our mores: a new type of moneyed pirate, suave rather than rugged; the use of sex as an anodyne in a sporting crowd; a relaxation of etiquette governing the companionship of boys and girls, a step he thought wholesome; a waywardness among women as a consequence of new freedoms. His own attitude toward women was neither puritanic nor Mediterranean, and later he was to debate with gravity their right to love without marriage.[19] That he knew the facts of life in the United States and respected honest literature is proved by his Introduction to David Graham Phillips's naturalistic *Susan Lenox: Her Fall and Rise* (1917), of which he said that no character "within the range of all fiction of all lands and of all times" had so overwhelmed him as had the heroine of Phillips's masterpiece. But in his own novels he assigned ideal characteristics to his favorites, condemned sexual irregularities, and was so sentimental, so fluent in the happy ending that he cannot be acquitted of the charge of having written to woo a magazine public.

No such insincerity can be detected in Margaret Deland, whose *The Awakening of Helena Richie* (1906) presented another woman who defied the moral law of a community. Mrs. Deland pleased her readers, and thereby jeopardized her position as a realist, by being in tune with their conventions. In an interview given the *New York Times* in 1905 (19 August) she called for truth in fiction and praised *The House of Mirth* because it fearlessly prescribed hopeless conditions which could have only an unhappy outcome. But Mrs. Deland, never so stern, softened the contours of Old Chester and its manners so that her Helena might be redeemed by means of a *deus ex machina* and of a little waif, and through the sieve of this preachment much of the strength of the novel trickles away. William Vaughn Moody was also troubled by the need in the twentieth century to abandon the puritanic yoking of sex with iniquity without simultaneously preparing the way for a

19. See his *The Common Law* (1911).

bouleversement of womanhood, and in his "The Great Divide" (1906) groped not too expertly for a solution to this problem. He transplanted his New England heroine to the far West, had her marry one of three would-be ravishers in order to save herself, and sent the couple back to her contrasting eastern home to win approval for her far from austere husband. The play was a New York hit, but Moody is reported to have dismissed it as "all rot." David Graham Phillips's *The Fortune Hunter* (1906) detailed a different peril for the American girl but did not handle it seriously. In it we have a mild megalomaniac who committed suicide after blundering in his search for a rich wife, a fantastic court trial, and rewarded patience and goodness. Written sketchily, the novelette is unworthy of Phillips.

No charge of either superficiality or of insincerity can be brought against Phillips's *Old Wives for New* and Robert Herrick's *Together*, both of which, published in 1908, are such venomous delineations of the leechlike American female as to unmask the full male resentment against the New Woman. Not hastening through a potboiler this time, Phillips plotted his novel warily, beginning with a prologue which is the most poetic thing he ever penned. The friezelike sculpturing of Sophy Baker under the waterfall, the lyrical treatment of the shy passion of Sophy and Charles Murdock convince us that he had a vivid remembrance of things past. But the idyllic temper quickly recedes. After marriage, progressively after her daughter grows up, Sophy relaxes into slovenliness of mind and body, becomes overweight, and of course, repellent to her husband, who nevertheless tries to remain loyal. But he cannot refrain from contrasting her with the chic women he meets nor can he eventually deny himself a brief and unrepented fling. "The master men," he reflects, "playing life as a game and using their fellow-men as pawns, would not go far if they included consequences to themselves in their calculations." After he falls in love with careerist Juliet Raeburn entanglements multiply in every chapter: there is a train wreck in which he is injured; Juliet nurses him in disguise; Sophy, stirred by a designing male secretary, has her face lifted, her dresses better styled, her exercises prescribed; Murdock asks for a divorce but is afraid that its shock may harm his pregnant daughter; Sophy's vanity prompts her to oppose a legal separation. When that vanity is sufficiently soothed by Blagdon's flattery Sophy agrees to a divorce and weds her secretary while Juliet claims Murdock in the end. *Old Wives for New* is far from being so flippant as its title. From first to last it is too melodramatic, too filled with hate for the possessive female, if not for all females, but it put squarely before the public the case of twentieth century man vs. woman. Juliet briefed it neatly when she defended Viola by saying: "She's just the average woman, selling herself because she's too lazy to work."

No brief synopsis of Herrick's *Together* can do justice to its mingling of muckraking and scorn for the new American woman, who, according to the author, looked upon marriage as a stepping-stone to Success, not motherhood. At the wedding with which the novel opens Fosdick remarks: "But love and marriage are two distinct and entirely different states of being,—one is the creation of God, the other of society. I have observed that few make them coalesce." The society Herrick describes is corrupted by greed and the restlessness of a new civilization; woman, heretofore the stable sex, has succumbed to both traits and according to Dr. Renault is too "refined," too self-intent, unwilling to bear children, false to nature, so avaricious that she whips her husband into the marketplace and so sexless that she loses him to some vital woman. To prove his contention that woman had become the Spender, a thing of man's lust and no longer his real mate, Herrick wrote a cruel story of disillusionments, suicide, and murders. The principal cause of unhappiness is the city; the remedy, a return to nature in both the physiological and the romantic senses in much the manner D. H. Lawrence was to propose. "The city delusion," declares Dr. Renault, who operates a cure for sick souls, "is one of the chief idiocies of the day." And so Margaret Pole, the one normal woman in the novel, finds peace

for a time by living with a man not her husband, then renounc-
ing him to prove that she had felt love, not mere desire, and
by settling in a small Vermont village afar from the snares of
a metropolis. Herrick repeated this Wordsworthian theme in
The Master of the Inn (1908), a vignette with a secret worked
into its design. Here again is the physician who runs a health
resort in New England with a therapy consisting of manual
labor, out-door play, communal bathing, simple food, and
man-to-man talk in the nature of a confessional. To the Inn
come invalids "from the cities where the heat of living
scorched them, where they had faltered and doubted the goodness of life." The best things about this short story are the
art with which Herrick evoked the healing spirit of New
England hills and the dramatic revelation at the end.

Another unpleasant woman is found in Booth Tarkington's
The Guest of Quesnay (1908), but in the same writer's *The
Conquest of Canaan* (1905) a heroine helps a near-outcast
establish himself in a community. Three other books, written
by women but neither attacking nor defending their sex, are
remembered because their authors had already distinguished
themselves or were going to attain fame: Willa Cather's *The
Troll Garden* (1905) heralded a talent not full-grown; Mary
Wilkins Freeman's *The Shoulders of Atlas* (1908) came close
to absurdity in sounding a Victorian warning; Ellen Glasgow's
The Ancient Law (1908) fell short of success in presenting an
American Jean Valjean.

The American writer most discussed in the better magazines
throughout the interval from 1900 to and including 1910 was
Henry James. This was not, of course, owing to a widespread
liking for his work, and the pages about him did not approach
in number those of the present Jamesian revival. He was mentioned and analyzed simply because no critic could disregard
the quantity and quality of his output and because the novels
of the major phase provoked decided reactions. In 1905 the
special reason for noticing James was that he paid a visit to
this country and was for the first time persuaded to give a
public lecture, one on "The Lesson of Balzac" before the Con-

temporary Club of Philadelphia.[20] In that year Joseph Conrad, contributing an appreciation of James to the January *North American Review*, called him an historical writer; Gertrude Atherton in *The Argonaut* (6 February) praised his "marvellous psychology"; and William C. Brownell in the April *Atlantic Monthly* dubbed him "the most thorough-going realist of even current fiction." In *Putnam's Monthly* for July, 1907, H. G. Dwight stressed James's Americanism, saying that his characters revealed the depths of American nature. The dissenters, particularly the humorists, concentrated upon James's style. Charles B. Loomis's gibe has already been quoted, and John Kendrick Bangs in the May *Bookman* for 1908 proposed a new verb to denominate a clouded expression, "to jame." No barbs, however, could lessen James's pleasure in the New York Edition of his novels and tales which began to appear in 1907 and which was to be one of the handsomest sets ever to reward a living author.

As intimated, the American theater, responding to the criticism that it was too flagrantly commercialized and awake to current ideas, showed an increasing earnestness. It was still obliged to rely upon audience appeal, to stage such plays as "The College Widow," "The Music Master," and "The Girl of the Golden West" in 1905, Richard Harding Davis's "The Dictator" in 1906, "The Man from Home" and "Brewster's Millions" in 1907, and "Little Nemo" in 1908. It also continued to rely upon the star system, lighting the names of David Warfield, Blanche Bates, George Fawcett, Margaret Anglin, and Fay Davis among others, upon novelties like the hiring of James Corbett to play in Bernard Shaw's "Cashel Byron's Profession," and upon the tours of celebrated foreign thespians like Sarah Bernhardt and Ellen Terry.[21] In doing

20. See Marie P. Harris, "Henry James, Lecturer," *American Literature*, XXIII, 301-14.

21. One of the old stand-bys, Richard Mansfield, died 30 Aug., 1907. Some others who died in that year: Josiah Flynt Willard (20 Jan.), T. B. Aldrich (19 March), Ian Maclaren (6 May), J.-K. Huysmans (13 May), Augustus Saint-Gaudens (3 Aug.), Edvard Grieg (4 Sept.), Mary J. Holmes (6 Oct.), Francis Thompson (13 Nov.).

these things it had defenders. Marc Klaw accepted the argument that the theater existed to satisfy public demands; James E. Metcalfe supported this view in *The Atlantic Monthly* for December, 1905, by declaring that the theater should please not the best persons but the most; and James L. Ford repeated in *The Reader* for November, 1906, that drama must appeal to the crowd. But in trying to please the many, producers did accept from playwrights manuscripts of topical interest and of an intellectual quality somewhat removed from the comedy of George Ade and Booth Tarkington. One of these was the message-ridden "The Lion and the Mouse" (1905) of Arthur Hornblow, which had for protagonist a man with a name suspiciously like that of John D. Rockefeller and with a high-handedness associated popularly with the founder of Standard Oil. Watching this play, theater-goers learned how a multimillionaire might go about ruining a Supreme Court Justice who stood in his way but could hardly believe in a conversion effected by the heroine's steadfastness and her socialistic harangue in the last act. Moody's "The Great Divide" and Fitch's dramatization of "The House of Mirth" were on the boards in 1906; George Broadhurst's "The Man of the Hour" in the same year was concerned with the timely subject of political bosses and municipal corruption. In 1907 Alla Nazimova toured in Ibsen, and Augustus Thomas's "The Witching Hour" told how John Brookfield employed telepathy and hypnotism to win the acquittal of a man accused of a Poesque murder and to save himself—a play attesting that interest in the occult to which Hamlin Garland ministered in *The Shadow World* (1908) and Richard Harding Davis in "Vera, the Medium" (1908) and which Professor James Hyslop stimulated by his articles on psychic research.

Three dramas of 1908 held extra-entertainment values. Israel Zangwill's "The Melting-Pot" proposed that Jews instead of remaining a peculiar people allow themselves to be absorbed into American culture. Eugene Walter's "Paid in Full" presented a tight-fisted business man who generously refused to take advantage of a wife trying to save her husband from jail and incidentally criticized socialistic thinking. Charles Rann Kennedy's "The Servant in the House," a modern miracle play, held some of the sharpest satire to be directed by an American playwright against debased Christianity. The drama moves on two levels. Literally, with the scene laid in England, it has to do with the need to repair a church building and with the search of a daughter for a missing father she cannot remember; allegorically it says that the higher priesthood is likely to be self-seeking, that the church exploits and disdains laborers, that it nevertheless holds vicars of integrity who are troubled by the odorous "drains," and that wives sacrifice their husbands' uprightness to their own vanity. The Servant is a Christlike figure who as butler assumes the suggestive name of Manson and who, partly through supernatural insight and partly through personal magnetism, brings redemption and vision to the House. In the last act both the vicar and the workingman set themselves to cleaning out the foul cesspool, the "grave" infested with rats, upon which the church is built, so that the pollution which has emptied the building of worshipers may end. All this is heavy-handed, but it was sufficiently heart-stirring in 1908. One bit of dialogue was especially controversial. In the second act Robert Smith, the worker, says to Manson:

> Fifteen years ago me an' my like 'adn't got a religion! By Gawd, we 'av one now! Like to 'ear wot it is?
> Manson. Yes.
> Robert. Socialism! Funny, ain't it?
> Manson. *I* don't think so. It's mine, too.[22]

The moving finger wrote no more vital statistic in 1904 than the vote cast for Eugene V. Debs for president. Over four hundred thousand men gave him their suffrage and by so doing registered their dissatisfaction with the established politico-economic system. That they should do so in the administration of a liberal chief executive like Theodore Roose-

22. Charles Rann Kennedy, *The Servant in the House,* New York, 1908. p. 56.

velt is a fact of such considerable historical importance that it must be cited here, and because socialistic ideas entered more and more into our literature from that year until World War I a brief treatment of those ideas as held by Americans is obligatory.

There were so many kinds of socialists in the United States that it is possible only to write generally of what they advocated. They were, first of all, anxious not to be thought subversive; at the outset of an address a socialist was pretty sure to distinguish between what he believed and what anarchists and communists preached. In his opinion socialism was no more than a step forward in the evolution of democracy. He may not even have read *Das Kapital*, but he was familiar with condensations of and essays about Marx. Wishing to keep within our traditions, he did not emphasize class struggle too uncomfortably, he did not mention a dictatorship of the proletariat, and he was not likely to speak of the dream of a classless society. Having thus shrugged off the more radical and un-American aspects of Marxism, he advocated changes so diffuse and vague as scarcely to be called programmatic but which had a cogent appeal not only for the poor but also for the highly conscientious in any economic rank.

For American socialism addressed its propaganda to the materialist, to the idealist, and to the many who wavered between these classifications. It assured the worker that he was underpaid and overcharged, that he was forever being gouged by a non-partisan coalition of business men and political bosses and even some educators. It reminded him of the gargantuan Beef Trust, of the inquiries into the Tobacco Trust and the Oregon land scandals in 1905, of Standard Oil, of how in 1906 Chancellor James R. Day of Syracuse University defended that monopoly and charged Roosevelt with being an anarchist, and of how in the same year Paul Elmer More of Princeton University had written in the August *Bookman* that educating young men in the classics instead of in economics would help check "the present peril of socialism." It asked him what should be done about the rising cost of living and whether J. P. Morgan had not, as Upton Sinclair asserted in *The Metropolis* (1908), caused the panic of 1907. It spoke of discrimination against Japanese in California and Negroes in the southern states and made capital of lynchings, of race riots in Tennessee and in Mississippi in 1907, and of the proposal of Charlotte Perkins Gilman in *The American Journal of Sociology* in October, 1908, that "dangerous" Negroes be drafted into a labor army and given uniforms, music, ceremonies, titles.[23] It dared to call the courts subservient to finance and pointed to the Haywood-Moyer-Pettibone case and to the jail sentences given to Samuel Gompers and John Mitchell in 1908. It espoused public ownership of utilities, of some of the means of communication and transportation, the referendum and recall, income taxes, higher wages, better housing and safety devices for workers, and rather tentatively the elimination of interest, profit, and rent. It ridiculed the hope of "pie in the sky" and demanded a better earth. It called attention to the progress socialism had inspired in Scandinavia and Germany and quoted an enemy, Max Nordau, who confessed in 1905 that "in spite of its theoretical absurdity it has already in thirty years wrought greater ameliorations than all the wisdom of statesmen and philosophers of thousands of years."[24] It promised to do something concrete and at once about the obvious social inequalities and injustices, and it was so persuasive that it brought men of wealth like J. G. P. Stokes, Joseph Medill Patterson, and Robert Hunter to its conference in Norton, Connecticut, in March of 1905. And both the Republican and Democratic candidates for president in 1908 came out for an income tax.

For the Gnostic whose purse was not too much involved American socialism had an equal charm. "From each according to his ability, to each according to his need" was a beguiling slogan, though if one thought about it "ability" and "need"

23. Charlotte Perkins Gilman, "A Suggestion on the Negro Problem," *The American Journal of Sociology*, XIV, 78-85.
24. Max Nordau, "Socialism in Europe," *The Cosmopolitan*, XXXVI, 524.

were hard things to measure. Since socialists blamed capitalism
for war, crime, poverty, class violence, drunkenness, prostitution, and unemployment it followed that the victory of their
party should put an end to these undesirable things. They
were of the opinion that coöperation could supplant self-
assertion as a principal human motive, that our practical ethics
could be improved by an education which taught that a man
was his brother's keeper. Indeed, they adopted Jesus, and
named Him the first socialist. But being materialists, they had
to argue that the medieval worshiper of Mary and the romantic Giant Man of the nineteenth century had been superseded
by Economic Man, the sport of economic forces, that he had
nothing to hope for from supernatural agencies, that he must
create a heaven here, and that socialism would tend to take the
place of Christianity in moral leadership. Like Christians of
an earlier era socialists tendered the opportunity to attain
martyrdom in a good cause; Debs was accustomed to hint
to young men in his audiences that if they wished a place in
history they should champion unpopular ideas in which they
believed. All these things had an allure for the high-hearted
young and also for the troubled thinker who found nowhere
else to turn; essays on socialism as the logical substitute for
Christianity were frequent in magazines; in 1908 alone three
books by prominent ministers showed the drift toward
socialism as practical Christianity—Walter Rauschenbusch's
Christianity and the Social Crisis, R. J. Campbell's *Christianity
and the Social Order*, and Shailer Matthews's *The Church and
the Changing Order*.

Acquainted with the history of third parties in the United
States, socialists were resigned to the probability that they
would never win a national election. Debs said that he knew
he would not sit in the White House. But he and his followers
were sure that their doctrines would permeate the political
thinking of the whole people, that the two major parties
would be obliged to adopt socialistic planks. They therefore
built for a future, not merely a political future but also a
moral one, for just as they accepted and applied the principle

of evolution in economic history so they looked forward to an evolution of man's character. The fit man of the remoter past, they asserted, had been the one of physical prowess; the fit man of the twentieth century was the man of mental superiority; but the fit man in time to come, they predicted, would be the most moral one. This prophecy was another challenge to the idealist, aware of the possible growth of a new national tradition. Who, indeed, should be the man of the hour? Clergymen were still adumbrating the meek, selfless man of the primitive church, but in actuality the man of the hour had for centuries been literally the man on horseback, and now in the 1900's he was the Napoleon of finance, the captain of industry, the master rogue, the burly sinner, the man higher up, the man-who-can-do-things. Was not this man an evolutionary misfit, already an anachronism? Was not the man of the hour to be one who without the incentive of divine approval would live in brotherhood with all men, everywhere? It is not, of course, intended to suggest that the socialists had first conceived of this man, but it is necessary to indicate that this question agitated many of our writers of fiction and some of our poets and dramatists in Roosevelt's administrations.

In 1905 the hero of Octave Thanet's *The Man of the Hour*, wrestling with a split personality, finally turned from socialism to the side of "law and order," and Paul Cahart in Samuel Merwin's *The Road-Builders* was so much in favor of forthright individualism that he settled a strike by knocking down a cook with a piece of scantling. LeRoy Scott's *The Walking Delegate* told of the struggle within a union during which Tom Keating defeated Buck Foley, a grafting labor leader, and saved a strike; Jack London's non-fiction *The War of the Classes* told how he become a socialist. In 1906 Upton Sinclair's *The Jungle*, intended by him to be a socialistic novel, was read by the public as a muckraking tract; Davis Parry's *The Scarlet Empire* pictured a Utopia in reverse, with a regimentation enforced in the name of the state and with a consequent destruction of spiritual life; Jack London's "What

Life Means to Me" (March *Cosmopolitan*) reviewed his
return to his own class, the working class, and trumpeted his
confidence in its future and in the future of humanity; Edwin
Markham's "The Hoe-Man in the Making," a series of articles
running in *The Cosmopolitan*, described among other things
toil, poverty, and disease among two million child slaves and
commented that "even the churches are silent." Interestingly
enough, the Graustarkian novel could be affected by the question of the hour, for Ervin Wardman's *The Princess Olga* had
business stirring up a revolt against the throne of Crevonia.
In the July *Arena* Archibald Henderson found Howells disillusioned with socialism and failing to tell us "of ourselves,"
though he told "of our manners and our minds, of our humors
and of our principles, of our follies and of our absurdities,"
which would seem to come pretty close to telling us of ourselves. Mark Twain rejected any such animadversion by
declaring in *Harper's* for the same month that Howells was
without a peer in the sustained exhibition of great qualities.

As though to make his own notation upon this disagreement
Howells, seventy years old now, published in 1907 *Through
the Eye of the Needle* which, uninteresting as the document-
ing of a dream state, revealed no disillusionment with socialism. In that year Hutchins Hapgood's *The Spirit of Labor*
novelized his study of Chicago workingmen, Jack London's
The Road apprised readers of what treatment tramps could
expect at the back doors and in the city jails of the nation,
Charlotte Teller's *The Cage* made sympathetic use of the
Haymarket Riot, and Richard Barry's "Slavery in the South
Today" (March *Cosmopolitan*) blamed Standard Oil, a
Florida railroad, the turpentine trust, and the lumber trust for
horrors and corruption in the deep south. One of the better
novels of 1907 was Brand Whitlock's *The Turn of the
Balance*, dedicated to "Golden Rule" Jones. Its purpose was
to expose the tie-up among business men, politicians, and
administrators of justice, and to do this it traveled from the
rich and complacent, who approved of charity, to the poor
and beaten, who did not want it. Whitlock typed his char-

acters too generously: there are the society bud whose eyes are opened to the misery of the underpaid, the snobbish young man who disgraces his family, the hypocritical banker, the brutal policeman and the brutal detective, the worker victimized by his employer, the ambitious attorney, the good-hearted prostitute, the young man hounded into criminality by the law. More original are the idealistic young lawyer who often tires of his cases and is cynical about the even-handedness of justice, and the jailbirds and riff-raff of saloons whose habits, manners, and jargon Whitlock handled with unusual fidelity. The plot is steered too closely, but *The Turn of the Balance* has the right blend of indignation and compassion, the direct translation of experience that help to make enduring literature.

In 1908 "Paid in Full" yoked Jesus to socialism and Upton Sinclair infuriated adherents of the *status quo* with two novels, *The Metropolis* and *The Moneychangers*, portrait galleries of powerful social and financial figures easily identified. "The Lounger" in *Putnam's Monthly* for March thought the first of these was "the funniest thing that ever happened" because it painted all the wealthy as vicious, freakish, dishonest, and hypocritical, going to church to maintain a front and hiring only preachers who were men of the world. When two months later Jeannette Gilder in the same periodical denounced *The Metropolis* as preposterous because its author did not belong to the Four Hundred Sinclair retorted that he did not need to be a hippopotamus in order to write about hippopotami, and that anyway he was familiar with the circle he satirized. John Kendrick Bangs's attack upon *The Moneychangers* took the milder form of a parody called *Potted Fiction*. Henry L. Mencken's biographical-critical *The Philosophy of Friedrich Nietzsche* (1908) was also in the nature of counter-propaganda. Mr. Mencken had too much gusto to sympathize with the gloom in Nietzsche's personality, but like the Polish-German thinker he did like to prick the bubble of philistine contentment and he appreciated Nietzsche's confession that among "the rabble of today" he hated most the socialist. Although Mencken thought Nietzsche's idea that the Jews had conspired to perpetuate a slave philosophy was "sheer lunacy," and although he was shy about accepting the doctrine of eternal recurrence, he endorsed the morality of the Superman as grounded in historical and psychological truths and as inspiring in the best sense.

It is not possible to store in separate compartments the literature which had to do with socialism, with muckraking, with politics, with the glorification of the Strong Man, or with Americanismus, for the novels, short stories, and plays which dealt chiefly with one of these topics unavoidably made use of some or even most of the others. In 1905 Booth Tarkington thought of himself as a socialist, thought he had been elected to the legislature as a Republican, and the six stories included in his *The Arena* (1905) described so much vote-buying, ballot-tampering, graft, blackmail, slander, and corruption that they could have intrigued the socialist, the muckraker, and the sociologist, and Roosevelt objected to them as discouraging the better people from entering politics. Similarly, Elliott Flower's eight stories in *Slaves of Success* (1905) exposed simultaneously the venality of politicians and the money madness which led men to betray their friends and their honor. However, five novels can safely be classified as political: David Graham Phillips's *The Plum Tree* (1905), Mary Dillon's *The Leader* (1906), I. K. Friedman's *The Radical* (1907) and Winston Churchill's *Coniston* (1906) and *Mr. Crewe's Career* (1908). The first of these, autobiographical in form, is an explication of the "dominion of great business interests over politics." Its presumptive writer, Senator Harvey Saylor, has as a young lawyer nearly crushed by a local boss changed his "line of battle," allowed himself to be bought by the Power Trust, and making an adjustment to "tactics of Life—as it is" attained such influence that he became a president-maker until at last his career shrivelled into failure. Not unrelieved failure, however, for his wife, whom he had married for money and prestige, having died, Saylor won the woman he had always loved.[25] The second novel made a hero of William Jennings Bryan under the name of John Dalton. The radical in the third was Bruce McAllister, a United States senator fighting for a child labor law in a congress which, together with the Supreme Court, was controlled by an invisible government of Big Business; the novel failed because the author attempted a lightness of touch with a hand that became all thumbs and because situations and dialogue were threadbare.

By 1907 Winston Churchill's political experience had converted him from an historical romancer to a realistic novelist of reform, and his two above-mentioned books are among the better ones of their kind, although some reservations must be made about *Coniston*. Churchill's Afterword to this novel suggests that he intended it to be a protest against arbitrary political power, but the protest is half-hearted in total effect since Jethro Bass is a lovable "boss" in the David Harum tradition as a character, and the bulk of the story is allotted to the love of Cynthia Wetherell and Bob Worthington. *Coniston* is a political novel because the stuttering Jethro rather incredibly becomes boss of his state, because of an outstanding comic account of the woodchuck session of the legislature, and because of the narrative of a battle between railroad interests and Bass, who fights this time only for a sentimental reason. The popularity of the novel must be traced to its conversational style of the b'gosh school, its warm human feeling, its romance sugared to the current taste, and its central character, illustrating that perennial favorite, the diamond-in-the-rough. *Mr. Crewe's Career*, dedicated to "the men who in every State of the Union are engaged in the struggle for purer politics," is also of uneven quality as fictional art. It is good in its reporting of the means by which

25. The expression "plum tree" is said to have originated in a telegram from Matthew S. Quay to his broker. In the novel Burbank has been identified as McKinley, Saylor as Mark Hanna. Scarborough bears some resemblance to Beveridge.

the United Northeastern Railroads masters politicians and legislators, good in its characterization of farmers, but its use of the monopolist's daughter as heroine, of the corporation counsel's son as hero, and of the egoistic Humphrey Crewe as candidate for governor seems today trite and at times trivial. Churchill's conclusion was that the railroad's policies represented an outworn stage in economic revolution, that new conditions were bringing new attitudes, and that a fresh day of conscience was dawning in American politics—the day of Theodore Roosevelt.[26] In both novels Churchill pulled his punches. As man and as storyteller he was bound to the tradition of gentility, of expected sentimentalism, of equally expected confidence in a brave world to come, and while that tradition gave him an audience in the years when it flourished, the reactionary nature of American politics from 1908 to 1912 and the horrors of World War I reduced his public as they must have lessened his will to write.

Novels of the marketplace, which Mary Moss (*The Atlantic Monthly*, May, 1905) thought a significant development in our fiction, were likely to be made of sterner stuff. David Graham Phillips's *The Deluge* (1905), a muckraking novel *par excellence*, gives us Matthew Blacklock, a Napoleonic financier who despises "wishy-washy" persons and runs roughshod over his opponents. After he marries Anita Ellersly, who has "preposterous notions of her superior fitness," the couple live at cross purposes until Blacklock learns the lesson of social responsibility, defies and defeats the Seven who dominate Wall Street, and discovers in the last chapter that his wife has loved him for a long time. In Phillips's *The Second Generation* (1907) Arthur and Adelaide Ranger, grown children of a self-made rich man, are almost disinherited in his will because he has seen money and education

26. Coniston was Croyden, New Hampshire; Jethro Bass was a Ruel Durkee. Bass does not greatly resemble real bosses like Penrose, Lodge, Odell, Murphy, Dick. *Coniston* and *Mr. Crewe's Career* stood at the top of the best-seller lists for their respective years; indeed, Mr. Churchill from 1899 to 1914 was one of the most popular American writers.

in the effete east make them snobbish and idle. But they have force, too, and fight their way upward from comparative poverty to fulfillment and comfort, although Adelaide's progress is hastened by a murder. The book is full of Phillips's anger at the dry-rot caused by too much money, at the social climber, at many women. A speech by Dr. Schulze conveys the feeling which Phillips put into all his serious books:

"Mankind found this world a hell, and is trying to make it over into a heaven. And a hell it still is, even more of a hell than at first, and it'll be still more of a hell—for these machines and these slave-driving capitalists with their luxury-crazy families are worse than wars and aristocrats. . . . Some day the world'll be worth living in—probably just about the time it's going to drop into the sun."

The same author's *Light-Fingered Gentry* (1907), sententiously and cynically written, came directly out of the scandals involving three large insurance companies in 1905 and 1906. Its Horace Armstrong, divorced by his wife Neva because he had married her for money, goes to New York to head an insurance company and to follow the sharp practices of the corporation, for he has learned that "as all the world knows, the eternal verities are kept alive solely by the hypocrites who preach and profess them." All the business men in the metropolis are pictured as corrupt, cowardly, vulgar; their wives, driving their husbands into thievery and rascality, are childless, tasteless, extravagant—the married man "in his own home, just as downtown . . . was not a man but a purse." But Armstrong, big, moody, brusque, masterful even with women, and, naturally, a westerner, turns honest, fights the "system" which is to blame for all that is wrong, cleans up the C.A.D., and wins back his estranged wife. Thus submitting to the American wish to have tragedies end happily, Phillips nevertheless recorded his opinion that "Heart and his younger brother, Mind, are two newcomers in a wilderness of force. They fare better than formerly; they will fare better hereafter; but they are still like infants exposed in the wilderness."

Henry M. Hyde's *The Buccaneers* (1905) was another chronicle of lying and trickery in trade, with the church impotent to arbitrate or reform. The hero of Robert Barr's *The Speculations of John Steele* (1905) was ruined by the Soap Trust. Charles Klein's novelization of *The Lion and the Mouse* (1906) followed the play closely. Edwin Lefèvre's *Sampson Rock of Wall Street* (1907) let us see another man of iron will, not a mere money-grabber but a developer of a continent. Francis Lynde's *Empire Builders* (1907) likewise took a nineteenth-century attitude toward the financier and private initiative. Arthur Jerome Eddy's *Ganton & Co.* (1908) had for hero a meat-packing tycoon who was gruff, irritable, unsparing of self or others, who had no illusions about the ways of the world and its inhabitants, but who was at bottom kind and generous. And the J. Rufus Wallingford of George Randolph Chester's *Get-Rich-Quick Wallingford* (1908) was so amusing in his effrontery, vanity, and quick-fire imagination that he had to be carried through several succeeding volumes.

However, the canonical idea of the man of the hour is to be found in Robert Herrick's novel of Packingtown, *The Memoirs of an American Citizen* (1905). This novel also adopts the autobiographical point of view, but does it successfully in as much as it is not only good self-revelation but also careful delineation of a credible character. Van Harrington looks at himself candidly, and the result is a portrait of a man who seems wholly unprincipled except to himself. A boyhood experience supplies the motivation for Harrington's future conduct, which is essentially beyond good and evil, for this Strong Man reasons much as Nietzsche did:

To my mind there was something childish in the use of those words "better" and "worse." Every age is a new one, and to live in any age you have got to have the fingers and toes necessary for that age. The forces which lie in us and make those triumph who do triumph in the struggle have been in men from the beginning of time. There's little use in trying to stop their sweep, or to sit and cry like Dround by the roadside, because you don't like the game. For my part, I went with the forces that are, willingly, gladly, believing in them no matter how ugly they might look. So history reads: the men who lead accept the conditions of their day. And the others follow along just the same; while the world works and changes and makes itself over according to its destiny.[27]

And to the mentioned Dround, Harrington gives warning that "There are no morals in business that I recognize except those that are written on the statute book. It is dog eat dog, Mr. Dround, and I don't propose to be the dog that's eaten" (p. 148). In this naturalistic philosophy he is encouraged by Mrs. Dround, who shares his will to power. "I always liked despots," she tells him.

"And, as a matter of fact, despots—the strong ones—have always really done things. They do today—only we make a fuss about it and get preachy. No, my friend, don't hesitate! The scrupulous ones will bow to you in time." [28]

Looking back over his life Harrington confesses frankly to bribing stockholders, tampering with councilmen and legislators, forcing competitors to the wall with rebates, buying judges, purchasing a seat in the United States Senate. Yet in spite of his stony realism one cannot help liking him at times for his loyalty to friends, his generosity to a brother and to a hostile preacher, his impulse to enlist as a soldier, and above all, his realization at the end that his rise to power had cost him the respect of the few idealists whose good opinion he valued.

The different kinds of hero invented consistently by writers between 1904 and 1909 reveal more than authors' predilections; they reveal also a painful if quiet division of opinion that confused American society throughout the decade. With

27. Robert Herrick, *The Memoirs of an American Citizen*, New York, 1905, p. 148.
28. *Ibid.*, p. 254.

an inescapable puritanic background the majority of Americans were impelled to try to formulate and live up to an ideal of character and were greatly troubled because the compulsions of event and thought had altered the old ideal and made necessary the selection of another. Obviously the man of the hour would not be the hero of Graustarkian and historical romances nor could he be in anything like fullness the exotic of either a Jack London or a Robert W. Chambers tale. There remained five types that might give meaning to both present and future: the Shepherd, the Servant who with saint-like austerity led others to the good life; the Thoreauvian individualist, occasionally appearing in Herrick's novels and often a doctor, who found himself and helped others by turning from the world of men and living at peace in nature; the Master Rogue who trampled weaklings underfoot while amassing vast material possessions; the financial pirate who mellowed, perhaps repented as the rogues of eighteenth century English picaresque romances mended their ways; and the sad but indomitable reformer, usually a lawyer, who like Gordon Marriott of *The Turn of the Balance* believed that social justice would arrive tardily but surely if informed and honest men would roll up their sleeves to work for it and would remember, as Whitlock wrote on the last page of the novel, that "Love, the great law of life, would one day, in the end, explain and make all things clear." Whoever the man of the hour would be, it was certain to the troubled minds of the early 1900's that he would possess great strength, great will; at no other time has American literature been so preoccupied with the morality of personal force and with heroes obsessed with the drive to success. There is not a neurotic among them, scarcely a sick one, although they may sometimes exhaust themselves by the fury of their battle for wealth and place. Even then they would have been ashamed to speak of having "nerves."

The muckrakers, reaching their heyday in 1906, favored the reformer as man of the hour, and by 1905 had already stirred up such unrest that George W. Alger complained in *The*

Atlantic Monthly for August about the "literature of exposure," saying that it was too severe on humanity, that it had no
salve for the "social sores" it described, that it was not constructive, and Richard Le Gallienne suggested that the Rough
Rider had been followed by the rough writer. In that year
Charles Edward Russell arraigned the Beef Trust in the February *Everybody's Magazine*, and in the November *Cosmopolitan* Ray Stannard Baker began a series of articles called
"The Railroads on Trial." [29] In 1905, too, the muckrakers
began to get results: the larger railroads stopped giving passes
as favors to politicians, Armour and others were indicted for
conspiracy to restrain trade, Charles Evans Hughes made his
national reputation by investigating insurance companies before a committee in Albany, and President Roosevelt in his
annual message to the congress in December asked for the
enactment of a pure food and drugs law.

Then in February of 1906 Upton Sinclair awoke to find
himself famous because of the publication of *The Jungle*, first
printed serially in the socialist paper, *The Appeal to Reason*.
This young author had not hesitated to pose as his man of the
hour a composite of Jesus and Shelley, and moved by what
he believed to be their principles and by his socialistic faith,
had spent seven weeks in Chicago observing the life of workers in the packing plants. His findings he put into *The Jungle*,
which he intended to be an attack upon wage slavery but
which horrified the public rather by its unvarnished details
of the slaughtering of animals and the packing of meat and of
the working and living conditions of exploited foreign laborers—it was easier to get excited over the falling off of a frozen
ear or the stirring of a man into a vat of lard than over the
oration with which the novel ends, and Sinclair wrote wryly
to *The New York World* that he had aimed at heart and mind
and hit the stomach. This misfire, however, made *The Jungle*
one of the most sensational successes of the decade, not only
because of its sales and of the discussion it provoked but also

29. In 1907 Mr. Baker took the pen name of David Grayson for his
Adventures in Contentment.

because Roosevelt read it, sent for the author, and thereafter pressed for the passage of the meat-inspection bill which Beveridge introduced into the Senate and of the Pure Food and Drug Act of 30 June, 1906, which prohibited the adulteration of foods and the false labelling of drugs. Eight meat packers made a joint reply to the findings of the Neill-Reynolds Report upon the industry, but that document justified *The Jungle*.

Objections to Sinclair's novel have come from three directions. One, that of the interests involved, has been indicated. Another was offered at the time by critics who for whatever reason thought the story offensive to good taste, and here *The Bookman*, never losing an opportunity to belittle Sinclair's writing, was representative; Frederic T. Cooper, reviewing *Ganton & Co.* in that magazine for December, 1908, alluded to *The Jungle* as "reek and slime," and exactly a year later its "Chronicle and Comment" column reported that "In this country Mr. Upton Sinclair's *The Jungle* is now merely a strong and unpleasant memory, and its author has been relegated to an obscurity from which he will with difficulty emerge." The third objection is still with us, as *The Jungle* is still with us and is by way of becoming a minor classic. Critics who insist that propaganda has no place in literature berate Sinclair's work upon that score, quite overlooking the fact that all literature is propaganda, that an anthology of "pure poetry," as an extreme example, is propaganda for pure poetry. The question is justly not whether literature may contain propaganda but whether the agitprop in *The Jungle* damaged this novel as form and as narrative, and the answer must be affirmative. The declamatory final chapter, like the inevitable endings of the proletarian novels of the 1930's, is uplifting but it is also artificial, an arbitrary re-channelling of the narrative flow, a piece of rhetoric instead of a logical continuation of story, and throughout most of the book the woes piled upon Jurgis and his family are so concentrated as to assault the imagination. However, this damage is too slight to spoil the complete effect. *The Jungle*, with an argument now out of date, remains one of the most heartrending accounts in fiction of what ignorant and helpless human beings have endured.[30]

By March of 1906 Roosevelt also thought that the literature of exposure might do more harm than good, and certainly the first installment of David Graham Phillips's "The Treason of the Senate" in *The Cosmopolitan* for that month, based upon the research of Gustavus Myers, could have been expected to undermine confidence in the highest legislative body of our government. On the seventeenth of March the president made an allusion to the muckrake at a dinner of the Gridiron Club, and on the fourteenth of the following month while laying the cornerstone of an office building for the House of Representatives he quoted Bunyan and denounced the muckrakers, arguing that if everything were painted in black no color would be left to apply to genuine rascality.[31] Ten days later William Howard Taft followed suit by attacking the muckrakers in a speech at Yale University.

In 1907 *Engineering News* (10 January) admitted that the number of accidents had seriously hurt public trust in railroads, and in August Judge Kenesaw Mountain Landis fined the Standard Oil Company of Indiana $29,240,000 for accepting rebates contrary to law.[32] Two books of that year ranged in opposite camps with respect to the muckraking movement: Thomas W. Lawson's *Friday the Thirteenth* told how Bob Brownley made a billion dollars through speculation and James R. Day's *The Raid on Property* defended the trusts and censured Roosevelt. Charles Edward Russell wrote the most provocative muckraking literature in 1908. His "Trinity Church; A Riddle of Riches" (*Cosmopolitan* for May) disclosed that this famous church owned from thirty-nine to one

30. Sinclair invested royalties from *The Jungle* in a project for communal living at Englewood, N.J., which disbanded when Helicon Hall burned in 1907. A young janitor at the Hall was named Sinclair Lewis.

31. In the same speech the president startled his hearers by advocating income and inheritance taxes.

32. Mr. Rockefeller commented upon the fine that Judge Landis would be a long time dead before it was paid. The fine has never been paid.

hundred million dollars' worth of real estate in the city, much of it in squalid and unsanitary slum tenements, and his *Lawless Wealth* collected the illuminating articles he had printed in *Everybody's Magazine* between 1902 and 1904 under the title of "Where Did You Get It, Gentlemen?" Joseph Medill Patterson's mediocre novel *A Little Brother of the Rich* (1908) received attention because it seemed to be an exposé from within the circle of the moneyed few. This sketch of muckraking activity during four years should not close without mentioning that partly as a result of the noisy publicity the first American capitalist to be sent to prison received his sentence on the sixth of November, 1908.

The death of Grover Cleveland on the twenty-fourth of June, 1908, was another reminder to the Democrats that they had urgent need for a candidate who might win in the presidential election of the following November.[33] George Harvey had as far back as 1906 been booming Woodrow Wilson for the nomination, and Bryan had been keeping in the public eye by editing *The Commoner*. William Howard Taft, who had been Roosevelt's trouble-shooter for a half dozen years, seemed in line for the Republican choice even by 1907, the year in which Gifford Pinchot, raising the question of conservation of natural resources, first attracted wide notice. The Republican Convention nominated Taft and Sherman; the Democratic one gave Bryan his third nomination. Roosevelt was again one of the big issues of the campaign; so were the matters of corporation contributions to political parties and the dictatorial rule of Speaker Joseph Cannon. Bryan, standing left of center, championing guarantees to National Bank depositors, flogging the trusts, capitalizing upon the panic of the preceding year, still impressed most Americans as irresponsible, and the prediction of the straw vote polled by *The Literary Digest* was borne out by the tally of the votes which

33. Some others who died in 1908: Edward MacDowell (23 Jan.), Ouida (25 Jan.), Joel Chandler Harris (3 July), Bronson Howard (4 Aug.), Victorien Sardou (8 Nov.).

closed a campaign producing one novel, now scarcely remembered: *The Big Fellow* by Frederic Palmer was about Taft.
One month before the election the Banker's Association of
America, meeting at Denver, had condemned proposals for
postal savings banks and a Federal guarantee of bank deposits
and had listened with mixed reactions to an address in which
Woodrow Wilson declared that the "issue is now joined, or
about to be joined, between the powers of accumulated
capital and the privileges and opportunities of the masses of
the people." Mr. Taft, pledging himself to carry out the
policies of his predecessor, had no idea how uncomfortable
that joining was to be.

V

The Twist of the Root

If history teaches anything it is that for as long as we have had knowledge of him the man called common has doggedly been fighting his way upward from slavery, ignorance, and exploitation to a form of society in which he may secure rights to life, liberty, and the pursuit of happiness, and that this battle has progressed unsteadily, with periods of advance for him and intervals of regression. For all that William Howard Taft sponsored much progressive legislation and that his Department of Justice prosecuted the trusts more vigorously than the preceding administrations had done, history has enrolled him among the leaders in a reactionary span and for that reason is inclined to justify his political defeat in 1912. It is true that Taft was by temperament, conviction, and training a conservative and that his four years in office were on the whole disappointing to a liberal, but history has sometimes made him a whipping-boy for the sins of his class and for the confused reaction of which he was a convenient symbol.

The cards were stacked against Taft from the start. He succeeded one of the most popular presidents the United States has ever had, and because he was non-dramatic, judicial, reluctant to engage in controversy, it seemed that he must in every way be a weak contrast to Theodore Roosevelt. Even before Taft's inauguration persons and circumstances were at work to cause a break between the two men, and when the rift came in a couple of years it was something inherent in the full situation and beyond the control of either. But it naturally redounded to the discredit of the new president. Any successor to the Rough Rider would have been a disappointment to the man in the street, and when Taft's policies and actions were generally assessed as reactionary, opposition to him, composed of criticisms ranging all the way from David Graham Phillips's belief that he was a willing tool of Wall Street to a widespread prejudice to the effect that he was too fat and too good-natured to be an effective chief executive, quickly coagulated.

The fact is that before 1912, before the Progressive Party had even been thought of, Theodore Roosevelt as a public educator had brought into the open a split within the Republican Party at the time when the muckrakers, backed by William Randolph Hearst, S. S. McClure, and Frank Leslie, had also brought into the clear a split within the entire middle class. From that day to the present the labels Republican and Democrat have had less meaning than the terms conservative and liberal, the division resting simply upon the question as to how far individuals may be trusted to regulate their own greed and to what extent police action of some kind may be required to circumscribe free enterprise and to enlarge the public welfare. There was in 1909 nothing new about this difference in opinion. What was new was the publicity given to it, the franker admission that politics and ethics must cope with the problem of a more equitable distribution of national income and that this was a matter of conscience which might transcend partisan allegiance. It was fatal for Taft's political future that he failed to understand this cleavage, that he therefore gave the impression of standing still, if not of approving the reaction against democracy which Woodrow Wilson had sighted in 1901. Popular resentment against huge corporation wealth and low wages, the waste of luxury and the high cost of living, the hand-in-glove friendship among Big Business and politicians and the courts, the seizing by private interests of national resources—a resentment fanned by the muckrakers, by Judge Ben Lindsey's *The Beast* (1910), and by Roosevelt, who knew how to use it in support of his ambitions—converged upon the president and forced him out of office after one term.

In 1910 *The Wall Street Journal* estimated the country's wealth at $125,000,000,000, but more and more working men came to believe that they had produced this wealth only to receive a mere trickle from it; in the same year it was estimated that 262,490 corporations had a net income of $3,125,480,000, arrived at, some workers began to suspect, through means like those employed by the Sugar Refining Company, much impugned in 1909. The Payne-Aldrich Tariff Act, passed in 1909, later stigmatized by Woodrow Wilson as the most conspicuous example ever afforded of the willingness of the Republicans to extend special favors to business, might, the common man thought, be to blame for high prices; the dismissal of Gifford Pinchot from the Forestry Service in 1910 looked like a repeal of Roosevelt's conservation program; the fact that in 1909 seventeen of the ninety-two members of the Senate were millionaires was turned into a wry joke; the re-election of Joseph Cannon as Speaker of the House in the same year meant a continued overruling of the will of the people; the charges against Senator William Lorimer weakened confidence in lawmakers chosen by state legislatures; Taft's opposition to woman suffrage on the grounds that women did not wish it and that if they had it they would be hoodwinked by an undesirable type of politician seemed but a figure in the illiberal pattern.

Opposition in congress to that pattern, at first aiming to curtail the power of Uncle Joe Cannon and to moderate the provisions of the tariff bill, crystallized with speed, and was led in the House by Victor Murdock and George W. Norris, in the Senate by Jonathan Dolliver, Robert M. LaFollette, Albert B. Cummins, Knute Nelson, and Albert J. Beveridge. These were the first Insurgents, excoriated by Cannon, watched uneasily by Taft, who helped to bring about the retirement of the last-named. Opposition outside congress was led by Democrats, by independent Republicans, by labor unions, by socialists, by the muckrakers, by suffragettes, and presently by Roosevelt. William J. Gaynor, running on a reform platform, was elected mayor of New York City in 1909. Woodrow Wilson, delivering the Phi Beta Kappa address at Harvard in the same year, urged an integration of life in college, and a little later, speaking to the graduates of the Hartford Theological Seminary, confessed that "It is a very confusing age for a man of conscience" and called upon the church to supply needed spiritual strength; the next year he won commendation by battling for a democratic Graduate School at Princeton University; by the fall of that year he was a definite possibility for the presidential nomination from his party. In California Hiram W. Johnson, attacking the influence of the Southern Pacific Railroad in state politics, won a Republican nomination and the governorship. Coal miners in Pennsylvania went on strike in August of 1909, and a year later a strike of streetcar employees in Columbus, Ohio, was so lawless that the mayor of the city had to summon two thousand volunteers to help the police and Governor Judson Harmon ordered one thousand members of the National Guard to the capital city to protect life and property. On the first of October, 1910, the building of the *Los Angeles Times* was blown up with a loss of life of fifteen. In that year Judge Elbert Gary's grant of one day of rest in seven to 200,000 workers in U. S. Steel seemed a concession wrung from unwilling authority. The socialists turned Taft's blunders, the popular restlessness, and attempts at suppression to their own profit and, encouraged by the selection of Aristide Briand as the first socialistic premier of France, in 1910 elected Emil Seidel mayor of Milwaukee by a large majority and Victor Berger as the first socialistic congressman. Jack London gave them readable if unoriginal propaganda in his *Revolution* (1909).

As for the muckrakers, who all along had been trying to make government less the expression of the Will to Power and more the functioning of a social contract enforced by a social conscience, they achieved some concrete successes in

1909 and 1910 and then by one of the contradictions of the period and without Theodore Roosevelt's lifting a finger to save them went down before the might of the interests they had done much to chasten. *Collier's Weekly* was in the front of the attack on Taft and Richard Ballinger in 1909; Mark Sullivan's criticism of congressional bureaucracy in the same magazine helped to solidify opposition to Cannon; Ray Stannard Baker's *The Spiritual Unrest* (1910) explained how the church, bolstered by the privileged class, was losing the people, and how new attempts were being made to give Christianity a practical social value; Gustavus Myers' *A History of the Great American Fortunes* (1910) purported to lay bare the financial misdeeds of the plutocrats. In March of 1910 with *Success* continuing to bring the Speaker of the House under fire, the Insurgents took from him the right to designate the members of the Rules Committee and excluded him from it; in April Charles Evans Hughes was appointed to the Supreme Court as a recognition of his skill in prosecuting the insurance companies in New York; in November the House of Representatives held a Democratic majority and Nelson Aldrich lost much of his authority in the Senate. In that year Reginald Wright Kauffman's *The House of Bondage* played up the white slave traffic, another aspect of commercialism which the muckrakers spread before the eyes of shocked readers, and Charles Edward Russell's series of articles contributed to *The Cosmopolitan* under the title of "What Are You Going To Do about It?" proved to be the last important muckraking effort, the first two of the papers dealing with graft in Albany and Pittsburgh respectively, the latter two with scandals touching the Illinois legislature. After that the Muckraking Movement collapsed gradually, the end coming about through a variety of causes including a slackened public interest, the fact that some of the magazines concerned were threatened with the withdrawal of profitable advertising, and the literary aspirations of the men who had been in the front rank of this journalistic crusade.

Political action on the part of women was almost necessarily confined to a speeding up of their agitation for the vote, and in May of 1910 they staged their biggest demonstration in New York, ending with speeches in Union Square; in the same year Washington became the fifth state to grant them the ballot.[1] Anne Morgan and Mrs. O. H. P. Belmont proved that "society" could participate in economic disputes by taking up the cause of striking shirtwaist girls in New York City in 1909. Some other items in the news suggested that male prerogatives were toppling, for in 1909 women competed in auto races from Philadelphia to New York and Selma Lagerlöf won the Nobel Prize for Literature; in 1910 Josephine Preston Peabody took a prize offered by the Stratford Theater with her poetic drama, "The Piper." And in 1909 Gertrude Stein could publish in *Three Lives* stories devoted altogether to women, one of them a Negress.[2]

The banners of suffragettes and the orations of Dr. Anna Howard Shaw worried Taft and his conservative following not at all. But the publicity given to Roosevelt's doings and the constant comparisons, explicit and implied, between king and kingmaker were irritating omens to both the president and his friends. It seemed that all Americans and almost all Europeans were on the *qui vive* as the ex-president, intent on big-game hunting, sailed to Africa before the Tafts had got fairly settled in the White House, that they eagerly pored over photographs of the safari which appeared in *Hampton's Magazine*, fretted over the lack of news from the Dark Continent, accepted Selig's Chicago-made movie "Hunting Big Game in Africa" as an authentic travelogue, and bought *Scribner's Magazine* to read Roosevelt's reporting on his adventures. When that explorer returned to civilization in March of 1910 by way of Khartoum he was greeted with great enthusiasm, and thenceforward the press headlined from day to day his trium-

1. The preceding states to do so were Wyoming (whose territorial constitution gave suffrage to women, a provision carried over into the state constitution in 1890), Colorado (1893), Utah (1895), Idaho (1896).

2. A minor but interesting example of feminine independence in 1910 was Laura Jean Libbey's brief tour of the vaudeville stage. See Louis Gold, "Laura Jean Libbey," *The American Mercury*, XXIV, 47-52.

phal progress through the cities of the Old World and the public utterances whereby, to the irreverent delight of his countrymen, he advised foreign nations upon the management of their domestic and external affairs; in one of his more thoughtful addresses he proposed at Christiana an armed international "league of peace." Back in the United States the Old Guard Republicans, anticipating the effect all the adulation might have upon the volatile ex-president and upon their own fortunes, awaited his homecoming with a trepidation warranted by the outcome, for Roosevelt, quickly sizing up the situation in New York State, reëntered politics with the purpose of rebuking and reforming the standpatters, and when in the late summer he went on a speaking tour of the western states, espousing the political philosophy he called the New Nationalism, it was already plain that he meant to challenge Taft's leadership. From then on the Roosevelt-Taft relation was that melancholy, and as it proved, fateful one of a deepening hostility between former friends. In the midst of all the commotion Roosevelt did not forget to maintain his reputation as a literary man: besides his printed accounts of his expedition he let it be known in an essay on great books in *The Outlook* (30 April, 1910) that he did not care for the Five-Foot Shelf of Charles W. Eliot, and in 1910 he published *African Game Trails*.[3]

The American political novel did not in the last two years of the decade have the vitality which might have been expected as a consequence of the issues and emotions involved in the actual political scene; indeed, its decline from the time of Theodore Roosevelt's administrations until the present is one of the lesser mysteries of our literature for the historical romance, the sentimental tale, the novel of outdoor adventure have never gone out of fashion and even the Graustarkian fabulum showed signs of life as recently as 1927. In 1909 Ellen Glasgow's *The Romance of a Plain Man* was another treatment

3. Two years earlier another strenuous statesman, the English Winston Churchill, had published *My African Journey*.

of the crumbling of the ante-bellum caste system in Virginia and of the Strong Man who learns the value of self-sacrifice. Hutchins Hapgood's *The Anarchist Woman* (1909) was the first serious attempt in our fiction to understand the revolutionary mind, and William R. Hereford's *The Demagog* (1909) drew upon the career of Hearst. Upton Sinclair's *Samuel the Seeker* (1910), not very enlivening propaganda for socialism, told how Samuel Prescott came to see the light that the author kindled. As companionable and as instructive in the techniques of politics as any of the above was Henry Miller's *The Man Higher Up* (1910), in which the red-headed Bob McAdoo by dint of fists, courage, and intelligence rose from Steeltown slums to the governor's mansion and, of course, earned the love of the heroine after a stern test of character.

But if the political novel drooped in 1909 and 1910 so did American literature in general. It was as though when Theodore Roosevelt left Washington some virtue had gone from American pens and printing-presses, and although this aside may originate only in fancy it is true that the novel languished, that the Strong Man previously described began to fade from the pages of narrative, that the conflicts most convincingly and fervidly plotted were those between men and women, and that critics searched for the cause of what they thought was a spell of literary invalidism. *The Atlantic Monthly* for November, 1909, had an explanation and a recommendation:

To our taste for the mediocre, too many of our clever writers are content to cater. Eager to please, more eager to earn money, easy-going, obliging, they fail to reach out toward their best, and settle comfortably to their lucrative, third-rate work. The writing of fiction as an art has suggested itself to but few among us; writing as a paying profession has suggested itself to a vast number. . . . We need greatly more writers who do not care merely to succeed, but are content to watch closely and interpret wisely, who are original enough to eschew the fashion that has brought money and over-easy applause.[4]

4. "English and American Fiction, a Review and a Comparison," *The Atlantic Monthly*, CIV, 681-82.

G. Lowes Dickinson, writing in the *Cambridge Review* (December, 1909) thought to burrow more deeply by alleging that "For America there is, broadly speaking, no culture... there is no life for its own sake." In *The Outlook* for 24 November, 1910, H. W. Boynton took a tory line to the effect that we had no crying need for new literary masterpieces and could "shift very well with the old ones for a decade or two." William Dean Howells praised Robert Herrick in *The North American Review* for June, 1909, claiming for his work universal qualities, but next year in his *My Mark Twain* he revealed a glimpse of his dissatisfaction with current writers by hailing Clemens as the Lincoln of our literature.[5] *The Nation* was of similar mind when (28 April, 1910) it selected James and Mark Twain as our chief writers. However, James's health was beginning to fail in 1909, and his *Julia Bride* was not one of his major productions, nor did Mark Twain's telling points against William Shakespeare as the author of the plays *(Is Shakespeare Dead?)* and his incomplete *Extract from Captain Stormfield's Visit to Heaven* (both in 1909) warm either the hearts or the minds of his following. And most commentators upon our letters, especially those who had hoped that sentimentalism might be evaporating from our books, were distressed as Florence Barclay's *The Rosary* moved to the top of the best-seller list for 1910.

If Robert Herrick's *A Life for a Life* appeared in 1910 to be a distinguished novel it was only because of the author's honesty of purpose, morose insights, and writing skill—things which gave him an advantage over most of his colleagues. Internal evidence suggests that Herrick meant to exhibit the universal qualities which Howells had attributed to him, for this novel is a kind of Divine Comedy, with Alexandra Arnold the Beatrice, the uncaptured vision of ideal love, and with Wethered the Virgil leading Hugh Grant through the Purgatory and the Inferno of factory, slum, and bank. Unfortunately, *A Life for a Life* is also a kind of *Barriers Burned*

5. This much-quoted appositive is found in *My Mark Twain: Reminiscences and Criticisms*, New York, 1910, p. 101.

Away for its climax coincides with a great civic disaster—the San Franscisco earthquake and fire of 1906—its characters are phantoms, and its love passages preposterous. It is also a kind of muckraking novel with poorly disguised, acridly distilled figures of big business, politics, and education. A prelude of three chapters sets the key of American life as a battleground on which victory goes to the swift and strong, as in a boys' baseball game; after that the hero, Hugh Grant, is shown going to the City to achieve that success for which Americans in those years strove with a blind intensity unique in our history. On his first night in the metropolis he is warned by the Anarch, whose story is as melodramatic as anything in E. P. Roe's romance of the Chicago fire, that modern industry was concerned with satisfying pointless or harmful desires and that the City attracted and swallowed its millions like a Moloch. More bracing is the exhortation of Miss Arnold, a banker's daughter, who phrased the rationale of her kind by reminding Grant:

"Men must fight for something. And the best win—that is all. My father won. I have always lived with strong people, who could rise above the shoulders of the crowd. They are leaders because they cannot help themselves. They make life what it is for all of us, and then make it better,—slowly,—better, more interesting, more worth living, more full of sensation. They harness the clouds. They make bread for the rest of us to eat. They make beauty, luxury, power—all that I love!" (p. 233)

Hugh Grant adopts this creed and by it rises in the world, but always at his side is the Anarch to argue that the poor are being robbed of the things that would make their lives meaningful in order that a few may have those things. This is one application of Herrick's title. But there is another, for the Anarch foresees a time of pillage and bloodshed in which the present order will be destroyed as the only way in which to secure justice, and this retribution in the future requires another interpretation of *A Life for a Life*. What is to come after this revolution the Anarch does not know, and the whole book suffers as social critique from the same inconclusiveness. Forty years after publication, its principal worth lies in the relevance to its time and in a passionate indictment of a world turned into a Gehenna of cruelty and greed and corruption.

Much less grim was Robert Grant's story of an old Bostonian going down before the new man of force and commercial astuteness, *The Chippendales* (1909). And much less forbidding, of course, were the historical romances which ministered to the love of excitement and change. In 1909 the twenty-first printing of Robert Neilson Stephens' *An Enemy to the King* (1897) proved that there was still an eager audience for the doubleted hero *sans peur* and almost *sans reproche*, yet writers of this type also seemed afflicted with the nervelessness we have noted, and little of their output deserves attention. F. Marion Crawford's *The White Sister* (1909), not purely historical, was reviewed as the movie material which it was; his last novel, *Stradella* (1909), was grounded on the life of the Italian composer. After another excursion into the smart set in *The Danger Mark* (1909), in which he again introduced the theme of "inherited" alcoholism, Robert W. Chambers returned to his first love with *Special Messenger* (1909), a novel of the Civil War which adapted the exploits of the famous Union spy Belle Boyd, and another routine novel of the same conflict, *Ailsa Page* (1910). Emerson Hough's *54-40 or Fight* (1909) put to use the Washington of President Tyler and the Oregon country of the disputed boundary line to hold up a stereotype plot. John Reed Scott's lackadaisical *The Impostor* (1910) was a tale of colonial Annapolis *à la Beaucaire* for its swordsman hero turned out to be the Earl of Doncaster and therefore eligible for the hand of Martha Stirling.[6] Inexplicably the Graustarkian fantasy had an edge over the historical novel in the number of sales, if not in quality, chiefly because of the popularity of McCutcheon's

6. After the success of Jeffery Farnol's *The Broad Highway* (1911) the historical novel went into an eclipse in this country. In the 1920's Rafael Sabatini brought it back into favor, but Hervey Allen's *Anthony Adverse* (1933) and Margaret Mitchell's *Gone With the Wind* (1936) must receive credit for restoring the type to its former popularity.

third volume in the saga of his Balkan fairyland, *Truxton King* (1909); this time a rebellion against the throne imperilled the life of the young heir until his rescue by a dashing American.[7] Another animated but vacuous specimen was Harold Mac-Grath's *The Goose Girl* (1909). Anthony Partridge's *The Kingdom of Earth* (1909), William T. Eldridge's *An American Princess* (1909), and Henry C. Rowland's *In the Service of the Princess* (1910) must have very few readers today.

Nor is it likely that the best sellers of 1909 and 1910, overwhelmingly American in authorship, are now much read, although an occasional seeker for adventure in print may pick up Rex Beach's story of the canning industry in Alaska, *The Silver Horde* (1909), and the many admirers of Mary Roberts Rinehart will check her three novels on the lists for those two years: *The Man in Lower Ten* (1909), *When a Man Marries* (1909), and *The Window at the White Cat* (1910). Neither Richard Harding Davis nor Jack London was now selling in the top brackets, but in those years the latter turned out two works of fiction still borrowed from the library or purchased in reprint editions. Each of these, as must be expected of London's writing at that time, combined social criticism with narrative and each was an admission of disillusionment and dejection. In *Burning Daylight* (1910) Elam Harnish found gold in Alaska, became a financier in the States, fell in love at forty, and then unconvincingly gave up a fortune and went off to live the simple life on a ranch.[8] *Martin Eden* (1909), freely autobiographical in its details of aspiration, heroic struggle, and creative frenzy in the life of a young writer and in its scoffing at alleged bourgeois standards, is less credible in telling of Eden's literary achievements and of Ruth's unworthy change of mind. Nor is it altogether persuasive as a study in

7. McCutcheon's further Graustark novels were *The Prince of Graustark* (1914), *East of the Setting Sun* (1924), and *The Inn of the Hawk and Raven* (1927). The last is the best written of the six and should be read first to follow the chronology of the dynasty which Yetive represented.

8. Two other contemporary novels whose heroes renounced wealth were Herrick's *A Life for a Life* and William Allen White's *A Certain Rich Man* (1909).

satiety, for although one can believe in Martin Eden's exhaustion it is not easy to accept the soul sickness of one so young. All of London's better books—and this is one of them—exert the great charm of a boyish eagerness for life as experienced through action; *Martin Eden* likewise extends for the melancholy the spell of an American brand of Wertherism and for lovers of Jack London it extends the fascination of a die that had been irrevocably cast, for there can be little doubt that when London put his hero to dreaming of rest in the South Seas and then at the end sent him crawling through the porthole of the "Mariposa" he was himself mortally hurt by discovering the emptiness in fame, money, friendship, and love—those rewards for which he had toiled with an energy superhuman and pitiful. *Martin Eden* must be read with a compassion proper to the intimate touching of a man's life, which is how London probably meant it to be taken, but the curious may find in it a parable of the self-destruction of the Superman or of the physical and mental collapse of the too-ambitious intellectual whom Max Nordau had accused of degeneration. Placed beside it, Richard Harding Davis's *The White Mice* (1909), a romance of intrigue, hairbreadth escape, and love in the Caribbean, is entertainment for an idle day.

The hero of Francis Lynde's *The Taming of Red Butte Western* (1910) saved a railroad from being looted. Herbert Quick's poor novel, *Virginia of the Air Lanes* (1909), part love story, part science fiction fantastically conceived and fantastically written, sprinkled with airship names like aëronats, aëronefs, helicopters, told of a monopoly in the air lanes won by Theodore Carson, inventor of an airship combining the speed of a present-day jet plane and the stability of a helicopter and can be remembered only as one of the first works of fiction to be written about the heavier-than-air type of plane. The machine in the sky was still viewed skeptically by a public that had now accepted the automobile as a vehicle rather than as a racing car and that was buying Henry Ford's Model T in 1909 because the average cost of other autos was

$2,126. While roads were being built so that cars might be driven more easily and speedily it was regretted that the horseless carriage had killed 917 persons and crippled 3,293 in 1910, and some moralists began to include it with the moving picture as a new corrupter of youth. At any rate, it was now so manifestly a tool and a pleasure of the twentieth century that C. N. and A. M. Williamson's *Lord Loveland Discovers America* and *The Motor Maid*, both published in 1910 and both pursuing their well-tried formula, appealed to the many readers who could share or hope to share in the joys and mishaps of motoring.

A fictional character who was to attain a divinity then un-guessed was a cowboy in Clarence E. Mulford's *Bar 20* (1907) and *Hopalong Cassidy* (1910). Hamlin Garland's *Cavanagh, Forest Ranger* (1910) made a case for conservation enforced by Federal rather than State authority and appropriately carried an introduction by Gifford Pinchot. Harold Bell Wright's sentimental problem novel, *The Calling of Dan Matthews* (1909), was one of the signs that American fiction had turned away from localism, but Alice Brown's stories in *Country Neighbors* (1910) were pure local color, with deft and kindly portraits of rustic folk in a beautiful New Hampshire setting. Montague Glass's humorous tales about Potash and Perlmutter in *The Saturday Evening Post* treated sympathetically a race that was to supply much material for fiction and drama in the years to come.

The reasons for the decline of the political novel at the end of the decade are not apparent. Certainly there was still need to expose and to satirize improper conduct in governmental affairs, but it may be that both muckrakers and novelists, often identical, believed that for the time enough had been said, that there was no need in flogging a horse nearly dead. It may be, as previously suggested, that when the clamor of Roosevelt's incumbency had subsided and the enthusiasm generated by his example had died down the political novel experienced a natural deflation. Or it may be that the novelists, a bit tired of their subject and sensing the reaction from reform, turned willingly to a topic which was not new but which they were to handle with a frankness and a choler that demonstrated how far behind the young century had left Victorian reticence and feeling. Whatever the reason, Winston Churchill, who had moved from the historical romance to the novel of politics, and David Graham Phillips, who doubled as muckraker and novelist and who, apart from his potboilers, had been trying to present the whole aspect of the United States, changed tactics in 1909 and 1910 and concentrated their attacks upon a single front. So did the genteel James Lane Allen.

One of the Charles Dana Gibson drawings likely to be hung in the American home was called The Eternal Question, so named because the hair of the famous Girl, sweeping from pompadour to a long curl upon the neck, shaped itself into an unmistakable interrogation point. Like most of what men had to say about women, whether in fun or seriousness, the pen and ink sketch conveyed an undertone of hostility. It intimated the immemorial masculine surmise that the purposes, thoughts, and behavior of the female are not set in rationality, but by 1909 this familiar admission of helplessness before feminine personality had a new tone, one of exasperation and sometimes of a virulence but little tempered. The cause for this was not merely that woman had now become man's competitor rather than his helpmeet, or that her emancipation permitted her to shed the modesties and disabilities of the immediate past. It was rather because woman as a competitor for wealth and prestige was not playing by the rules that man had devised, that like the colossus of business and the politician she was too often disregarding good faith and honesty while she brought into play her peculiar weapons of marriage, adultery, and divorce with which the twentieth century seemed to arm her. Just as the hero had under the criticism of the "realists" faded out of our best fiction so now the heroine was vanishing from life and literature, and Churchill, Phillips, Herrick, and other writers, perhaps resenting her disappearance out of deeply personal instead of literary reasons, turned

upon the New Woman with a harshness that comes as a surprise to anyone who too confidingly looks back upon the early
years of this century as distinguished by a chivalry now lost.
The resentment, it is true, had been rising since the Civil War,
but never before had it been displayed so unreservedly as
Phillips showed it by his novels of 1909 and 1910. Indeed, few
American writers have released more animus in trying to
puncture the legend of fair women.

The New Woman had been cradled in the major social
transformations of the nineteenth century. The first of these
was the Industrial Revolution, which practically eliminated
the family as an economic unit, perhaps self-supporting, and
which made the women of the middle and lower classes potential or actual breadwinners. It also produced those fortunes
which some women coveted no less than did most men, fortunes which women, especially those well-placed, had a chance
to win by bargaining in Vanity Fair. One result of the mercenary marriage was an increase in the number of divorces in
the United States; there were over 25,000 in 1886, over 72,000
in 1906, and since this figure was twice that representing the
number of divorces in all the remaining Christian world, and
since divorce in our country was chiefly an urban phenomenon and the recourse of the well-to-do, it was logical
to see a connection between industrialism and the divorce
problem. A second major social change involved a throwing
off of the restraints of traditional religious conceptions, notably those by which rewards and punishments were distributed in eternity, women were subordinated to men, and
marriage constituted a sacrament. The third great mutation
was that of an irresistible process of social and individual
liberation, a groundswell making for democracy, whereas at
the top was that reaction against democracy which rendered
the era perplexing and paradoxical. Because of this strong
undercurrent of rebellion and readjustment women by 1910
had largely rejected marriage as a career in martyrdom and
had asserted a right to personal freedom comparable to the

right to economic freedom which they had barely won. None of these changes brought the anticipated happiness; each was therefore grist for the novelist's mill. The wealth and leisure and position for which women battled often burned down into the ashes of boredom; separation and divorce left psychic wounds which healed slowly; liberty entailed restlessness and the high frustration of loneliness. The Girl in the Eternal Question might have been drawn with two profiles, since she faced both ways. In her anger at being trapped in this predicament the New Woman was likely to become sadistic as well as selfish, and it was this combination of traits, this suicide of the romantic heroine, which evoked the condemnations of Herrick, Phillips, and others. Hers was a wanton cruelty, sometimes an ignorant one produced by the "education" against which Phillips inveighed—the training of a girl for "success" in wedlock as her brother might be groomed for success in a brokerage concern. James Lane Allen, breaking away almost entirely from the trend and manner of his earlier writing, was going to examine a biological reason for woman's disquiet and in so doing to scuttle his popularity and injure his reputation.

Because of its title and its intention, Winston Churchill's *A Modern Chronicle* (1910) invites comparison with William Dean Howells' *A Modern Instance* (1882). The latter, an excellent example of what Howells meant by realism, is a meticulous study of a middle class marriage that came to grief because its commonplace, spoiled young husband and wife never gained to emotional maturity, one of them morally heedless, the other possessive. Howells handled their failure and the expedient of divorce with all the honesty of which he was capable, yet he could not hide his distaste for what was in the 1880's an extreme solution, nor his belief that Bartley and Marcia had brought disaster upon themselves with little help from society. *A Modern Chronicle* did not so much scrutinize the institution of marriage as it did the individual who uses the institution and the custom of the country to further her own interests. At the same time Churchill phrased some current doubts about marriage when he wrote:

> One of the burning and unsolved questions of to-day is,—will it survive the twentieth century? Will it survive rapid transit and bridge and Woman's Rights, the modern novel and the modern drama, automobiles, flying machines, and intelligence offices; hotel, apartment, and suburban life, or four homes, or none at all? Is it a weed that will grow anywhere, in a crevice between two stones in a city? Or is it a plant that requires tender care and the water of self-sacrifice? Above all, is it desirable? (p. 173)

These queries were more than incidental for Churchill's method in this novel was mildly Zolaesque; he sought to stress in the story of Honora Leffingwell the parts played by heredity and environment. That being so, he held her father accountable for Honora's charm and irresponsibility, her mother for ambition and impulsiveness—"nearly every important act of her life," Honora once admitted to herself, "had been precipitate." Though she was from childhood captivating to all men she was not a twentieth century version of *la belle dame sans merci,* for the motive which led her to think she was in love with Howard Spence and to marry him was disciplined and also strengthened by the milieu into which marriage took her, so that she was moved by the cool amorality of Trixton Brent and swept into divorce and re-marriage by the head-strong "Viking," Hugh Chiltern. Through all of these chapters Honora is believably complex in her force and weakness, refinement and passion, modernity and old-fashioned "character," and to this credibility Churchill added a quiet wit and veracity in dialogue, a natural handling of what on the stage would have been called business, an understanding of the *mores* in revolution, and an unobtrusive appeal to the American conscience that make *A Modern Chronicle* one of the best novels of the last half of the decade. Only in the creation of the faithful Dobbin, Peter Erwin, and in the happy ending did he surrender unconditionally to literary convention and to his own idealism.

In 1909 and 1910 David Graham Phillips published four works of fiction about women and marriage whose values, as well as the intensity of his feelings about his subjects, can best be determined by discussing them in a climactic rather than in a chronological order. *White Magic* (1910) is a tedious novel in which Beatrice Richmond, who announces that she is "not one of those milk-and-water, cowardly women who have to wait until they're loved before they begin to give what they call love," tries in a long debate to convince a god-like young painter that he is enamored of her and that love will not destroy his art. Her effort hardly seems worth while, and the story would sound more like Robert Chambers at his worst than like Phillips if it were not for the portrait of a ruthless financier, for characteristic complaints about the education of a girl of the upper middle class and about the weakness of rich young men, and for arguments against marriage which may have been those of the author as well as of Roger Wade. *The Fashionable Adventures of Joshua Craig* (1909), which might have been entitled The Taming of the Snob, is in its alternate layers of muckraking and of analysis of the new American heroine recognizably a work by Phillips. It begins with an arraignment of the rich and the politicians in Washington, where most of the scene is laid and where Craig, another superman from the West intent upon the conquest of the capital, is so boastful, so crude that he is a public joke, yet so able and incorruptible that he is appointed an assistant to the Attorney-General of the United States. "I don't want money," he tells his best friend, "I want power—to make all these snobs with their wealth, these millionaires, these women with their fine skins and beautiful bodies, bow down before me—that's what I want!" Adventuring into society, he is a bull in the Sèvres shop, outspokenly accusing new acquaintances of being "sycophantic, idle, useless." To this "mighty, inevitably prevailing, Napoleonic" man Margaret Severence, a compound of cynicism and sweetness, is attracted because she is sick of the snobbish, greedy, and treacherous circle within which she moves and because she surmises that he will go far. From Chapter XIII on the narrative sinks almost to burlesque in language and situation as Margaret marries Craig and plans on her honeymoon to surrender only if he will return to Washington as Attorney-General. She reckons without her Petruchio, who employs moonlight, an indomitable will, and some unorthodox maneuvers to bend her to his wish to go back to his native State and run for governor. This paltry novel was the fateful one which led directly to the killing of Phillips by a deranged man who thought that the author had been maligning a sister.

The Husband's Story (1910) had more matter and more art. To attain focus while he sacrificed perspective Phillips made this novel the autobiography of Godfrey Loring and thus pointed up the peevishness, inefficiency, vanity, untidiness, and wastefulness of his wife, whom the husband assumes to be typical.

The truth is [Loring is presumed to write] that while she is sitting still, playing with a lapful of artificial flowers of fake culture, like a poor doodle-wit, the American man is growing away from her. She knows nothing of value; she can do nothing of value. She has nothing to offer the American man but her physical charms, for he has no time or taste for playing with artificial flowers when the world's important work is to be done.... All the while she hugs to her bosom the delusion that she is the great soul high sorrowful (p. 45).

Later, when the unequal division of labor which is their marriage comes to the issue of a divorce opposed for the time by Edna Loring, the husband reflects:

Love is generous, is considerate, finds its highest pleasure of self-gratification in making the loved one happy. Such a conception of love never entered her head—and how many American women's heads does it enter? (p. 398)

And Loring's bad opinion of his wife is strengthened by a conversation with his misogynist friend Armitage, who remarks: "I have only one strong feeling—and that is my contempt for woman—the American woman," and continues:

"The sex question! That's the only question worth agitating about. Until it's settled—or begins to be settled—and settled right, it's useless to attempt anything else. The men climb up. The women they take on their backs become a heavier and heavier burden—and down they both drop—and the children with them. Selfish, vain, extravagant mothers, crazy about snobbishness, bringing up their children in extravagance, ignorance, and snobbishness—that's America to-day!" (p. 154)

The point of view from which this story is related, and which seems to be pretty much Phillips's, assured a minimizing of the husband's contribution to failure, but the reader will find him guilty of too complete an absorption in himself and his ambitions, guilty of folly in not keeping a firmer grip upon household affairs especially as they related to the rearing of his daughter, guilty of an austere spurning of sentiment. In such items as the trip to Europe, the entrance of Prince Frascatoni, the wavering over divorce, the untimely illness of the wife, the comments upon the English, and the finding of the right woman for the husband this novel has an interesting resemblance to *Dodsworth* (1929), but Phillips's writing hand was doubled into a fist whereas Sinclair Lewis's held its pen in nervous fingers. No fiction has more forthrightly stated the case against the American woman who chooses a mate because of his money-making potential, who regards marriage as the ladder up which she climbs into the society page, who is willing to sell her daughter in the nuptial bazaar, and who maddeningly goes the way of egotism while convinced of her unselfishness, purity, and delicacy; none of Phillips's bottled more of his wrath against the ordinary sensual female.

Yet *The Hungry Heart* (1909) is the best of his novels published in his lifetime.[9] We learn from Phillips's biographer that the ubiquitous but not always safe guide, Frank Harris,

9. *Susan Lenox: Her Fall and Rise*, which in spite of repetitiousness deserves to rank with the work of Dreiser and James T. Farrell in the history of American naturalism, was published posthumously in 1917. Phillips was shot on 23 Jan., 1911, and died the following night.

declared he would "rather have written *The Hungry Heart* and the *Light Fingered* [*sic*] *Gentry* than *Anna Karenina* itself" [10] and H. L. Mencken was sufficiently impressed with *The Hungry Heart* and *The Husband's Story* to hail Phillips in the January, 1911, *Smart Set* as "the leading American novelist." Today *The Hungry Heart* is so nearly forgotten that the three most useful histories of American fiction do not mention it, and because of this neglect a brief synopsis, inadequate though it must be, seems justified.

The Hungry Heart is an American version of "A Doll's House" carried to situations more dramatic and searching than the slamming of a door. Richard Vaughan, marrying the beautiful Courtney Benedict, takes her to his home in the Midwest, where the clash between the two begins almost at once. For Vaughan, believing that his bride is a "good woman," that she is "all woman" and therefore content with her part as wife, mother, and housekeeper, neglects her while he buries himself in his chemical laboratory. But Courtney wishes also to cultivate her mind, to share his real life with him, and when he laughs this off and develops into something of a tyrant in the conventional masculine style her mind "teemed with the thoughts that in this age of the break-up of the old-fashioned institution of the family force themselves upon every woman endowed with the intelligence to have, or to dream of, self-respect" (p. 54). Then the husband installs in the house a young scientist, Basil Gallatin, to help him in his experiments, and we have a masterly study of the slowly growing infatuation between him and Courtney, each trying to idealize the other, each speaking of "real love" and of its rightness and needs, with the wife so frankly aware of the sexual implications that at his first overtures she tells him to return to his "old haunts" for a few days. "You'll come back cured," she assures him. She is aware, too, of the dark corridors in her own nature, and when she becomes Gallatin's mistress she

---

10. Isaac F. Marcosson, *David Graham Phillips and His Times*, New York, 1932, p. 307.

does not deny herself to her husband, this being a necessary, hateful deceit. "Somehow," she informs her lover, "I seem to delight in shocking myself—and you. Loving you is—all sorts of pleasures and pains. I want them all!" In their apologies to themselves and to each other we hear sensualists fiddling on the strings of sentimentalism, but Courtney, who throughout behaves with unexpected honesty, presently detects a false note, so that when her husband discovers the affair and Basil offers to redeem her through marriage she replies: "We women have got to stop being canary birds if we're to get real self-respect—or real consideration" (p. 419), and she goes on: "I'm done forever with the kind of romance and idealism we were brought up on. I'm going to build as high as I can, but I'm going to build on the ground" (pp. 420-421).

In this crisis the husband conducts himself with dignity and at last with humility, saying that he is glad for what has happened since it has awakened him, has saved him from becoming "a dust-dry, routine plodder, getting more and more useless every day," with narrowing intellectual interests. Having learned his lesson, he indulgently permits Courtney to remain in the house and to work beside him in the laboratory, where she is surprisingly apt. Ultimately she comes to see how big her husband is, how small the man to whom she had given herself, and when Basil again urges marriage, reminding her that the only excuse for what she has done is her love for him, she scandalizes him by her rejoinder:

"On the contrary, my only excuse is that I was swept away by my craving for love—for what Richard in our brief honeymoon had taught me to need."
"For God's sake!" he cried. "How *can* you say such things?"
"Because they are the truth," she answered with quiet dignity.

And a moment later she asks:

"Do you know what would happen if I married you? ... I see you know what would happen. The same thing again."
"Courtney!—Good God!"

The denouement comes in a melodramatic scene in which the lover proves himself a coward, but Courtney, before returning to her husband's arms, tells him that she regrets nothing: "That experience with him—it helped me toward learning how to live." And he assures her it has taught him. So both discover that "the wise make of their mistakes a ladder, the foolish a grave."

The Hungry Heart does not have the richness of thought and feeling that we expect of the best European novels, but it has enough of feeling and thought, enough of story-telling skill to rise above most American fiction of the decade. Eschewing the elocutionary construction, Phillips for the first time showed a fixity of purpose and application resulting in that suspense which he deemed indispensable to narrative, and resulting in a coherence of all elements, a *legato* which brings into close harmony the characters as believable persons, appropriate to their setting, tortured by their codes, and commanding the reader's sympathy. This is not to say that *The Hungry Heart* might not have been improved. As a study of marriage it is neither acute nor final, for Phillips was always unsubtle. He could not have meant that adultery is to be recommended as a specific for an unhappy couple, yet that is the way out of the condition he plotted, with a forgiveness at the end which, if not forced upon the husband by the author, at least seems at odds with his background and temper. One must conclude that the ending is extracted from Phillips's inner romanticism, from that store of sentiment which most Americans reserved for a buried life, rather than from the factors implicit in the circumstances. Phillips always had trouble with the endings of his books; this time he did discard his too-easy cynicism.

It is not necessary to underline the courage required to write *The Hungry Heart*. Phillips did more than inspect fearlessly an institution still regarded by the great majority as sacrosanct. He struck at man's fatuous assumption of mental superiority to woman. He deprecated the clinging vine. He totally dismissed the Nietzschean concept of woman as breeder, and for the first time in American literature he pre-

sented sex candidly as a call of nature, needing no poetic
camouflage and deserving no apology. He did not remove the
fig leaf from woman, but he did reveal her, to adapt the phrase
of Heinrich Heine, naked beneath puffed sleeve and long
skirt, and this he did with both taste and passion, things which
do not always easily unite. He proved, that is to say, how
possible it is to write about adults in an adult way, with no
prurience but with no concession to censorship, his probing
remorseless, his knowledge extensive, his integrity proof
against any temptation to lower his theme to pornography.
The Hungry Heart may have done something to bring about
a better understanding between men and women, a more
mature attitude toward wedlock, and if it did its current
neglect is one of the puzzling injustices in the history of our
letters.

James Lane Allen surveyed marriage from a different angle
in his remarkable *The Bride of the Mistletoe* (1909), which
anticipated a present-day interest in the uses of myth, symbol,
and anthropology in fiction. The point of this compact tale is
that sex is a concern of youth and young manhood, woman an
incident in a man's career, middle age a time for readjustment
of wife to husband. To make this point tactfully Professor
Ousley at his wife's insistence reads to her a lecture in which
he unriddles the primitive significance of the Christmas tree,
of its ornaments, of the mistletoe, and in a flash of intuition
she sees what she has meant to him and why he has been
neglecting her for his studies. Confronted with the fact that
he needs her less than he did she first reacts in anger, resolving
to quit the house forever, but through a night of vigil she
becomes reconciled to the inevitable decline of passion. Only,
for a moment she allows her thought to wander to a neighbor,
the family doctor who, she realizes, loves her. The abuse
which this slender *nouvelle* brought down upon a once-
popular author demonstrates the reverence in which marriage
was held at the opening of the century. Reviewers called it
a bastard form of writing, said it failed to make sense, denounced it as sordid, as cruel reading for women, as unfit for

la jeune fille, as ridiculous, as gauze-veiled eroticism, and *The Congregationalist* (24 July, 1909) went so far as to declare that "the book reminds one of the performance of a man half drunk." Readers today can still find the story elusive but they will not reject it as indecent, and they may take pleasure in the attempt to peer into then unlighted recesses of human conduct and in the writing itself, which is as coldly effective as though the pages had been frosted by the winds blowing about the professor's house on that Christmas Eve.

The Bride of the Mistletoe was to be the first volume of a trilogy. The second volume was *The Doctor's Christmas Eve* (1910), a near-static novelette in which the counterfeit peace of Doctor Birney's family is broken by the innocent remark of a little son, whose death at the end brings father and mother together in a tentative solution to their alienation. In this sequel Allen meant to say that a marriage based upon physical attraction alone cannot long endure, a text which seems harmless enough, but again reviewers summoned hostile epithets, berating this story as decadent, mawkish, morbid, and absurd. Daunted by the reception given to these attempts James Lane Allen left the trilogy unfinished and gave no public hint as to how he would have completed it or what his unifying purpose had been.[11]

In 1909 and 1910 the American theater, commendable for its growth in responsibility to its audiences, often employed the topics current in American fiction: the occultism which satisfied the craving of some minds for certainty with respect to a future life, the battle of the sexes, race antagonism, the class struggle, the personality of the *entrepreneur,* the lure of the big city. Two events gave a special fillip to the stage in those years; one, the visit of Sarah Bernhardt in October of 1910, the other, the opening of the New Theatre in New York on the sixth of November, 1909, with E. H. Sothern

11. For an interpretation of Allen's intention see Grant C. Knight, "Allen's Christmas Trilogy and Its Meaning," *The Bookman,* LXVIII, 411-15, or Chapter V in the same writer's *James Lane Allen and the Genteel Tradition,* Chapel Hill, 1935.

playing in "Antony and Cleopatra." The New Theatre also presented in its first season John Galsworthy's impartial handling of the labor question, "Strife," and Edward Sheldon's "The Nigger," in which Philip Morrow, learning that he had Negro blood, sacrificed his career and his sweetheart for the sake of race.[12] In 1909 Johnston Forbes-Robertson appeared as another redeemer in Jerome K. Jerome's "The Passing of the Third Floor Back," Margaret Anglin was leading lady in "The Awakening of Helena Richie," and George Fawcett played the dominating father and man of business in "The Great John Ganton." The first-night audience at Clyde Fitch's "The City" must have expected at the end of a palpitating second act in which, among other sensational things, they first heard "God damn" included in dialogue on an American stage, to see a satire on the familiar social climber who comes from a small town to make his way in the metropolis.[13] But the anticlimactic third act made it clear that Fitch intended to construct a problem play, focused melodramatically upon a young man whose father had set off a chain reaction of dishonorable deeds for which the son and daughter paid the penalty. Much of this exciting play was critical of Big Business and of a society whose wealth made it careless of moral standards, but at bottom "The City" was a preachment on the visitations of parental sin.

Eugene Walter's "The Easiest Way," another success in 1909, likewise carried its social commentary: John Madison charged Brockton, a stock manipulator, with living unproductively off the toil of others, and the furious speech in which Laura Murdock accused Brockton of framing her showed, as did the constant advice of Elfie St. Clair, the consciousness among women that they must either victimize men or be victimized by them. But the difficult artistic undertaking the

12. With respect to what was called "the Negro question" it may be recalled that Jack Johnson's defeat of Jim Jeffries at Reno on the Fourth of July, 1910, precipitated riots over the United States.

13. The profanity is also printed in *Plays by Clyde Fitch* (Memorial Edition), New York, 1915, p. 580.

playwright set himself in this drama was to win understanding for a heroine who left a rich protector for a worthy man whom she loved, only to learn that she could not support poverty and must return to the provider of comforts. It was an unsympathetic if pitiful part, and that it came off well was a tribute to Frances Starr, who more than Mr. Walter made the frail actress heroine credible; in the reading Laura's decision seems too quickly made, Brockton's wealth too theatrical, and Elfie a bold stereotype.

William Vaughn Moody's "The Faith Healer," another production in 1909, is a confused and sentimental play with characterization too heavily inked, good dialect, an interesting first act, and a weakening hold upon the attention unless one can pretend not to guess the outcome. It is confused because it seems at various times an Easter miracle play, a play whose subject is the conflict between science and mysticism, a play about a man with a mission who is diverted from his purpose by the eternal Eve, a play contrasting faith and good works, a play in which an erring woman is transfigured. It is sentimental because the Faith Healer, a kind of Vanamee, has some speeches that are too pretty and because he unbelievably recovers his power in the last act. In this instance, with Moody again trying to see woman as both divine and earthy without doing damage to his idealization of her, his reach for symbol and truth and theme so exceeded his grasp that in the end "The Faith Healer" looks like capitalization of a widespread but passing fad for psychic research.

Drama for 1910 can be fairly summed up by noting that the greatest success was "Get-Rich-Quick Wallingford," this marking a decline as startling as it is inexplicable. National pride was hurt when Frederick S. Converse's "The Pipe of Desire," hope of music-lovers who wished opera in English, failed at the Metropolitan Opera House that year, and it remained for an Italian, Giacomo Puccini, to compose the best opera on an American story, "The Girl of the Golden West," which had its première on the tenth of December, 1910, at the Metropolitan. That pride was mollified by the visit of the Metropolitan Company to Paris in May and by the realization that the sale of the assets of the Manhattan Opera Company to the Metropolitan a month earlier would insure an institution whose resources would have world-wide respect. In two other ways the Metropolitan demonstrated that it was keeping abreast of the times: in 1910 the production of Tschaikowsky's "Pique Dame" signalized the first appearance of Russian opera in the United States, and a broadcast of "Cavalleria Rusticana" led the way to a new use of a recent invention and to a further publicizing of the voice of Enrico Caruso.

Not too much can be said for other types of American writing in the last two years of the decade. Ezra Pound was received appreciatively in London in 1909, but on this side of the Atlantic Robert Service's *Ballads of a Cheechako* (1909), appealing to many of the same readers who thrilled over the tales of Jack London and Rex Beach, and James Whitcomb Riley's verses celebrating boyhood and farm seemed poetic enough to a large public which gave little heed to the founding of the Poetry Society of America in 1910, and which showed too small an interest in John Lomax's collection of western ballads, *Cowboy Songs* (1910). This anthology was published with the encouragement of such unlike—and in two instances one is tempted to say unlikely—authorities as Barrett Wendell, George Lyman Kittredge, and Theodore Roosevelt. Today it is a permanent addition to American literature, with some of its songs reaching through concert and radio performances a popularity which supports Professor Wendell's tribute to them as compositions "straight from the heart of humanity."

In 1910 Edwin Arlington Robinson, sad with the knowledge that he had failed to win either critical or popular approval and with the memory of privations caused by poverty, felt already outdistanced and old. But this feeling that he was a Watcher by the Way strengthened his forbearance for the odd gifted persons characterized in his *The Town down the River* of that year—persons who had also stumbled or halted on the journey to self-fulfillment, men and women who were sometimes wastrels, sometimes sinners, sometimes like Miniver Cheevy aliens in a materialistic civilization, but who were wise in their assertion of individuality, in their refusal to reduce the angles of personality so as to fit into a high place. As in *Captain Craig* the poet's voice was pitched in a minor strain but was never tremulous and never unkind; Robinson's understanding of these failures, his recognition of kinship with them, of a sharing in the fugitive dream which can never be told, tempered his irony with that reserve which alone can render it functional. In classic spareness, in a near approach to mockery, in the rejection of common illusions and in their faint self-pity the stanzas may owe something to A. E. Housman. But Robinson's humanity was warmer. It was no accident that the opening poem in the volume should have been about Abraham Lincoln ("The Master"), a patient Titan misunderstood and derided by lesser men who could not perceive greatness in a gentle and humorous guise, and it was not too strange that after his praise of the democratic president Robinson could in "An Island" invest so contrasting a figure as Napoleon with pathetic grandeur because that conqueror had at least aspired magnificently. For this was one more testimony to the wavering of the contemporary American between respect for justice and admiration for power for its own sake. Yet in its indirect way *The Town down the River* is throughout its length a protest against materialism, against the creed of success and the use of the dollar as yardstick, and this protest, indicated by a dedication to Theodore Roosevelt, is manifest in the last poem, "The Revealer," a eulogy of Roosevelt as the man who had broken open the door of privilege, and a call, not too hopeful, for all of us to carry on the battle against reactionary politics. Though some reviewers still complained about obscurity, this was the first of Robinson's books to receive anything like approving notices, a fact to be attributed not so much to the championship of Roosevelt and other influential friends as to the sensing that here was genuinely original lyric poetry, neither Whitmanesque nor politely sentimental in the magazine fashion.

In the realm of non-fictional prose a Bryn Mawr professor, Albert Schinz, denied in his *Anti-pragmatism* (1909) that pragmatism was a philosophy and asserted that it was a form of opportunism which would triumph in the United States not because it was true but because it was false; readers generally passed this by in favor of the quiet essays in David Grayson's *Adventures in Friendship* (1910). William C. Brownell's smoothly written *American Prose Masters* (1909) pleased the academic world with its chapters on accepted writers; today we note that although it gave acute and sensible treatment to Fenimore Cooper it ignored, in line with criticism of that day, the contribution of Herman Melville. All forms of American writing in 1909 and 1910 seemed held in a state of suspension, with nothing very new in subject or method, and the student does not need to have much imagination in order to feel that in those two years our literature was holding its breath, was caught in a lull while it awaited fresh themes, untried approaches, new techniques in the hands of younger authors. Van Wyck Brooks, realizing that a literary era was passing, predicted in *The Wine of the Puritans* (1909) that satire would flourish in our expanding culture and make lively the years to come.

Anyone who reads the newspapers and periodicals of those two years may also suspect a pause in national and international politics as well as in the growth of our arts. It was a brief period of indecision, of wary footwork and sparring between conservative and insurgent factions. In our foreign diplomacy we upheld the Monroe Doctrine but practiced something called for the first time "dollar diplomacy." At home, and in a much restricted area of example, William Winter resigned from *The Tribune* in 1909 because it would not print his remonstrances against the Theater Trust, yet the New York stage had just been offering plays which had dramatic merit as well as Broadway drawing power; Josef Hofmann wrote in the *Ladies' Home Journal* for September, 1909, that musicians could get a good education in this country, yet our opera companies and orchestras preferred artists of foreign training; C. Lewis Hind, disapproving of the Ashcan School, thought in the *International Studio* a year later that our painting required something more subtle than "hustle and bustle and smokestacks"; President Taft and his assistants subscribed to liberal principles while the administration swung steadily to the right and Theodore Roosevelt, dictating editorials for *The Outlook* in 1910, wondered how he could be honest without being critical of the man he had put into the White House. Everywhere, here and abroad, was contradiction; everywhere a misleading appearance of peace accomplished through reaction. The *status quo* seemed in no danger. No eye was clear enough to see what impended, no Cassandra warned in the marketplace that mankind was about to experience an ordeal generated by a selfish use of power and force. No thinker was aware of how deeply the roots of fate were being twisted as the first ten years of the twentieth century became the property of the historian, or of how terribly the challenge to democracy was to be hurled and answered.

Indeed, the newspaper reader in 1909 and 1910 might easily have believed that the most important news of the time lay in the dispute between Frederick Cook and Robert A. Peary as to which had discovered the North Pole. The continued anti-Japanese feeling in California was dull by contrast, and Louis Bleriot's flight in a monoplane across the English Channel in less than thirty minutes in July of 1909 and the willingness of our War Department in the same year to believe that Orville Wright's airplane might be of some use received much less space in newsprint. With characteristic libertarian sentiment Americans cheered the deposing of Abdul Hamid II in April, 1909, and of Manuel of Portugal in September, 1910, but they had little perception of the deep stirring of the common man, East and West, nor did they understand how fully the Great Powers were adopting the philosophy of Captain Alfred Mahan, how the race to build super-Dreadnoughts was to reach a crisis when the navies of Germany and Japan became threats to the balance of national interests, how Secre-

tary Meyer's announcement in February of 1910 that he
intended to make our navy the mightiest in the world had to
lead to Japan's resolve to enlarge its fleets. Andrew Carnegie
went on pouring out millions for the creditable purpose of
banishing war as a means of settling international discords,
but in 1909 the Czar of Russia paid visits to Germany,
England, and Italy which were not mere pleasure trips, and in
August of the next year the Japanese set in train a long fatality
by annexing Korea.

On the sixth of February, 1909, Marcella Sembrich sang
her farewell in the Metropolitan Opera House, and the rival
Emma Eames followed her example a week later. Then the
American stage lost one of its greatest visitors when Helena
Modjeska died on the eighth of April, one day before F.
Marion Crawford died at Sorrento and two days before the
death of Algernon Charles Swinburne at Putney. George
Meredith died in May; Edward Everett Hale and Sarah Orne
Jewett in June; Edward H. Harriman laid down the scepter
of his railroad empire in September, five days after the last
curtain had fallen for Clyde Fitch. Richard Watson Gilder
and Father John Tabb died one day apart in September. The
day after Christmas it was Frederic Remington who was gone.
    Tom Platt survived the loss of his political sway until the
sixth of June, 1910. In April came the news of the death of
Björnstjerne Björnson. In the same month, with Halley's
comet hanging like a folded white fan in the sky, Mark Twain
died, as he had foretold; his "The Turning Point in My Life,"
summing up the mechanistic philosophy he had expounded in
his dialogue *What Is Man* (1906), had appeared in *Harper's
Bazar* the preceding February. The short reign of Edward VII
came to an end on the sixth of May, and O. Henry, planning
a novel to be called *Truthful*, left it forever unfinished on the
fifth of June. The deaths of Florence Nightingale in August
and of Julia Ward Howe in October left gaps in English and
American life respectively and called for reminiscences of the
middle of the nineteenth century. Then American art lost

Winslow Homer and John La Farge in the autumn, and American poetry gave up the promising William Vaughn Moody at the age of forty-one. In November Leo Tolstoi, driven from his home by endless bickerings over property and alleged favoritism, breathed his last in the house of a railroad official at Astapovo and was buried without Christian rites. Thomas Hardy, venerable enough to be forgiven for the shocks he had administered to his generation, received the Order of Merit in the summer; Henry Adams, lonelier than ever now that Hay and La Farge were in their graves and "Harry" James ill in England, lived on in Lafayette Square with his memories and his disdain; James himself mourned the loss of his brother William (who died on the twenty-sixth of August) with whom he had sometimes disagreed in both good and bad humor, and mourned, too, the passing of an age which both had helped to make memorable.

But a new era, a new generation were at the threshold. In the fall of 1910 Woodrow Wilson, using a political machine for his own ends, was elected governor of New Jersey while a small-town editor named Warren G. Harding failed to secure equal distinction in Ohio. A taciturn, not too successful lawyer, Calvin Coolidge, became mayor of Northampton in that year; the name of Herbert Hoover, a little known engineer who had accumulated a fortune in Asia, appeared on a book titled *Principles of Mining;* an ambitious scion of a notable family, Franklin Delano Roosevelt, took his seat in the Senate of New York State. The class of 1910 at Harvard included Walter Lippmann, T. S. Eliot, Heywood Broun, John Reed, Robert Edmond Jones; the president's son, Robert A. Taft, graduated in that year from Yale.

History was writing Finis to one full volume and was turning the white page of another.

In its more formal aspects criticism is a debate with the past and the future, a re-assessment of the values estimated by former writers and a challenge to the judgment of those to come. Enough has been quoted from time to time throughout this book to make it plain that reviewers and critics between 1900 and 1911, and even many of the novelists and playwrights themselves, were dissatisfied with the quality of our literature produced within that period. Their disappointment, it is true, did not extend to such pieces of fiction as *The Octopus* and *The Pit*, *The House of Mirth* and *The Deliverance*, *The Call of the Wild* and *The Sea-Wolf*, *The Son of Royal Langbrith*, and the stories of O. Henry, and despite reservations the discerning bookmen took pride in the late novels of Henry James and in the printing of the New York Edition. Likewise, the specialists who reviewed *Pragmatism*, *The History of the Standard Oil Company*, *The Life of Reason*, *The Theory of Business Enterprise*, and *Folkways* did so with respect, realizing that these were volumes which would have long life and validity within their particular areas of thought, and poetry-lovers read the verses of William Vaughn Moody with something more than lukewarm enthusiasm. Yet the decade had a flat taste to men eager for literary masterworks, and by contrast with the 1880's, which saw the publication of so many notable American novels, and the 1890's, which resounded with the battle between "romanticists" and "realists" and which took excitement from the rise of Stephen Crane, it offered them only a little to tease the appetite and nothing to satisfy the demand, so typical of the day, for a Great American Novel. That there was no clamor for a Great American Play or for an American epic suggests strongly enough that criticism then did not so much as hope for such achievements. And no one dreamed of nominating an American candidate for the Nobel Prize for literature.

Now American critics and reviewers have all through our literary history employed a surprisingly fair set of values for the judging of books, especially books of fiction. They have, of course, made serious errors of omission and of commission, but in proportion to the number of cases brought before them they have demonstrated a judgment both sound and sensible. A contributor to *The Bookman*, it must be remembered, who wrote kindly of a story by McCutcheon or by the Williamsons had no illusions about the worth of that tale; he knew the differences between it and a novel by James or by Edith Wharton, but he also considered the purpose of the popular work and the service it could render to a certain kind of reader, and while he was somewhat dismayed by the outpouring of sub-literary narratives he was enough of a humanist to give a place to the poor things that were our own, the stories of "escape" that supplied legitimate reasons for reading. Today it is impossible not to sympathize partially with the ruefulness of the majority of critics in the interval we have been studying. But it is nonetheless necessary to file a dissenting opinion in some particulars, necessary to point out that while they were justified in commending the books just named and in lamenting the general low level of appreciation and of output, they did fail to estimate properly a few volumes and some of the aspects of the literature of their time, they did not go deeply enough into the causes of what they felt was a prevailing mediocrity, and they did, lacking sufficient perspective, mistake a plateau for a plain.

They cannot fairly be blamed, to be sure, for having failed to give rank to *Sister Carrie*, to *The Education of Henry Adams*, to *Mont-Saint-Michel and Chartres*; these were volumes whose manner of publication made difficult a wide and immediate critical evaluation. But their coolness toward *Captain Craig* convicts them of obtuse conservatism, their antagonism toward *The Jungle* suggests that like some magistrates of a different kind of court they could follow a line which was also that of vested authority, and their treatment of James's novels of the major phase even when it was deferential seems today to be so superficial as to be almost uninformed.

The truth is that when the critics mourned the artistic unfruitfulness of their decade they had in mind chiefly the imbalance set up by the mass of books composed to please a large uncritical public, insubstantial works that supported Henry James's aspersion that we were "the disinherited of art." In a period when values had come more and more to be fixed by cash equivalents it did look as though genius were following trade, as though writers were prostituting their talents in the market-place and as though the choice rewards went most often to the least deserving, so that there was constant temptation to pander to common taste. Actually, as we can see, the years from 1900 to and including 1910 produced their quota of books of a permanent luster, but for the contemporary these books must have been well-nigh buried under the landslide of merely popular fiction scribbled by men and women whom David Graham Phillips derided as "stupid, unthinking writers."

According to the plaintiffs in those years the cause of the imbalance was, simply, Americanismus. They alleged that the dead hand of profit-making lay heavily upon the theater and the publishing houses, that writers surrendered their artistic principles in order to share in the big money, that these writers submitted their manuscripts to the magazines which paid most for contributions and to the publishers who understood how to take advantage of the Age of the Best Seller, and that they deliberately shaped their writing to mercenary ends. There is so much evidence, direct and indirect, to bolster these charges that they cannot be dismissed. But at the same time an historian must protest that even the offending best sellers had some worth, that the weakness of our drama did not grow from the root of all evil alone, and that to offer Americanismus as an explanation of the overall literary character of the decade is to fall into a great simplification indeed.

Francis W. Halsey in *Our Literary Deluge* (1902) reminded his contemporaries that books were no longer addressed to a handful of readers, that the revolution in printing and distribution had inevitably brought not only expanded markets but also a lowering of literary standards. Mr. Halsey's recording of an obvious fact was wrapped within the equally obvious foil of an aristocratic prejudice far from worn through today. To defend the popular literature here would mean an entrance into a lengthy digressive controversy, but intimations of such a defense have already been given: this kind of writing provided a therapeutic relaxation of the will (badly needed in the era of Theodore Roosevelt), permitted an escape from the strait-jacket of routine, stimulated the fancy and the invention, often bulwarked the morals of persons not given to abstract thinking, frequently conveyed encouragement through its cheerfulness and its happy ending, and in short was invariably good fun and therefore its own excuse for being. Books, like persons, can be loved even when they are not great. To read experimentally among the popular novels of that day is often to reawaken an appreciation for innocence and for sheer narrative, to rouse nostalgia for an era when Cupid's arrow was not a phallic symbol but the dart of love and when the novelist dipped his bucket not into the roiled water of the unconscious but into the spring of exciting action. More concretely, it may be proposed that the hope of writing a best seller sent many a young man or woman into authorship, and that while this resulted in a plethora of mediocre books it also increased the chances for the development of genuine ability; the opportunity to make money with the pen can be abused and, contrariwise, turned to good account. That Americans jumped at the opportunity is indicated by the fact that of the 110 best sellers for the period under study only fourteen were written by foreigners.[14] It is easy to believe that this practice in writing led to praiseworthy achievements in the following decades.

The drama assuredly suffered during the decade from the ambitions of the box-office and, probably, from the overlordship of a theater trust. But it had other limitations. It was still constricted by its picture-frame psychology and by its longstanding tendency to be too theatrical; it had not yet learned from Chekhov and Hauptmann that naturalness is more dramatic than staginess, that affectations and over-writing dim the footlights. As for the poetic dramas, they did not in spite of many commendable lines and scenes have enough of either good poetry or good drama, and their unwillingness to deal with contemporary social problems set them too far apart from the actualities of the age and seemed to give their verse

14. A Canadian, Sir Gilbert Parker, was the non-American most frequently represented in the lists of best sellers.

an inflated quality not far from extravaganza. Olive Dargan's *Semiramis, and Other Plays* (1909), for example, revealed that author's partiality for the late Elizabethan dramatists and her skill with the majestic and passionate measure, but her interest in the queen of Palmyra and the Empress Carlotta and Edgar Poe lacked sufficient relevance for the reader of that year, and William Vaughn Moody's hope to explain the interdependence of God and man and the reconciliation of the two in his trilogy *The Masque of Judgment* (1900), *The Fire-Bringer* (1904), and *The Death of Eve* (unfinished) ended in frustration. Metaphysical thinking had gone out of fashion in a pragmatic period. Toward the end of the decade the theater did, as we have noted, tighten both its social message and its dramaturgy, but "with the failure of Moody's *Faith Healer*, the false dawn of the new American drama was over," [15] and years were to pass before the Little Theater and Eugene O'Neill were to compete successfully with Broadway and to inaugurate a period of dramatic distinction.

But above everything else, the character of American writing between 1900 and 1910 was determined by the nature and movement of the transition through which our literature and our society were then passing. Since literary taste changes about every ten years it is true that almost every decade is an unfolding of some kind, but the one we are studying was peculiarly and strikingly so because it encompassed the passing from "romanticism" to "realism." The 1890's had seen the crisis in this passing, one brought about largely through the reading of foreign books and through the impingement upon the artistic consciousness of such things as imperialistic adventures, the wretchedness of the poor, the revolt of the farmer, the weakening of religious authority, the warfare between employer and laborer, and the spread of scientific knowledge. The early years of the twentieth century were those of development from this turning-point. By 1900 the realists had won the right to express themselves in their own way, yet

15. Emery E. Neff, *Edwin Arlington Robinson*, New York, 1948, p. 150.

almost all of them retained so much of the old faith as to con-
fuse their purposes and techniques and to impart to the literature of the interval an ambivalence that is typical and damag-
ing. Their dilemma was confessed with simple candor by Booth
Tarkington:

I thought in my youth that life could be got into books with
prettier colors and more shaping than the models actually had;
and I fell in with a softer, more commonplace and more popular
notion of what a story should be. Where that acceptance definitely
stopped in me was "Beauty and the Jacobin" [1912].[16]

What this means, in so far as it is also true of Tarkington's
fellow-writers, is that the romantic belief in man's essential
goodness was being given up grudgingly, that there was still
hope (or at least the habit) of reconciling romantic and realistic attitudes, and that it was for many penmen a relief to think
that the economic system could be blamed for the existence
of evil. The conflict in representative novels was often, therefore, no longer between man and fate, or man and nature, but
between man's ethics and the morality of capitalism, with the
medieval devil supplanted by a Strong Man who was not so
much an evolutionary symbol as a survival of the Byronic hero
and who dominated our literature in this era as he never had
before and never has since. This thematic conflict was the
strongest and most prevalent sign of the novelist's wavering
in central point of view, of his uncertainty as he shed the
illusions of the nineteenth century and made use of new discoveries about human behavior. Because southern society accepted these discoveries reluctantly and disapproved of the
changing times the literature of the South in this decade was
noticeably impoverished.

The novelist's awakening to facts was quickened by his reading of foreign authors, and in his selection of them lies another
sign of the transition through which our literature was passing.
For in the 1890's our young men had tried to write like Steven-

16. Booth Tarkington, "The World Does Move," *The Saturday Evening
Post*, CC, 121.

son or Kipling or, toward the end, like Zola. In the early 1900's the models shifted largely from British to French, although Arthur Wing Pinero still served dramatists who, like Fitch and Richard Harding Davis, dealt in the well-made social comedy. The newer English or Irish luminaries, Wells, Shaw, Arnold Bennett, Galsworthy, Yeats, did not yet light the highway for American writers; the guidance was supplied by Balzac and Flaubert and Maupassant and Zola, with Eugène Brieux and Paul Hervieu becoming mentors for dramatists who had formerly learned from Ibsen, Björnson, and Strindberg. The art of Maupassant was reflected in what was dry, cool, and small-scale in the writing of Robert Herrick, and in the compression of O. Henry and the aloof irony of Ellen Glasgow, who also learned virtuosity from Flaubert. But the French novelists whose influences were farthest in reach were Balzac and Zola—Balzac, "the first not only to see his people, physically and morally, in their habit as they lived, with all their personal hobbies and infirmities, and make the reader see them, but to draw his dramatic action as much from the relation of his characters to their houses, streets, towns, professions, inherited habits and opinions, as from their fortuitous contacts with each other," [17] and Zola, whose philosophy of determinism was so attuned to the scientific information of the new century and so in keeping with its explanation of social forces that it penetrated our literature at many points and expanded in many directions. The admiration of James for Balzac is well known, and Edith Wharton and James Lane Allen were not far behind in their esteem for the author of the *Comédie humaine*; as early as his drafting of *Vandover and the Brute* Frank Norris had experimented with the handling of repulsive details in the way that had made Zola a scandal among his own countrymen, and Theodore Dreiser was soon called the American Zola; while a host of minor writers, some of whom had read no French novels, drifted in the stream whose bed had been widened and deepened by the currents of foreign realism

17. Edith Wharton, *The Writing of Fiction*, New York, 1925, p. 5.

and naturalism. These shifts in taste and technique, demonstrations of a period of transition, brought with them contradiction and mistrust, perhaps even a sense of guilt, which help explain some of the literary deficiencies of the decade, for naturalism was fundamentally hostile to the American doctrine of freedom of choice, genteel manners could be relinquished only with regret in some quarters, and so involved were the definitions of romanticism and realism that Balzac attributed to Walter Scott the beginning of the methodology of the realist and Frank Norris looked upon Zola as the fountain-head of romanticism.

Not even Theodore Dreiser could divest himself wholly of the romantic spirit, which informed some of his short stories and was otherwise crystallized in his pity for fated characters, but he accepted and illustrated in all his novels up to *The Bulwark* (1946) the principles of biological and economic determinism; he was, indeed, the only one of his contemporaries who made almost complete the transit from older outlook to newer, and therein lies his permanent importance in American literature. Frank Norris and Jack London had also learned to exploit the elemental in nature and in man and had applied the Darwinian hypothesis to their fiction; London in his propaganda taught that rich and poor were caught in the vise of an economic system; but both men were at heart unreconstructed romantics and thereby divided artists. London was, in truth, the most serious casualty of the transition for he could not take the long leap over the gap separating American romanticism from French naturalism. Like Herman Melville he thought of the white man as the fiercest of animals, but he could not, as Mark Twain did, conceive of man as lower than beasts in the moral scale and he rejoiced in a struggle which was essentially anarchic. London's instinct was to feel life as chaos and battle and to exult in the strength which produced both, but his intelligence, which was not of the most acute, tried to rationalize instinct, to fit jagged pieces into a design, and so he found laws operating in the vast spaces of the far North: the law of natural selection, the law of Eskimo and

Indian whereby iron sank in water and women obeyed men, and the law of the white man, enforced by stalwart Mounted Police. Since London's eye was not single, since he could not decide whether he was a disciple of Nietzsche or of Marx, he compromised a narrative gift originally distinguished by vigor, freshness, and dramatic proficiency, and eventually wrote some of the poorest novels of the day.[18] The quandary into which he floundered was not, to be sure, the only cause of his failure. He lacked intellectual range and was insensitive to much in human nature. When his experience no longer supplied material for creation, when his invention lagged, he fell back upon plagiarism, upon assistance from others, upon a pathetic *fortissimo*, and at that point his downward course accelerated.

Historical romancers were but little affected by the new trends in literature or by contemporary events; they continued to enshrine the trinity of heroine, hero, and villain, only slightly altered by concessions to realistic characterization. And the cluster of humorists excelled in sharing a comic spirit congenial to the temper and the power of the United States. But almost all the writers of fiction who made as much as a half-hearted trial at representing the actualities were obliged to take into account those compulsives and events which comprised the major portion of the history of their time. The first of these, which they appropriated through feeling rather than through analysis, was the world-wide reaction against democracy, proved by international struggles for power in which "inferior" peoples were subjugated, by the growth of monopolies in this country and abroad, by the concentration of political privilege in the hands of the wealthy, by an unfair treatment of the Negro in the United States, by the high regard for the colossus in business, and by the tendency to confide too willingly in the leadership of magnetic Strong Men like Wilhelm II and Theodore Roosevelt. All this, as we have seen, inspired a counter-revolution conducted by anarchists, socialists, trade unionists, and liberals of various types. Then there were also the

18. Read, for example, his *The Little Lady of the Big House* (1916).

armament race, with its attendant rivalries in scientific invention; the increasing importance of the machine and the regimentation of habits under the discipline of advertising; the economic liberation of woman and the consequent readjustment of man's relation to her. These were the phenomena which could not be ignored by the honest intelligent novelist or dramatist, but they were also the phenomena which he not infrequently wished to observe and report with a glancing eye. When he looked at them steadily he was likely, as Mark Twain and Henry Adams did, to believe he had discovered revolution preparing disaster and hence to fall into a pessimism new to America.

Because of the overwhelming pressure of these events and circumstances upon the collective creative mind it is not hazardous to reason that American literature would have acquired from 1900 to 1910 a heavy sociological emphasis even without the examples of the *Comédie humaine* and the Rougon-Macquart series. The preparation for this change had also been made by the protestants against the excesses of the Gilded Age, by the able, patient leadership of Howells in the battle for realism, by the cumulative effects of the sharpened warfare between classes during the 1880's and 1890's, by the veritism of Hamlin Garland, and by the contributions of many writers now assigned to lowly seats in the literary hierarchy. That groping concern with the unconscious which had given glory to the fiction of Hawthorne and Melville and Poe, that idealized topography which in their narratives had betrayed the unfulfilled wishes of the true romantic, were now pretty nearly abandoned in favor of an examination of the more easily observed forms of personality and of the surface of American society. There was as yet no collectivization in the American novel—the individual was still of paramount interest there —but it became the favorite occupation of the writer to study that individual with respect to external rather than internal tensions, to relate him to the men Emerson had called "gladiators of power," to new concepts of justice, to the emancipated woman. This occupation was in fact almost a duty from which there was small chance to escape. Willa Cather did escape, but even James and Mrs. Wharton, those inheritors of strong romantic impulses, came sporadically to terms with the requirements of the transition and wrote about the problems implicit in easier divorce and easier money, and in *The Ivory Tower* James might have written a novel to please both socialist and muckraker. Ellen Glasgow progressed from romance to the Comedy of Virginia; Winston Churchill and Upton Sinclair graduated from the historical tale to the novel of social criticism; and in their respective fashions *Pragmatism* and *Folkways* were tokens of a change in dogma. The American writer was for the time losing what James called a "taste for the intangible." The zeal to save souls had turned into an enthusiasm for saving the body of the United States. So imperious was this urge, whetted by the example of President Roosevelt, that, as we noted, the American novelist not infrequently participated directly in politics, learning much from the participation and sometimes sacrificing too much time and energy to it; Brand Whitlock, for one, admitted that it was his fate to vacillate between politics and literature.[19]

In so far as they brought the nature of this transition into clear focus without having the genius either to comprehend it or to translate it into great art, the typical novelists of the first decade of the twentieth century were Robert Herrick and David Graham Phillips. Both told—as Frank Norris and William Allen White were telling with less persistence—what it cost to succeed in this country, what bankruptcy of character came to men and women for whom life had no meaning beyond the satisfaction of desire. Living in Chicago where he could not fail to be impressed by the enormous material power which alarmed James upon his visit there, Herrick was especially diligent in showing how greed and the craving for success undermined the honor of professional men; Phillips, whose residence was in New York City, attempted to make a whole out of American life, to bring its threads together into a heavy

19. Brand Whitlock, *Forty Years of It*, New York, 1914, p. 69.

tapestry depicting the rout of American character, with, however, a hero who often fought his way through temptation to
a personal victory. Both novelists beheld marriage as a tourna-
ment of wills in which each partner fought for power in one
form or another, both marked that the matriarch was dispos-
sessing the patriarch, both—like Norris and Jack London and
Dreiser—rebelled against the encroachment of women upon
male prerogatives. Both thought that competition for wealth
and prestige had brought society to the brink of moral failure,
and both came near attacking business not because it was too
big and too ruthless but simply because it was business; Phillips,
indeed, seemed as far as his fiction was concerned to hate
money. Both left to us invaluable records of the storms and
stresses experienced by our society as it moved from the cal-
lousness of the Gilded Age to a consciousness of its sins, as it
became aware of the debilitating effects of Americanismus and
bestirred itself in a search for health. Both rejected the romantic attitude in fiction with a casualness which measured
their contempt.

Yet for all their perceptiveness, their knowledge, and their
moral intensity these two novelists did not quite make the
grade. Recently Lionel Trilling offered the shrewd observation that "At the heart of Herrick there is deadness and even
a kind of malice"—the latter part of this accusation probably
arising from the fact that Herrick strikes one as having taken
pleasure in the weakness of his characters.[20] Behind Herrick
and Phillips is a spiritual emptiness, especially noticeable in the
instance of Phillips, who was emphatically three-dimensional.
A novelist is not required to solve problems, but the great
novelist must have a view of the real world made up of man's
purpose and man's destiny and must also have a sensitiveness
to the fate of humanity, a consciousness of sharing in that lot,
a humility, therefore, and a pity that is also love. There is much
too little of these things in Herrick and in Phillips. One need
not find fault with their acquaintance with human behavior or

20. Lionel Trilling, "The Roots of Modern Taste," *The Partisan Review*,
XVIII, 522.

question their strictures upon the contemporary economic set-up, but one must ask whether the correction of that system would automatically produce justice, whether man knows what justice is, and whether he deserves it. The willingness of Jonathan Edwards to be damned if that were God's will was a matter utterly alien to the speculations of these two novelists, who were essentially almost as materialistic as the burly individuals they arraigned and who were likewise creatures of a time when Americans were discarding their old fondness for abstractions. It is true that in reading Phillips one is oppressed by the compulsion to recognize the loneliness of human individuality and the prevalence of something like original sin, the latter being identified with the lust for power which so openly beset Americans in the decade we are examining. But he made little use of these items. The tantalizing opportunity to universalize his moods and observations was there but it was not grasped.

It was not grasped because Phillips—and to a smaller degree, Herrick—was a man of limited intellectual and emotional range and because he was a man in a hurry. Neither of them created a character to live long in the memory, for, the message being so important to each of them, their personae tended to become types: the Strong Man, the young fellow who does not have the stamina of his elders, the doctor or architect who tampers with the ethics of his profession, the worthless rich clubman, the Griselda who brings her husband back into the path of rectitude, the wife who is wastrel and tyrant, the politician who markets his integrity. Phillips, pacing outside his characters and seeing them from that point of view, gave them appearances and motions and words but gave as though he were writing for a newspaper and so fell short of that rare art which is almost life itself. Even his Susan Lenox was to be but the embodiment of a thesis instead of a believable victim like Clyde Griffiths. And most of Phillips's characterizations droop with a shallowness forced upon his writing because he was trying as soon as possible to free himself from journalistic routine; he could not afford the dogged industry through which Theodore Dreiser documented the histories of his financiers and his little people.

It may well be that Phillips, as his biographer informs us, wrote novels because he believed that through them he would gain a larger and more receptive audience than he would through his magazine articles and that he could thus prod governments into constructive legislation and honest administration.[21] This would account in part for the monotony of his plots, the plainness of his style, the sincerity of his tone, all constructing an effect of realism as true and sometimes as dull as the stenographic report of an average conversation. Herrick's prose has more patina, but whatever claims these two men have to the title of artist—and this holds true for the community of novelists who had a similar program—rests upon their rendering of the image of the American man of their day.

But if their places as artists are something less than secure, Herrick and Phillips and the considerable number of writers who criticized American society in this interval of transition without fully understanding the forces at work foreshadowed clearly a turn to satire in our literature when the heat of the moment had somewhat died down. And they had an effect upon American history which cannot yet be fully calculated. Supported by those Gracchi of the press castigated by Roosevelt as muckrakers they prevented the transfiguration of the Strong Man into a cultural hero. In so doing they split the middle class, not along the Hamilton-Jefferson line where it had been split for a century, but along the line of individual conscience. In this way they were largely responsible for the rise of the independent voter whose rôle has been decisive in recent national politics, the voter willing to experiment with the New Freedom, the New Deal, the Fair Deal. The reforms which the writers advocated helped to reinforce the American will to fight in 1917 even when those reforms were in arrears of what the Germans had accomplished in the same sphere of social legislation, for they were an earnest of what could be

21. Isaac F. Marcosson, *David Graham Phillips and His Times,* New York, 1932, p. 272.

done through democratic processes of education and popular voting. If year by year it is getting harder to tolerate unrighteousness in legislatures and executive offices and judicial chambers, if it is getting harder for the business man and the politician and the journalist to shirk responsibility to the public they profess to serve, if it is getting harder to justify aggressive war and the exploitation of the weak, and if this change is good, then we owe a great debt not only to Eugene V. Debs, William Jennings Bryan, and Theodore Roosevelt but also to the novelists, the playwrights, the poets, the essayists, and the muckrakers who were awake to the dangers of the twentieth-century reaction against democracy. Most important of all, these authors accepted and underlined the duty which American penmen assumed before the Republic was born: the duty to demand the right to express freely their ideas, their opinions, and the facts as found. In the long run their courage may prove to have had more value to us all than pure art could have had.

BIBLIOGRAPHY

INDEX

Bibliography

Aaron, David. *Men of Good Will: A Story of American Progressives.* N. Y., 1951.

Abbott, Lyman. *Reminiscences.* Boston, 1915.

———. *Silhouettes of My Contemporaries.* N. Y., 1921.

Adamic, Louis. *Dynamite.* N. Y., 1931.

Adams, Brooks. *America's Economic Supremacy.* N. Y., 1900.

———. *The Law of Civilization and Decay.* N. Y., 1895.

Adams, Charles F., Jr., Adams, Henry. *Chapters in Erie and Other Essays.* Boston, 1871.

Adams, F. U. *Conquest of the Tropics.* Garden City, 1914. A story of the United Fruit Co.

Adams, Henry. *Letters of Henry Adams, 1892-1918* (ed. Worthington C. Ford). Boston, 1938.

———. *The Education of Henry Adams.* N. Y., 1907.

Adams, James T. *Henry Adams.* N. Y., 1933.

———. *The Adams Family.* Boston, 1930.

Addams, Jane. *Twenty Years at Hull House.* N. Y., 1910.

Ahnebrink, Lars. *The Beginnings of Naturalism in American Fiction.* Cambridge (Mass.), 1950.

Alden, Henry M. *Magazine Writing and the New Literature.* N. Y., 1908.

Aldrich, Mrs. Thomas B. *Crowding Memories.* Boston, 1920.

Alger, George W. *Moral Overstrain.* Boston, 1906.

Allen, Frederick. *The Big Change.* N. Y., 1952.

———. *The Great Pierpont Morgan.* N. Y., 1949.

Allen, Philip L. *The Triumph of Righteousness in High Places.* N. Y., 1906.

Anderson, Thornton. *Brooks Adams: Constructive Conservative.* Ithaca (N. Y.), 1951.

Andreas, Osborn. *Henry James and the Expanding Horizon.* Seattle (Wash.), 1948.

Andrews, Kenneth R. *Nook Farm, Mark Twain's Hartford Circle*. Cambridge (Mass.), 1950.

Atherton, Gertrude. *Adventures of a Novelist*. N. Y., 1932.

Badè, W. F. *The Life and Letters of John Muir*. Boston, 1923-24.

Baker, Ray S. *Woodrow Wilson; Life and Letters*. Vol. II. Garden City, 1927.

Baldwin, Charles E. *The Men Who Make Our Novels*. N. Y., 1919.

Ballou, Jenny. *Period Piece: Ella Wheeler Wilcox and Her Times*. Boston, 1940.

Bangs, Francis K. *John Kendrick Bangs, Humorist of the Nineties*. N. Y., 1941.

Barnard, Ellsworth. *Edwin Arlington Robinson: A Critical Study*. N. Y., 1952.

Barnett, James H. *Divorce and the American Divorce Novel, 1858-1937*. Phila., 1939.

Barrow, Edith M. *News and These United States*. N. Y., 1952.

Barrus, Clara. *The Life and Letters of John Burroughs*. Boston, 1925.

Baym, Max I. *The French Education of Henry Adams*. N. Y., 1951.

Beach, Joseph W. *The Method of Henry James*. New Haven (Conn.), 1918.

Beach, Rex. *Personal Exposures*. N. Y., 1941.

Bean, Walton. *Boss Ruef's San Francisco*. Berkeley (Calif.), 1952.

Beard, Charles, and Beard, Mary. *The Rise of American Civilization*. N. Y., 1930.

Bebel, August. *Women under Socialism* (trans. Daniel De Leon). N. Y., 1904.

Beer, Thomas. *Hanna*. N. Y., 1929.

Begbie, Harold. *The Life of General William Booth*. N. Y., 1920.

Bennett, Mary. *Elizabeth Stuart Phelps*. Phila., 1939.

Bennett, Mildred. *The World of Willa Cather*. N. Y., 1951.

Berg, Leo. *The Superman in Modern Literature*. London, 1916.

Bikle, Lucy. *George W. Cable*. N. Y., 1928.

Bining, Arthur C. *The Rise of American Economic Life*. N. Y., 1949.

Bishop, Joseph B. *Theodore Roosevelt and His Time*. N. Y., 1920.

Blake, Nelson M. *A Short History of American Life*. N. Y., 1952. Particularly Part III.

Blum, Daniel. *A Pictorial History of the American Theatre, 1900-1950*. N. Y., 1950. Mostly a history of the New York stage with illustrations.

Blum, John M. *The Republican Roosevelt*. Cambridge (Mass.), 1954.

Bogan, Louise. *Achievement in American Poetry, 1900-1950*. Chicago, 1951.

Bogart, Ernest L. *An Economic History of the United States*. N. Y., 1907.

Bok, Edward. *The Americanization of Edward Bok*. N. Y., 1920.

Bolles, Blair. *Tyrant from Illinois: Joe Cannon's Experiment with Personal Power*. N. Y., 1951.

Bosanquet, Theodora. *Henry James at Work*. London, 1924.

Boutroux, Émile. *William James* (trans. Archibald and Barbara Henderson). N. Y., 1912.

Bowers, Claude. *Beveridge and the Progressive Era*. Boston, 1932.

Boynton, Percy. *Some Contemporary Americans*. Chicago, 1924.

Bridge, James H. *Millionaires and Grub Street*. N. Y., 1931.

———. *The Inside History of the Carnegie Steel Company*. N. Y., 1931.

Britt, George. *Forty Years—Forty Millions: The Career of Frank A. Munsey*. N. Y., 1935.

Brogan, Dennis. *The American Character*. N. Y., 1904.

Brooks, John G. *The Social Unrest; Studies in Labor and Socialist Movements*. N. Y., 1903.

Brooks, Van Wyck. *New England: Indian Summer*. N. Y., 1940.

———. *Sketches in Criticism*. N. Y., 1932.

———. *The Confident Years, 1885-1915*. N. Y., 1952.

———. *The Wine of the Puritans; A Study of Present-Day America*. N. Y., 1909.

Broun, Heywood, and Leach, Margaret. *Anthony Comstock, Roundsman of the Lord*. N. Y., 1927.

Brown, E. K. *Willa Cather: A Critical Biography*. N. Y., 1953.

Brown, George R. *The Leadership of Congress*. Indianapolis, 1922.

Brownell, William C. *American Prose Masters*. N. Y., 1909.

Bryan, W. J., and Bryan, Mary. *The Memoirs of William Jennings Bryan*. Phila., 1925.

Burke, Billie. *With a Feather on My Nose.* N. Y., 1949.

Burnett, Constance B. *Five for Freedom.* N. Y., 1952.

Burnett, Vivian. *The Romantick Lady: The Life Story of an Imagination.* N. Y., 1927. About his famous mother.

Burr, Anna R. *Weir Mitchell: His Life and Letters.* N. Y., 1927.

Burton, Richard. *Literary Likings.* Boston, 1908.

Busbey, L. White. *Uncle Joe Cannon: The Story of a Pioneer American.* N. Y., 1927.

Butt, Archibald. *Taft and Roosevelt; The Intimate Letters of Archie Butt.* Garden City, 1930.

Calverton, V. F. *The Liberation of American Literature.* N. Y., 1932.

Canby, Henry S. *Turn West, Turn East.* Boston, 1951.

Cargill, Oscar. *Intellectual America.* N. Y., 1941.

Carlson, Oliver. *Brisbane, a Candid Biography.* N. Y., 1937.

———, and Bates, Ernest. *Hearst, Lord of San Simeon.* N. Y., 1936.

Carnegie, Andrew. *The Autobiography of Andrew Carnegie.* N. Y., 1920.

———. *The Empire of Business.* N. Y., 1902.

———. *The Gospel of Wealth, and Other Timely Essays.* N. Y., 1900.

Carson, N. B., and Colson, E. S. *Myrtle Reed.* N. Y., 1911.

Caruso, Dorothy. *Enrico Caruso, His Life and Death.* N. Y., 1945.

Cary, Elisabeth. *The Novels of Henry James.* N. Y., 1905. The first full-length study of James.

Casson, H. M. *Cyrus Hall McCormick: His Life and Work.* Chicago, 1909.

Chamberlain, John. *Farewell to Reform.* N. Y., 1932.

Charnwood, Godfrey. *Theodore Roosevelt.* Boston, 1923.

Charteris, Evan. *John Sargent.* London, 1927.

Clemens, Samuel L. *Mark Twain's Autobiography.* N. Y., 1924.

Cleveland, F. A., and Powell, F. W. *Railroad Promotion and Capitalization in the United States.* N. Y., 1909.

Cleveland, R. M., and Williamson, S. T. *The Road Is Yours.* N. Y. A survey covering all phases of motoring in the U. S.

Clymer, Floyd. *Treasury of Early American Automobiles.* N. Y., 1951.

Cody, William F. *The Adventures of Buffalo Bill.* N. Y., 1904.

Cohn, David L. *The Good Old Days.* N. Y., 1940.

Coleman, McAlister. *Eugene V. Debs: A Man Unafraid.* N. Y., 1930.

Commager, Henry S. *The American Mind: An Interpretation of American Thought and Character Since the 1880's.* New Haven (Conn.), 1950.

Commons, John R., and others. *History of Labor in the United States.* N. Y., 1918.

Connolly, Christopher. *The Devil Learns To Vote.* N. Y., 1938. A story of Montana.

Connolly, Margaret. *The Life Story of Orison Swett Marden, a Man Who Benefited Men.* N. Y., 1925.

Cook, Frederick A. *My Attainment of the Pole.* N. Y., 1911.

Cooper, Frederic T. *Some American Story Tellers.* N. Y., 1911.

Cortissoz, Royal. *John La Farge: A Memoir and a Study.* Boston, 1922.

Cowie, Alexander. *The Rise of the American Novel.* N. Y., 1948.

Cowley, Malcolm. *After the Genteel Tradition.* N. Y., 1937.

Croly, Herbert. *Marcus Alonzo Hanna.* N. Y., 1912.

Crosby, Ernest. *Golden Rule Jones, Mayor of Toledo.* Chicago, 1906.

Daggett, Stuart. *Chapters in the History of the Southern Pacific.* N. Y., 1922.

Daiches, David. *Willa Cather; A Critical Study.* Ithaca (N. Y.), 1951.

Dakin, E. F. *Mrs. Eddy: The Biography of a Virginal Mind.* N. Y., 1929.

Daly, Joseph. *The Life of Augustin Daly.* N. Y., 1917.

Daniels, Josephus. *The Life of Woodrow Wilson, 1856-1924.* Phila., 1924.

Darrow, Clarence. *The Story of My Life.* N. Y., 1932.

Davies, Acton. *Maude Adams.* N. Y., 1901.

Davis, Oscar K. *Released for Publication: Some Inside Political History of Theodore Roosevelt and His Times, 1898-1918.* Boston, 1925.

Davis, Robert, and Maurice, Arthur B. *The Caliph of Bagdad.* N. Y., 1931. About O. Henry.

DeCastro, Adolphe. *Portrait of Ambrose Bierce.* N. Y., 1929.

Deland, Margaret. *Golden Yesterdays.* N. Y., 1941. The second volume of two autobiographical works, it ends with 1917.

Dell, Floyd. *Upton Sinclair: A Study in Social Protest.* N. Y., 1927.

DeMille, George. *Literary Criticism in America.* N. Y., 1931.

Dennett, Tyler. *John Hay: From Poetry to Politics.* N. Y., 1933.

Depew, Chauncey. *My Memories of Eighty Years.* N. Y., 1922.

DeVoto, Bernard. *Mark Twain's America.* Boston, 1932.

———. (ed.). *Mark Twain in Eruption.* N. Y., 1940.

Dewey, George. *Autobiography of George Dewey.* N. Y., 1913.

Dickinson, Asa. *Booth Tarkington.* Garden City, 1926.

Dorfman, Joseph. *Thorstein Veblen and His America.* N. Y., 1934.

Dorr, Rheta C. *Susan B. Anthony: The Woman Who Changed the Mind of a Nation.* N. Y., 1928.

Downer, Alan. *Fifty Years of American Drama, 1900-1950.* Chicago, 1951.

Downey, Fairfax. *Portrait of an Era as Drawn by Charles Dana Gibson.* N. Y., 1936.

———. *Richard Harding Davis: His Day.* N. Y., 1933.

Doyle, Arthur C. *The History of Spiritualism.* N. Y., 1910.

Dreiser, Helen. *My Life with Dreiser.* Cleveland (Ohio), 1951.

Dreiser, Theodore. *A Book about Myself.* N. Y., 1922.

Dudley, Dorothy. *Forgotten Frontiers: Dreiser and the Land of the Free.* N. Y., 1932.

Duffy, Herbert S. *William Howard Taft.* N. Y., 1930.

Dupee, Frederick W. (ed.). *The Question of Henry James.* N. Y., 1946.

Dyer, Walter A. *David Grayson, Adventurer.* N. Y., 1926.

Earnest, Ernest. *S. Weir Mitchell, Physician and Novelist.* Phila., 1950.

Edgar, Pelham. *The Art of the Novel from 1700 to the Present Time.* N. Y., 1933.

Egbert, Donald, and Persons, Stow (eds.). *Socialism and American Life.* Princeton, 1952.

Elias, Robert H. *Theodore Dreiser, Apostle of Nature.* N. Y., 1948.

Ellis, Elmer. *Mr. Dooley's America: A Life of Finley Peter Dunne.* N. Y., 1941.

Elson, Louis C. *The History of American Music.* N. Y., 1925.

Erskine, John. *Leading American Novelists.* N. Y., 1910.

Farrar, Geraldine. *The Autobiography of Geraldine Farrar: Such Sweet Compulsion.* N. Y., 1938.

Faulkner, Harold U. *The Quest for Social Justice, 1898-1914.* N. Y., 1931.

Ferguson, DeLancey. *Mark Twain: Man and Legend.* Indianapolis, 1943.

Fields, Annie. *Charles Dudley Warner.* N. Y., 1904.

———. (ed.). *Letters of Sarah Orne Jewett.* Boston, 1911.

Filler, Louis. *Crusaders for American Liberalism.* N. Y., 1939.

Firkins, Oscar. *William Dean Howells: A Study.* Cambridge (Mass.), 1924.

Fish, C. R. *The Rise of the Common Man.* N. Y., 1927.

Flory, Claud. *Economic Criticism in American Fiction.* Phila., 1935.

Flower, B. O. *Progressive Men, Women and Movements of the Past Twenty-Five Years.* Boston, 1914.

Flynn, John T. *God's Gold: The Story of Rockefeller and His Times.* N. Y., 1932.

Flynt, Josiah. *My Life.* N. Y., 1908.

Foley, Richard N. *Criticism in American Periodicals of the Works of Henry James from 1866 to 1916.* Washington (D.C.), 1944.

Follett, Helen, and Follett, Wilson. *Some Modern Novelists.* N. Y., 1918.

Foner, Philip S. *Jack London, American Rebel.* N. Y., 1947. A collection of London's revolutionary writings, with a preface of 130 pp.

Ford, Henry J. *Woodrow Wilson, the Man and His Work: A Biographical Study.* N. Y., 1916.

Ford, James L. *Forty-Odd Years in the Literary Shop.* N. Y., 1921.

Gabriel, Ralph H. *The Course of American Democratic Thought: An Intellectual History.* N. Y., 1940.

Garden, Mary, and Biancolli, Louis. *Mary Garden's Story.* N. Y., 1951.

Garland, Hamlin. *My Friendly Contemporaries.* N. Y., 1932.

———. *Roadside Meetings.* N. Y., 1930.

Geismar, Maxwell. *Rebels and Ancestors.* Boston, 1953.

Gerould, Katherine F. *Edith Wharton: A Critical Study*. N. Y., 1922.

Gilder, Rosamond (ed.). *Letters of Richard Watson Gilder*. Boston, 1916.

Gilman, Lawrence. *Edward MacDowell: A Study*. N. Y., 1909.

Goldman, Emma. *Living My Life*. N. Y., 1931.

Goldman, Eric. *Rendezvous with Destiny: A History of Modern American Reform*. N. Y., 1952.

Gompers, Samuel. *Labor in Europe and America*. N. Y., 1910.

———. *Seventy Years of Life and Labor*. N. Y., 1925.

Goodrich, Lloyd. *John Sloan, 1871-1951*. N. Y., 1952.

———. *Winslow Homer*. N. Y., 1944.

Gorgas, Maria, and Hendrick, Burton. *William Crawford Gorgas: His Life and Work*. Garden City, 1924.

Gosnell, Harold. *Boss Platt and His New York Machine*. Chicago, 1924.

Grant, Robert. *Fourscore*. Boston, 1934.

Grattan, C. Hartley. *Bitter Bierce*. Garden City, 1929.

———. *The Three Jameses*. N. Y., 1932.

Gray, James; Brodbeck, May; Metzger, Walter. *Men, Ideas, and Judgments, 1900-1950*. Chicago, 1952.

Green, Harold E. *Towering Pines*. N. Y., 1943. A biography of John Fox, Jr.

Greene, Graham. *The Lost Childhood and Other Essays*. London, 1951. Five papers on Henry James.

Griffin, Martin, Jr. *Frank R. Stockton: A Critical Biography*. Phila., 1939.

Hale, Edward E. *Memories of a Hundred Years*. N. Y., 1902.

Hall, Ernest. *The Satirical Element in the American Novel*. Phila., 1922.

Halsey, Francis W. *Our Literary Deluge and Some of Its Deeper Waters*. N. Y., 1902.

Hamilton, John J. *The Dethronement of the City Boss*. N. Y., 1910.

Hampton, Benjamin. *A History of the Movies*. N. Y., 1930.

Hansen, Harry. *Midwest Portraits*. N. Y., 1923.

Hapgood, Hutchins. *A Victorian in the Modern World*. N. Y., 1939.

Hapgood, Norman. *The Changing Years*. N. Y., 1930.

Harper, Ida H. *The Life and Works of Susan B. Anthony*. Indianapolis, 1898.

Harrison, Charles. *Clarence Darrow*. N. Y., 1931.

Hart, James D. *The Popular Book*. N. Y., 1950.

Hartwick, Harry. *The Foreground of Fiction*. N. Y., 1934.

Harvey, Rowland H. *Samuel Gompers: Champion of the Toiling Masses*. Berkeley (Calif.), 1935.

Hatcher, Harlan. *Creating the Modern American Novel*. N. Y., 1935.

Hawthorne, Hildegarde. *Harold Bell Wright: The Man Behind the Novels*. N. Y., n.d. (pamphlet).

Haycraft, Howard. *Murder for Pleasure: The Life and Times of the Detective Story*. N. Y., 1941.

Haynes, Frederick E. *Third Party Movements Since the Civil War*. Iowa City, 1916.

Hendrick, Burton J. *The Age of Big Business*. New Haven (Conn.), 1919.

———. *The Training of an American: The Earlier Life and Letters of Walter H. Page, 1855-1913*. Boston, 1928.

Henry, David D. *William Vaughn Moody: A Study*. Boston, 1934.

Henry, Robert S. *This Fascinating Railroad Business*. Indianapolis, 1942.

Hibben, Paxton. *The Peerless Leader, William Jennings Bryan*. N. Y., 1929.

Hicks, Granville. *John Reed: The Making of a Revolutionary*. N. Y., 1936.

———. *The Great Tradition*. N. Y., 1933.

Hill, Howard C. *Roosevelt and the Caribbean*. Chicago, 1927.

Hillquit, Morris. *A History of Socialism in the United States*. N. Y., 1903.

Hoffman, Frederick. *The Modern Novel in America, 1900-1950*. Chicago, 1951.

Holbrook, Stewart H. *The Story of American Railroads*. N. Y., 1947.

Holliday, Robert C. *A Chat about Samuel Merwin*. Indianapolis, 1921.

———. *Booth Tarkington*. N. Y., 1918.

Howells, William Dean. *My Mark Twain*. N. Y., 1910.

Howgate, George W. *George Santayana*. Phila., 1938.

Hughes, Glenn. *A History of the American Theater, 1700-1950.* N. Y., 1951.

Hume, Robert A. *Runaway Star: An Appreciation of Henry Adams.* Ithaca (N. Y.), 1951.

Hunter, Robert. *Poverty.* N. Y., 1904.

Hyslop, J. H. *Science and a Future Life.* Boston, 1910.

Iglehart, Ferdinand C. *Theodore Roosevelt: The Man as I Knew Him.* N. Y., 1919.

Ireland, Alleyne. *An Adventure with a Genius: Recollections of Joseph Pulitzer.* N. Y., 1920.

Jacobs, Lewis. *The Rise of the American Film.* N. Y., 1939.

James, Henry. *Partial Portraits.* London, 1888.

———. Prefaces to *The Novels and Tales of Henry James.* N. Y., 1907-1917.

———. *The American Scene.* N. Y., 1905.

———. *The Letters of Henry James* (ed. Percy Lubbock). N. Y., 1920.

———. *The Middle Years.* N. Y., 1917.

James, Marquis. *Biography of a Business, 1792-1942.* N. Y., 1942. (Ins. Co. of North America.)

Jennings, Al. *Through the Shadows with O. Henry.* N. Y., 1921.

Jessup, Philip. *Elihu Root.* N. Y., 1938.

Johnson, C. O. *Borah of Idaho.* N. Y., 1936.

Johnson, Gerald W. *Incredible Tale: The Odyssey of the Average American in the Last Half Century.* N. Y., 1950.

Johnson, Robert U. *Remembered Yesterdays.* Boston, 1923.

Johnson, Tom L. *My Story* (ed. Elizabeth Hauser). N. Y., 1911.

Johnson, W. F. *Four Centuries of the Panama Canal.* London, 1907.

Jordan, David, and Kellogg, Vernon. *The Scientific Aspects of Luther Burbank's Work.* San Francisco, 1909.

Jordy, William H. *Henry Adams: Scientific Historian.* New Haven (Conn.), 1952.

Josephson, Matthew. *The President Makers, 1896-1919.* N. Y., 1940.

———. *The Robber Barons: The Great American Capitalists, 1861-1901.* N. Y., 1934.

Jusserand, J. A. Jules. *With Americans of Past and Present Days.* N. Y., 1916.

Kaufman, W. A. *Nietzsche: Philosopher, Psychologist, Antichrist.* Princeton, 1950.

Kazin, Alfred. *On Native Grounds.* N. Y., 1942.

Keller, Helen. *The Story of My Life.* N. Y., 1904.

Kelly, Fred C. *George Ade, Warmhearted Satirist.* Indianapolis, 1947.

——. *Miracle at Kitty Hawk: The Letters of Wilbur and Orville Wright.* N. Y., 1951.

Kemler, Edgar. *The Irreverent Mr. Mencken.* Boston, 1950.

Kennan, George. *E. H. Harriman: A Biography.* Boston, 1922.

Kennan, George F. *American Diplomacy, 1900-1950.* Chicago, 1951.

Kennedy, W. S. *The Real John Burroughs.* N. Y., 1924.

Key, Ellen. *Love and Marriage* (trans. A. G. Chater). N. Y., 1911.

Kipnis, Ira. *The American Socialist Movement, 1897-1912.* N. Y., 1952.

Kirk, Clara, and Kirk, Rudolph (eds.). *William Dean Howells.* N. Y., 1950. An anthology with an admirable introduction.

Knight, Grant C. *James Lane Allen and the Genteel Tradition.* Chapel Hill, 1935.

Kohn, Hans. *Force or Reason: Issues of the Twentieth Century.* Cambridge (Mass.), 1937.

Kolodin, Irving. *The Metropolitan Opera, 1883-1935.* N. Y., 1936.

La Follette, Belle, and La Follette, Fola. *Robert M. La Follette: June 14, 1855-June 18, 1952.* N. Y., 1953.

La Follette, Robert M. *Autobiography: A Personal Narrative of Political Experience.* Madison (Wis.), 1913.

La Follette, Suzanne. *Art in America.* N. Y., 1929.

Lane, Albert. *Elbert Hubbard and His Work.* Worcester (Mass.), 1901.

Lawrence, Margaret. *The School of Femininity.* N. Y., 1936.

Lawson, Thomas W. *Frenzied Finance.* N. Y., 1905.

Lee, Gerald S. *Inspired Millionaires: A Forecast.* Northampton (Mass.), 1908.

Leech, Harper, and Carroll, John C. *Armour and His Times.* N. Y., 1938.

Leisy, Ernest E. *The American Historical Novel.* Norman (Okla.), 1950.

Lewis, Edith. *Willa Cather Living.* N. Y., 1953.

Lewis, W. D. *The Life of Theodore Roosevelt*. Phila., 1919.

Lewisohn, Ludwig. *Expression in America*. N. Y., 1932.

Lichtenberger, James P. *Divorce: A Study in Social Causation*. N. Y., 1909.

Lindsey, Ben, and Borough, Rube. *The Dangerous Life*. N. Y., 1931.

Lindsey, Ben, and O'Higgins, Harvey. *The Beast*. N. Y., 1910.

Link, Arthur S. *Wilson: The Road to the White House*. Princeton, 1947.

———. *Woodrow Wilson and the Progressive Era*. N. Y., 1954.

Lloyd, Henry D. *Lords of Industry*. N. Y., 1910.

———. *Men, the Workers*. N. Y., 1909.

Lodge, Henry C. *Theodore Roosevelt*. Boston, 1919.

Lodge, Oliver. *Science and Immortality*. N. Y., 1910.

London, Jack. *Revolution, and Other Essays*. N. Y., 1910.

———. *The People of the Abyss*. N. Y., 1903.

———. *The Road*. N. Y., 1907.

———. *The War of the Classes*. N. Y., 1905.

London, Charmian. *The Book of Jack London*. N. Y., 1921.

London, Joan. *Jack London and His Times*. N. Y., 1939.

Longworth, Alice R. *Crowded Hours*. N. Y., 1933.

Lovett, Robert M. *All Our Years*. N. Y., 1948.

———. *Edith Wharton*. N. Y., 1925.

Lubbock, Percy. *Edith Wharton*. N. Y., 1947.

Lundberg, Ferdinand. *Imperial Hearst: A Social Biography*. N. Y., 1936.

Lutz, Alma. *Created Equal: A Biography of Elizabeth Cady Stanton, 1815-1902*. N. Y., 1940.

McCafferty, E. D. *Henry J. Heinz: A Biography*. N. Y., 1903.

McCloskey, Robert A. *American Conservatism in the Age of Enterprise*. Cambridge (Mass.), 1951.

McClure, S. S. *My Autobiography*. N. Y., 1914.

McCutcheon, John T. *John McCutcheon's Book*. Chicago, 1948.

McSpadden, Joseph W. *Light Opera and Musical Comedy*. N. Y., 1936.

McWilliams, Carey. *Ambrose Bierce: A Biography*. N. Y., 1929.

Madison, Charles. *American Labor Leaders: Personalities and Forces in the Labor Movement*. N. Y., 1950.

Madison, Charles. *Critics and Crusaders: A Century of American Protest.* N. Y., 1947.

Mahan, Alfred T. *The Interest of America in International Conditions.* Boston, 1910.

Manchester, William B. *Disturber of the Peace: The Life of H. L. Mencken.* N. Y., 1951.

Mandel, L. *Robert Herrick.* Chicago, 1927.

Mantle, Burns. *American Playwrights of Today.* N. Y., 1929.

Marchand, Ernest. *Frank Norris: A Study.* Palo Alto (Cal.), 1942.

Marcosson, Isaac. *Adventures in Interviewing.* London, 1920.

———. *David Graham Phillips and His Times.* N. Y., 1923.

Matthews, Basil J. *Booker T. Washington: Educator and Interracial Interpreter.* Cambridge (Mass.), 1948.

Matthews, Brander. *The Historical Novel and Other Essays.* N. Y., 1901.

Matthiessen, F. O. *Henry James: The Major Phase.* London, 1944.

———. *The James Family.* N. Y., 1947.

———. *Theodore Dreiser.* N. Y., 1951.

Meehan, Jeannette P. *The Lady of the Limberlost: The Life and Letters of Gene Stratton-Porter.* Garden City, 1928.

Mencken, H. L. *Heathen Days, 1890-1936.* N. Y., 1943.

Merriam, Charles E. *American Political Ideas, 1865-1917.* N. Y., 1920.

Millis, H. A. *The Japanese Problem in the United States.* N. Y., 1915.

Mitchell, John. *Organized Labor.* Phila., 1903.

Montagu, Ashley. *Darwin: Competition and Coöperation.* N. Y., 1952.

Moody, John. *The Railroad Builders.* New Haven (Conn.), 1919.

More, Paul E. *The Drift of Romanticism.* Boston, 1913.

Morris, Lloyd. *William James: The Message of a Modern Mind.* N. Y., 1950.

Morse, E. W. *The Life and Letters of Hamilton W. Mabie.* N. Y., 1920.

Moses, Montrose J., and Gerson, Virginia. *Clyde Fitch and His Letters.* Boston, 1924.

———. *The American Dramatist.* Boston, 1911.

——— and Brown, John Mason. *The American Theatre as Seen by Its Critics.* N. Y., 1934.

Mott, Frank L. *Golden Multitudes*. N. Y., 1947.
Myers, Gustavus. *A History of the Great American Fortunes*. Chicago, 1910.
———. *The History of Tammany Hall*. N. Y., 1917 (rev. ed.).

Neff, Emery E. *Edwin Arlington Robinson*. N. Y., 1948.
Neuberger, Richard L. *Integrity: The Life of George W. Norris*. N. Y., 1937.
Neuhaus, Eugen. *The History and Ideals of American Art*. Palo Alto (Cal.), 1931.
Nevins, Allan. *John D. Rockefeller*. N. Y., 1941.
———. *Study in Power: John D. Rockefeller, Industrialist and Philanthropist*. N. Y., 1953.
———. *The Emergence of Modern America*. N. Y., 1927.
Nevius, Blake. *Edith Wharton*. Berkeley (Cal.), 1953.
Neyhart, Louise. *Giant of the Yards*. Boston, 1952. About Gustavus Swift.
Nolan, Jeanette C. *James Whitcomb Riley, Hoosier Poet*. N. Y., 1941.
———; Gregory, Horace; Farrell, James T. *Poet of the People: An Evaluation of James Whitcomb Riley*. Bloomington (Ind.), 1951.
Norris, Charles. *Frank Norris, 1870-1902*. N. Y., 1914.
Norris, Frank. *The Responsibilities of the Novelist*. N. Y., 1903.
Nowell-Smith, Simon. *The Legend of the Master*. N. Y., 1948.
Nye, Russel. *Midwestern Progressive Politics*. East Lansing (Mich.), 1951.

O'Connor, Harvey. *The Astors*. N. Y., 1941.
———. *The Guggenheims: The Making of an American Dynasty*. N. Y., 1937.
O'Connor, William V. *An Age of Criticism, 1900-1950*. Chicago, 1952.
O'Gara, Gordon C. *Theodore Roosevelt and the Modern Navy*. Princeton, 1943.
Olcott, Charles S. *The Life of William McKinley*. Boston, 1916.
Orchard, Harry. *The Confessions and Autobiography of Harry Orchard*. N. Y., 1907.
Oursler, Fulton. *The True Story of Bernarr Macfadden*. N. Y., 1929.

Overton, Grant. *The American Nights Entertainment*. N. Y., 1923.
———. *The Women Who Make Our Novels*. N. Y., 1925.

Page, Rosewell. *Thomas Nelson Page: The Memoir of a Virginia Gentleman*. N. Y., 1923.
Paine, Albert B. (ed.). *Mark Twain's Autobiography*. N. Y., 1924.
———. *Mark Twain: A Biography*. N. Y., 1912.
Parrington, Vernon L. *The Beginnings of Critical Realism in America, 1860-1920*. N. Y., 1920. Vol. III of *Main Currents in American Thought*.
Parsons, Frank. *The Heart of the Railroad Problem*. Boston, 1906.
Pattee, Fred L. *A History of American Literature Since 1890*. N. Y., 1915.
———. *Side-Lights on American Literature*. N. Y., 1922.
———. *The Development of the American Short Story*. N. Y., 1923.
———. *The New American Literature, 1890-1930*. N. Y., 1930.
Paxson, Frederic L. *Recent History of the United States*. Boston, 1921.
Peary, Robert. *The North Pole*. N. Y., 1910.
Peck, Harry T. *Twenty Years of the Republic, 1885-1905*. N. Y., 1906.
Peltz, Mary E. *Behind the Gold Curtain: The Story of the Metropolitan Opera, 1883-1950*. N. Y., 1950.
Perry, Bliss. *A Study of Prose Fiction*. Boston, 1902.
Perry, Ralph. *The Thought and Character of William James*. Boston, 1935.
Persons, Stow (ed.). *Evolutionary Thought in America*. New Haven (Conn.), 1950. See Malcolm Cowley's essay "Naturalism in American Literature," pp. 300-333.
Pinchot, Gifford. *The Fight for Conservation*. N. Y., 1910.
Poole, Ernest. *The Bridge: My Own Story*. N. Y., 1940.
Pound, Ezra. *The Letters of Ezra Pound* (ed. D. D. Paige). N. Y., 1950.
Pusey, Merlo J. *Charles Evans Hughes*. N. Y., 1951.
Pyle, J. G. *The Life of James J. Hill*. N. Y, 1936

Quinn, Arthur H. *American Fiction: An Historical and Critical Survey*. N. Y., 1936.
———. *A History of the American Drama from the Civil War to the Present Day*. N. Y., 1927.

Quint, Howard H. *The Forging of American Socialism: Origins of the Modern Movement.* Columbia (S. C.), 1953.

Reed, Louis S. *The Labor Philosophy of Samuel Gompers.* N. Y., 1930.
Regier, Cornelius C. *The Era of the Muckrakers.* Chapel Hill, 1932.
Rhodes, James F. *The McKinley and Roosevelt Administrations, 1897-1909.* N. Y., 1922.
Rice, Alice Hegan. *Inky Way.* N. Y., 1940.
Riesman, David. *Thorstein Veblen: A Critical Interpretation.* N. Y., 1953.
Riis, Jacob. *A Ten Years' War.* Boston, 1900.
———. *The Making of an American.* N. Y., 1901.
———. *Theodore Roosevelt the Citizen.* N. Y., 1904.
Rinehart, Mary R. *My Story.* N. Y., 1931.
Roberts, Kenneth. *I Wanted To Write.* Garden City, 1949.
Roosevelt, Theodore. *The Letters of Theodore Roosevelt* (ed. Elting Morison). Cambridge (Mass.), 1951-52. Vols. III to VI deal with the years 1901-1909.
———. *Theodore Roosevelt: An Autobiography.* N. Y., 1913.
———. *The Strenuous Life.* N. Y., 1900.
Rose, Lisle. *A Survey of Economic Fiction, 1902-1909.* Chicago, 1938.
Russell, Charles E. *Bare Hands and Stone Walls: Some Recollections of a Side-line Reformer.* N. Y., 1933.
———. *Lawless Wealth: The Origin of Some Great American Fortunes.* N. Y., 1908.
———. *Stories of the Great Railroads.* Chicago, 1912.
———. *The Uprising of the Many.* N. Y., 1907.

Saint-Gaudens, Homer. *The American Artist and His Times.* N. Y., 1941.
Saloutos, Theodore, and Hicks, John D. *Agricultural Discontent in the Middle West, 1900-1939.* Madison (Wis.), 1951.
Santayana, George. *Persons and Places.* N. Y., 1944.
———. *The Middle Span.* N. Y., 1945.
Santos-Dumont, Alberto. *My Air-Ships.* N. Y., 1904.
Saxton, Eugene F. *Gene Stratton-Porter, A Little Story of Her Life and Work.* N. Y., n.d. (pamphlet).

Schlesinger, Arthur M. *New Viewpoints in American History.* N. Y., 1922.
———. *The Rise of the City.* N. Y., 1938.
Schreiner, Olive. *Women and Labor.* N. Y., 1911.
Seitz, Don. *The "Also Rans."* N. Y., 1928.
———. *Joseph Pulitzer: His Life and Letters.* N. Y., 1924.
Seltson, William H. *Metropolitan Opera Annals.* N. Y., 1947.
Sergeant, Elizabeth S. *Willa Cather: A Memoir.* Phila., 1953.
Seton-Watson, Hugh. *The Decline of Imperial Russia.* London, 1953.
Shafer, Robert. *Christianity and Naturalism.* New Haven (Conn.), 1926.
———. *Paul Elmer More and American Criticism.* New Haven (Conn.), 1935.
Shaw, Anna. *The Story of a Pioneer.* N. Y., 1915.
Shay, Felix. *Elbert Hubbard of East Aurora.* N. Y., 1926.
Simons, A. M. *Class Struggles in America.* Chicago, 1903.
Sinclair, Upton. *American Outpost: A Book of Reminiscence.* N. Y., 1932.
Skinner, Otis. *Footlights and Spotlights: Recollections of My Life on the Stage.* Indianapolis, 1924.
Smith, Albert E., and Koury, Phil A. *Two Reels and a Crank.* Garden City, 1952.
Smith, Bernard. *Forces in American Criticism: A Study in the History of American Literary Thought.* N. Y., 1939.
Smith, C. Alfonso. *O. Henry's Biography.* Garden City, 1916.
Smith, Cecil. *Musical Comedy in America.* N. Y., 1950.
Smith, Nora A. *Kate Douglas Wiggin as Her Sister Knew Her.* N. Y., 1925.
Snell, George. *The Shapers of American Fiction, 1798-1947.* N. Y., 1947.
Sothern, E. H. *The Melancholy Tale of "Me"; My Remembrances.* N. Y. 1916.
Spargo, John. *Syndicalism, Industrial Unionism and Socialism.* N. Y., 1913.
———. *The Bitter Cry of the Children.* N. Y., 1906.
———. *The Spiritual Significance of Socialism.* N. Y., 1908.
Sparks, Boyden, and Moore, S. T. *Hetty Green: A Woman Who Loved Money.* Garden City, 1930.

Speare, Morris E. *The Political Novel: Its Development in England and in America.* N. Y., 1934.

Spearman, Frank H. *The Strategy of Great Railroads.* N. Y., 1904.

Spender, Stephen. *The Destructive Element.* Boston, 1935. See Part I for Henry James.

Spiller, Robert, and Others. *The Literary History of the United States.* Vol. II. N. Y., 1948.

Stanton, Theodore, and Blatch, Harriot (eds.). *Elizabeth Cady Stanton as Revealed in Her Letters, Diary and Reminiscences.* N. Y., 1922.

Starr, Harris E. *William Graham Sumner.* N. Y., 1925.

Starrett, Vincent. *Buried Caesars.* Chicago, 1923. Chapters on half-forgotten popular authors.

Steffens, Lincoln. *The Autobiography of Lincoln Steffens.* N. Y., 1931.

———. *The Letters of Lincoln Steffens.* N. Y., 1938.

———. *The Shame of the Cities.* N. Y., 1904.

———. *The Struggle for Self-Government.* N. Y., 1906.

Steiner, E. A. *The Immigrant Tide, Its Ebb and Flow.* N. Y., 1909.

Stephenson, Nathaniel W. *Nelson W. Aldrich: A Leader in American Politics.* N. Y., 1930.

Stevenson, Adlai. *Something of Men I Have Known.* Chicago, 1909. Has a chapter on "The Lost Art of Oratory."

Stoddard, Lothrop. *Master of Manhattan: The Life of Richard Croker.* N. Y., 1931.

———. *The Rising Tide of Color against White World-Supremacy.* N. Y., 1920.

Stokes, George S. *Agnes Repplier, Lady of Letters.* Phila., 1949.

Stone, Irving. *Sailor on Horseback: The Biography of Jack London.* Boston, 1933.

Stone, L. A. *Emerson Hough: His Place in American Letters.* Chicago, 1925.

Storey, Moorfield. *The Philippine Policy of Secretary Taft.* Boston, 1902.

Stratton-Porter, Gene. *Let Us Highly Resolve.* N. Y., 1927.

Straus, O. S. *Under Four Administrations from Cleveland to Taft.* Boston, 1923.

Sullivan, Mark. *Our Times: The Turn of the Century.* N. Y., 1927.

Sullivan, Mark. *Our Times: The War Begins, 1909-1914.* N. Y., 1932. See pp. 440-532 for a personalized account of the break between Roosevelt and Taft.
———. *The Education of an American.* N. Y., 1938.
Sutherland, Donald. *Gertrude Stein.* New Haven (Conn.), 1951.

Tandy, Jennette. *Crackerbox Philosophers in American Humor and Satire.* N. Y., 1925.
Tarbell, Ida. *All in the Day's Work.* N. Y., 1939.
———. *The History of the Standard Oil Company.* N. Y., 1904.
———. *The Nationalizing of Business, 1878-1898.* N. Y., 1936.
Tarkington, Booth. *The World Does Move.* Garden City, 1928.
Taubman, Howard. *The Maestro: The Life of Arturo Toscanini.* N. Y., 1951.
Taylor, Deems; Peterson, Marcelene; Hale, Bryant. *A Pictorial History of the Movies.* N. Y., 1943.
Taylor, Walter F. *The Economic Novel in America.* Chapel Hill, 1942.
Tebbel, John. *George Horace Lorimer and The Saturday Evening Post.* Garden City, 1948.
———. *The Life and Good Times of William Randolph Hearst.* N. Y., 1952.
Thayer, William R. *The Life and Letters of John Hay.* Boston, 1915.
———. *Theodore Roosevelt: An Intimate Biography.* Boston, 1913.
Thomas, Augustus. *The Print of My Remembrance.* N. Y., 1922.
Throm, Edward L. (ed.). *Fifty Years of Popular Mechanics.* N. Y., 1951. A backward look at the magazine.
———, and Crenshaw, James S. *Auto Album.* N. Y., 1952.
Tracy, H. C. *American Naturalists.* N. Y., 1930.
Treadwell, Bill. *50 Years of American Comedy.* N. Y., 1951.
Trilling, Lionel. *The Liberal Imagination: Essays on Literature and Society.* N. Y., 1950.

Underwood, John C. *Literature and Insurgency.* N. Y., 1914.

Van Doren, Carl. *The American Novel.* N. Y., 1940 (rev. ed.).
———, and Van Doren, Mark. *American and British Literature Since 1890.* N. Y., 1925.

Van Doren, Mark. *Edwin Arlington Robinson*. N. Y., 1927.

van Dyke, Tertius. *Henry van Dyke*. N. Y., 1935.

Van Vorst, Mrs. John, and Van Vorst, Marie. *The Woman Who Toils*. N. Y., 1903.

Veblen, Thorstein. *The Theory of Business Enterprise*. N. Y., 1904.

Villard, Oswald G. *Fighting Years*. N. Y., 1939.

———. *Prophets True and False*. N. Y., 1928.

Voegelin, Eric. *The New Science of Politics*. Chicago, 1952.

Wagenknecht, Edward. *Cavalcade of the American Novel*. N. Y., 1952. Excellent combination of scholarship and criticism.

Walbridge, Earle. *Literary Characters Drawn from Life*. N. Y., 1936.

Walcutt, Charles C. *The Romantic Compromise in the Novels of Winston Churchill*. Ann Arbor (Mich.), 1951.

Walker, Franklin. *Frank Norris: A Biography*. Garden City, 1932.

———. *San Francisco's Literary Frontier*. N. Y., 1939.

Warfel, Harry, and Orians, G. H. (eds.). *American Local Color Stories*. N. Y., 1941. Valuable Introduction.

Washburn, Charles G. *Theodore Roosevelt: The Logic of His Career*. Boston, 1916.

Washington, Booker T. *Up from Slavery*. N. Y., 1901.

Weber, Max. *The Protestant Ethic and the Spirit of Capitalism*. N. Y., 1950.

Wecter, Dixon. *The Hero in America: A Chronicle of Hero-Worship*. N. Y., 1941. Lively analyses of Roosevelt and Bryan in Chapter Fourteen.

———. *The Saga of American Society*. N. Y., 1938.

Weirick, Bruce. *From Whitman to Sandburg in American Poetry: A Critical Survey*. N. Y., 1924.

Werner, Morris R. *Bryan*. N. Y., 1929.

West, Ray B. *The Rise of Short Fiction in America, 1900-1950*. Chicago, 1952.

———. *The Short Story in America, 1900-1950*. N. Y., 1953.

Wharton, Edith. *A Backward Glance*. N. Y., 1934.

White, William A. *Masks in a Pageant*. N. Y., 1928.

———. *The Autobiography of William Allen White*. N. Y., 1946.

White, William A. *The Old Order Changeth: A View of American Democracy*. N. Y., 1910.
Whitlock, Brand. *Forty Years of It*. N. Y., 1914.
———. *The Letters and Journal of Brand Whitlock*. N. Y., 1936.
Wiggin, Kate Douglas. *My Garden of Memory*. N. Y., 1923.
Wilcox, Ella W. *The Worlds and I*. N. Y., 1918.
Wiley, Harvey W. *An Autobiography*. Indianapolis, 1930.
Williams, William A. *American-Russian Relations, 1781-1947*. N. Y., 1952.
Winter, William. *The Life of David Belasco*. N. Y., 1918.
Wish, Harvey. *Society and Thought in Modern America*. N. Y., 1952.
Wister, Owen. *Roosevelt: The Story of a Friendship, 1880-1919*. N. Y., 1930.
Wolfe, L. M. *Son of the Wilderness: The Life of John Muir*. N. Y., 1945.
Wood, Clement. *Bernarr Macfadden: A Study in Success*. N. Y., 1929.
Woodward, Comer C. *Tom Watson: Agrarian Rebel*. N. Y., 1938.
Wright, Harold B. *To My Sons*. N. Y., 1934.
Wyatt, Edith. *Great Companions*. N. Y., 1917.

Ybarra, T. R. *Caruso: The Man of Naples and the Voice of Gold*. N. Y., 1953.
Yellen, Samuel. *American Labor Struggles*. N. Y., 1936.

Zabriskie, Edward H. *American-Russian Rivalry in the Far East, 1895-1914*. Chicago, 1945.
Zink, Harold. *City Bosses in the United States*. Durham (N. C.), 1930.

INDEX